God Bless
the Pill

God Bless the Pill

THE SURPRISING HISTORY OF CONTRACEPTION AND SEXUALITY IN AMERICAN RELIGION

Samira K. Mehta

The University of North Carolina Press
CHAPEL HILL

This book was published with the assistance of
the Anniversary Fund of the University of North Carolina Press.

Designed by Lindsay Starr
Set in Quadraat Pro, Cabernet, and Cervo Neue
by Jamie McKee, MacKey Composition

Complete Library of Congress Cataloging-in-Publication
data is available at https://lccn.loc.gov/2025047085.
9781469693422 (cloth: alk. paper)
9781469693439 (pbk.: alk. paper)
9781469686653 (epub)
9781469693446 (pdf)

For product safety concerns under the European Union's General Product Safety
Regulation (EU GPSR), please contact gpsr@mare-nostrum.co.uk or write to
the University of North Carolina Press and Mare Nostrum Group B.V.,
Doelen 72, 4831 GR Breda, The Netherlands.

For my grandmother, Katherine Ruth Huffer Hotchkiss;

my mother, Linda Katherine Hotchkiss Mehta;

and my goddaughter, Daisy Boynton Melvin

And to the memory of my paternal grandmother,

Kaushalya Devi Chowla Mehta (ca. 1917–71), for whom

birth control would have made a world of difference

CONTENTS

ILLUSTRATIONS

PREFACE

I cannot remember a time when I was not interested in feminism. One of my parents' closest friends, a woman named Debbe Jacobs, worked for the Ms. Foundation and brought me a copy of the album *Free to Be . . . You and Me* when I was about three. I would sing along about how mommies could be almost anything they wanted to be, or how it was all right for boys to cry. I recall my mother objected to the poem about how everyone hated housework. While I suspect that my mother does hate it (as do I), my mother pointed out that for some of the women in the neighborhood, housework was a source of pride and accomplishment. From the very start, then, I grew up not only as a feminist but as one who understood that there were many points of view within feminism.

By the time I was in junior high school and high school in the 1990s, my feminism had become focused on reproductive health and sexual abuse. My father usually made himself very good snacks to eat while watching the PBS *Newshour*, and if you wanted to eat the nachos, you also had to watch the news, and so I watched the Senate hearings for Clarence Thomas's nomination to the US Supreme Court. My father taught me how to watch the proceedings and know that Anita Hill was telling the truth. "Look," my father said, "these are very embarrassing things, even for grown-ups. It is very hard for a Black woman to have to say these things, on the news, to a panel of white men. For the rest of her life, this is what people will think of first when they hear her name. No one would ever put herself through this if she were not both telling the truth and extremely brave."

I was on fire with rage about what it meant to be a woman in the workplace. Then we watched Operation Rescue target women's health clinics, and my father told me that abortion needed to be available and safe, but more importantly so did birth control. He also told me that his mother had no access to birth control, and so she had seven live births, two abortions—forced on her by my grandfather—and, my father assumed, many miscarriages.

My father's feminism was complicated. Later, my mother, knowing that his support for abortion might or might not extend to an ability to cope with sexually active daughters, told me that if I ever got pregnant, I should let her know, and "we would take care of it and not tell Daddy." She made sure that I knew that I had the right to say no to boys, but also that it was okay, if I believed that I was ready, to say yes.

My father was from India, and he never totally figured out how to talk—or not talk—about sex with my sister and me. When he took me to Costco before I left for what everyone still called freshman year at college in 1996, he insisted on buying a Costco-sized box of condoms. I was humiliated and told him that he was "not the mom." He was adamant—he worried that since I had been on the Pill since age twelve because of polycystic ovarian syndrome, I would think that, because I was not going to get pregnant, I was safe. He did not want me contracting HIV or anything else. He also told me that "the other girls might not have liberal parents," so I would need enough condoms to share. My father had not been to an American college. He did not know that there were condoms available for free in the dorm first aid kits and at the student health office. But he was determined not only to protect his own daughters, but to make sure that we could help our friends protect themselves.

At college, I started to put these tools into action. I volunteered at a hotline where we fielded calls about rape and about sexual health. I did clinic escorting at the Planned Parenthood with the Swarthmore College Pro-Choice Task Force, eventually learning to drive the sixteen-seater van and alternating weekends with my friend Caitlin. When my maternal grandmother found out that I was standing outside a Planned Parenthood in all weather, she sent me long underwear and a note about how you have to honor commitments, even once it gets miserable and cold. After college, I volunteered for Survivor Assistance, a spin-off of the Boston Area Rape Crisis Center. Sometimes after a particularly rough call, I would sleep on the couch so that my crying would not wake up my boyfriend. Eventually, I got better at dropping a wall between the calls and my emotions.

In my early twenties, I visited India. While I was there, I asked my father's older brother about my grandmother's cause of death. I knew that she had died in her fifties after what had been described as a long illness. Without a missing a beat, my uncle replied, "Papaji." Papaji was my grandfather. Later, I asked my mother whether my grandmother had died not of her illness but of domestic violence. My mother interpreted my uncle's comment as meaning that my grandfather had worn my grandmother out with the pregnancies, the babies, the miscarriages, the forced abortions, the emotional and likely

physical abuse, the exacting standards about his food and his tea, the sex
that she could not refuse, the anger that he visited on her children. My paternal grandmother's story made my father into a man who was fervent in
the feminism he wanted for his daughters and his nieces. Because of my paternal grandmother's story, I have always known that the cost of life without
feminism is unbearably high, and reproductive justice has long been at the
heart of my feminism.

In grad school, however, my activism dropped off. I still marched when
called for, still occasionally took a friend or classmate for a rape kit, a pregnancy test, or an abortion. My activism dropped off because I was busy,
but also because I felt like we had won—not against sexual violence, but at
least against antiabortion activism, which by extension blocks women from
birth control, Pap smears, prenatal care, and everything else that women's
health clinics provide. When I moved to Boston in 2000, the local Planned
Parenthood said that it did not need volunteers. When I moved to Atlanta, I
saw that there were protesters outside the women's health clinic around the
corner from my synagogue's offices. But the protests looked so small, so in-
effectual, that it felt like we had turned a corner. I did not foresee a day when
my goddaughter would have less bodily autonomy than I had.

When I started researching the role of religion in US birth control debates
ten years ago, I did not think this would be a controversial topic. Indeed, I
chose birth control over abortion because I was looking for something less
controversial. I also thought that because birth control was less polarizing,
this would be an interesting history to trace, a place where I could easily see
how mainstream feminism had changed and shaped mainstream religion.
I was excited to see how previous generations of feminists had created that
change, and also, if I am being honest, to see how my own work might be
part of that lineage.

This is a very different moment, and I have found a very different story
from the one I imagined. While this book will show that there was a great deal
of feminist activism through the middle and end of the twentieth century, it
will also show that that activism was much less determinative than the influence of more conservative forces within religious groups and broader society.
Women's growing access to birth control did not occur because religious
authorities and political figures embraced bodily autonomy, sexual pleasure,
and intellectual ambitions. Instead, religious advocacy for birth control grew
from a focus on the economic and emotional health of the heteropatriarchal
family. Even women's health was framed as important less because of a woman's right to health as an autonomous individual, and more because children

were better off with a healthy mother, and certainly better off if their mother did not die in childbirth. Religious advocacy for birth control was limited—if one's goal was the feminist liberation of women and others with the capacity for pregnancy. It was also fragile. The expansion of birth control access was dependent on people using birth control in ways that the more conservative elements of society saw as enhancing, rather than detracting from, the family.

As I share this book today, having written it for the most feminist of reasons, I must acknowledge that while such commitments can dictate the questions we ask, they cannot dictate the answers we find. For me, this reality is one of the hardest in practicing history.

ACKNOWLEDGMENTS

There are many, many people to thank in the decade-long process of bringing this book into the world. I hope that I have thanked everyone here, but if I have forgotten some, I beg their forgiveness.

Elaine Maisner became my editor at UNC Press for my first book, based on my dissertation, and she pushed me to think of this study has having a bigger, broader scope than that one. I thank her for believing in me, pushing me, and tirelessly championing me, even after retirement. When Elaine retired, Mark Simpson-Vos took over as my editor. He is a very different kind of editor than Elaine was, wonderful in an entirely different set of ways. I suspect that this book will be all the stronger for having had both of their hands on the project. Together, Elaine and Mark got me some of the most fabulous reviews one could hope to have, which is to say that while they were encouraging and complimentary, they also pushed me and the book to be so much more. Thank-you to the anonymous reviewers whose suggestions helped me make this work so much smarter than it was. Cate Hodorowicz took over at the final stages, and I would like to thank her, and the rest of the UNC Press team, including Helen Kyriakoudes and Erin Granville. They have been truly wonderful.

I owe much gratitude to the student researchers with whom I have worked over the years: Sayge Martin, Emma Breitmann, Daisy Fellows, Julia Lerone, and Doris Bryn Norrie. Amaya Rios was not technically a student research assistant, but she was nonetheless a very important conversation partner. Brook Wilensky-Lanford and Linda Hotchkiss Mehta have both contributed their immense editorial talents to this project. Thank you, Brook and Mommy, for making this book better than it would have been without you.

This project has been supported by the Cashmere Subvention Grant, which was, at the time that I received it, given out by the Association for Jewish Studies Women's Caucus for research in gender and sexuality studies. I thank the

Women's Caucus, the Gender Justice Caucus, and, most importantly, Laura Levitt for supporting the grant. The archival research for this project has been supported by a number of research grants for which I am deeply grateful. I have received The Rabbi Theodore S. Levy Tribute Fellowship from the American Jewish Archives, a New England Regional Fellowship Consortium Research Grant, a Rockefeller Archive Center Research Stipend, and a Sophia Smith Collection Travel-to-Archives Grant from Smith College. I have also received money from the Program in Jewish Studies at the University of Colorado Boulder to complete archival research. These funds have resulted in research at the aforementioned archives, and also at the American Jewish Historical Society, the Schlesinger Library, the Harvard Divinity School Library, the Presbyterian Historical Society, the Francis A. Countway Library of Medicine at the Harvard Medical School, the Yale Divinity School Special Collections, the Notre Dame University Archives, and the Library of Congress. I am grateful to the archival and reference librarians at all of these institutions. In addition, I am grateful to Gloria Korsman and Kerrie Harthan, Anthony Petro and Patrick McKelvey, Dana Herman and Jason Kalman, Chaos Golubitsky, and, most impressively, Rebecca Wingo, all of whom housed me during research trips.

There are many, many librarians who deserve more thanks than I can possibly share, both for their help in these archives and for more general reference assistance. Among them are Jennifer Barr and Charlene Peacock (Presbyterian Historical Society); Jennifer Fauxsmith, Sarah Hutchinson, and Ellen Shea (Schlesinger Library); Nanci Young (Smith College Archives); Gloria Korsman, Renata Kalnis, and Rebecca Villarreal (Harvard Divinity School Library); Megan Welsch (the University of Colorado Boulder); Edie Sandler, Mary Champagne, and Cheryl Adams (Library of Congress); and Kevin Schlottman (American Jewish Historical Society Archives). This book has taken long enough that not all of those librarians are with the institutions that I have listed here, and the names of some of the people who have provided wonderful help have been lost to email accounts that I no longer have. But it is a truth universally acknowledged that no good historical work could be done without archivists and reference librarians, and I thank them all. In particular, Tom Rosenbaum, z"l, was the face of the Rockefeller Archive Center for me. He held a wealth of knowledge about the collection and was a profound loss.

In addition to these archival fellowships, I benefited from two yearlong fellowships, one of which I used for research and incubating ideas and one during which I wrote the book. In 2016–17, I was the David B. Larson Fellow in Health and Spirituality at the Kluge Center of the Library of Congress. I did much of the groundwork for this book there, and also spent a lot of time protesting. I would like to thank Travis Hensley and Emily Coccia for their work supporting all the fellows, and some of my fellow fellows in particular: Amy Bride, Luis Campos, Alex Loktionov, Lanie Millar, Rosie Narayan, Alan Noonan, Christine Okoth, Tom Smith, Arun Sood, and Ruth Turner. I also served as a research associate, visiting associate professor of North American religions, and the Colorado Scholar in the Women's Studies in Religion Program (WSRP) at Harvard Divinity School. It would be impossible to say enough about the help and support that I received from Ann Braude and the incomparable Tracey Wall during my year with the WSRP (and, if we are being honest, during my HDS student days). I would like to thank them and my cohort of research associates, J. Jessica Fowler, Elena Herminia Guzman, S. Zahra Moballegh, Fareen Parvez, and Ashley Purpura in particular, for the workshopping of chapters. Thank you also to Catherine Brekus, Margaret Hamm, David Holland, Kama Lord, Dan McKanan, Shaul Magid, Kerry Maloney, Hussein Rashid, and Annette Yoshiko Reed for making the year at the HDS so warm and welcoming. The students in my Religion and Repro ductive Politics in the United States class at HDS were wonderful readers of the in-process manuscript and also just so much fun.

Many people have given me the opportunity to present my work and receive feedback from colleagues in the field. I would like to thank Dan Vaca and the graduate program in religion at Brown University; Tisa Wenger and the graduate program in American religion at Yale University; David Holland, Kelsey Hanson Woodruff, and the North American Religions Colloquium at Harvard Divinity School; Nick Underwood and the College of Idaho; Sally Promey and the Sensory Cultures of Religion Research Group at Yale University; Wallace Best, Seth Perry, Judith Weisenfeld, and the Religions in the Americas Workshop at Princeton University; Mary Hale and the Newberry Library; Wallace Best and the Program in Gender and Sexuality Studies at Princeton University; Rachel Gordan and the attendees of the Jewish 1950s Conference at the University of Florida; Matt Hedstrom and his grad students at the University of Virginia; and Peter Manseau and the Smithsonian National Museum of American History. Molly Jackson at The Conversation gave me a platform to explore some of the ideas in this book in print. I am grateful for the discussion about my work that occurred in all of these venues. The feedback that I received made the work much stronger, both in content and form. Many others invited me to give more formal talks, and those, too, honed my thoughts.

In addition, I would like to thank the following scholars for reading drafts of chapters at various points in this extremely long process, for sharing resources when asked (or when they saw something helpful), and for generally being part of the community of scholars who have supported this project: Ann Braude, Catherine Brekus, Pete Cajka, Jessica Cooperman, Emmanuel David, Rebecca Davis, Sarah Dees, Jamil Drake, Jack Downey, Gill Frank, Katharine Gerbner, Rachel Gordan, Marie Griffith, Rachel Gross, Matt Hedstrom, David Holland, Sarah Imhoff, Hilary Kalisman, Rachel Kranson, Adrienne Krone, Laura Leibman, Laura Levitt, Katie Lofton, Charlie McCrary, Lerone Martin, Deepti Misri, Celeste Montoya, Bethany Moreton, Hillary Potter, Shari Rabin, Hussein Rashid, Michal Raucher, Nora Rubel, Kristie Soares, Lauren MacIvor Thompson, Dan Vaca, Alexis Wells-Oghoghmeh, Judith Weisenfeld, Tisa Wenger, Heather White, and Robert Wyrod. Each of these readers offered generous feedback and careful attention that made me both a better writer and a better scholar. I would particularly like to note Matthew Cressler and Kate Dugan, who carefully read the sections on Catholicism. I would also like to thank Lerone Martin for being my emotional support texting buddy in the final stages of copyediting. Any mistakes, in content or grammar, are my own alone.

Anthony Petro read the entire manuscript before I submitted it, pushing me at once to be more precise and to make bigger and bolder claims. I am grateful to him for reading the work and for almost two decades of near-daily intellectual collaboration. His dissertation and first book on religion and the AIDS crisis are what made me interested in religion and medicine in the first place. The summer that I began my archival research for this project, I lived in Anthony's apartment for the summer. I was unemployed, and only later did I realize that Anthony had dramatically discounted the rent in order to fit my budget. He also came home a couple of times during the summer and filled the fridge with food that I like, rather than food that he likes. If I were to enumerate all of the other reasons I have to thank and appreciate Anthony, I would never stop writing, but I hope he knows what they are.

There are also academic communities that have supported me and this book, whether or not they read its pages. While I was at Albright College, Jennifer Koosed got me permission to take a fellowship at the Library of Congress, which is not really the Albright way. She, Rob Seesengood, Victor Forte, and Trudy Prutzman made the Chapel a wonderful place to work. In addition, I am grateful for the friendship and support of Bridget Hearon, Denise Greenwood, and Ian Rhile, the last of whom knows just what to say when a month of archival digging turns up nothing.

At the University of Colorado, I am fortunate to have two academic homes in Women's and Gender Studies and in Jewish Studies. I am grateful to both of those communities; many of my Women's and Gender Studies colleagues are listed above as readers, but many of them are also lovely and wonderful friends. I would like particularly to thank Julie Carr, my Department of Women and Gender Studies (WGST) chair, for her tireless support; Celeste Montoya, who served as my official mentor; and Alicia Turchette and Kai Blake-Leibowitz, the WGST staff who make the Cottage a wonderful place to be. Of late, I have been the director of the Program in Jewish Studies (PJS). I would like to thank Thomas Pegelow Kaplan for agreeing to be the interim director so that I could take the WSRP fellowship and PJS Executive Committee members Sam Boyd, Hilary Kalisman, Yonatan Malin, and Eli Sacks for being great to work with every day. John-Michael Rivera was dean of both the division of arts and humanities and the division of social sciences when I received the WSRP fellowship, and he was therefore the person who enabled me to go—thank you, J-M. It is a treat to have another scholar of American religion on campus, and I am so lucky that Debbie Whitehead is here. I appreciate that Phoebe Young, in the History Department, sees me as a historian. I would also like to thank Donna Axel, who officially helps with grant proposals, but who has also become one of my biggest cheerleaders.

It has been more than a decade since I left Emory, but my adviser Gary Laderman is always in my corner, as are Eric Goldstein and Wallace Best, my master's thesis adviser. All three of them take emergency phone calls, as do Tisa Wenger, Judith Weisenfeld, Laura Levitt, and Laura Leibman.

The act of being a spinster lady professor can be a lonely business, and so I would like to thank the people who are the backbone of my community and of my life. I am listing some of them in groups, but each of them matters to me more than I can say.

While I was working on this project, I was part of the Young Scholars in American Religion mentoring program, which has been the most special professional experience of my life, and a deeply personally significant one as well. I would like to thank Phil Goff and the Center for the Study of Religion & American Culture for organizing the program. I would also like to thank my mentors Sally Promey and Sylvester Johnson, and the members of my cohort: Joe Blankholm, Melissa Borja, Chris Cantwell, Matthew Cressler, Sarah Dees, Jamil Drake, Katharine Gerbner, Shari Rabin, and Alexis Wells-Oghoghmeh. Thank you for reading things when I ask you to; for putting me up in your homes when I blow through town, sometimes with animals; for wearing the things that I knit you; and for answering phone calls late at night or phone calls about power drills. Katharine commented that getting our cohort is like getting a family, and she is so right.

I would also like to thank my reading group, whose members have gotten together to read and share our lives for over five years. Each of them sees me and my love languages: Sarah Dees, who shows up literally and figuratively when her presence brings needed assistance or deep joy; Kate Dugan, who makes me feel deeply seen and whose commitment to friendship is part of the bedrock beneath my feet; Sarah Imhoff, who covers when my executive function fails, and who once commented that being knit for is one of her love languages—because she knows knitting is one of mine; and Adrienne Krone, who is always there on the other end of the phone, more or less no matter what, even though the phone is not her thing. I do not have words to say what you all mean to me.

In addition, the academy has gifted me with friends who are not neatly grouped together, but who are the warp and woof of my life. Rachel Gordan, thank you for more than twenty years of phone calls, postcards, and Zabar's bagels. Never love an institution, because it will not love you back, but I most certainly love many of the people: Brandon Bayne, Wallace Best, Dianne Betkowski, Jenny Caplan, Allison Covey, Karla Goldman, Eric Goldstein, Hilary Kalisman, Martin Kavka, Brett Krutzsch, Gary Laderman, Laura Leibman, Laura Levitt, Nora Rubel, Eli Sacks, Donovan Schaefer, Tom Smith, Dianne Stewart, Claire Sufrin, Miram Udel, Judith Weisenfeld, Tisa Wenger, Brook Wilensky-Lanford.

I would like to thank some friends who have made Colorado start to feel like home, but who have not otherwise appeared here: Jaime Koehler Blanchard, Andrew Chiacchierini, Gregg Drinkwater, Megan Friedel, Michelle Gaffga, Chaos Golubitsky, Ellie Emerich Hart, Alec Hart, Melissa Hoffman, Rachel Rinaldo, Honor Sachs, Charlie Sacks, Liz Sacks, Tova Sacks, Hope Saska, Haley Simpson, Brian Stephenson, Carol Thompson, Jamie Wallace, Brook Walters, Darryl Wiser, and Nate Wyrod. Thank you to the Sacks family and to Olivia and Greg Williams for storing my stuff when I went to Boston for the year.

Finally, I would like to thank Andrea Ajello, Matteo Ajello-McGlothlin, Yoshimi Azuma, LeeAnn Bambach, Calvin Hotchkiss, Sam Hotchkiss, Sara Hotchkiss, Josh Kidd, Susannah Laramee Kidd, Fran Lightsom, Cameron McGlothlin, Daisy Melvin, Jeremy Melvin, Sita Mehta Merchea and the Merchea men, Cathy Muller, Kwame Philips, Janna Said, Ely Sheinfeld, Shayna Sheinfeld, the Smith-Brown family, Candace West, and, most importantly, Daisy Jane Mehta, Linda Hotchkiss Mehta, and Quincy Hotchkiss Mehta for all of the love and support.

God Bless
the Pill

Introduction

When Alan Guttmacher, president of the Planned Parenthood Federation of America, delivered the 1970 commencement address at Smith College, he closed with a clarion call to the young women gathered before him. "I started this discourse like a historian," Guttmacher announced. "I conclude it like a preacher, not a preacher of religion, but a preacher of social behavior."[1] Guttmacher, a secular leader in the birth control movement, borrowed the power of religious authority to underscore the moral implications of the choice to use birth control. Other speakers in the same moment might have borrowed that religious authority to warn that birth control access caused sexual promiscuity among the increasingly empowered women graduates. But Guttmacher preached different values, and he was not the only one to frame his pro-birth-control message in religious terms. Indeed, the year before, the *New York Times* had referred to him as the "evangelist" of birth control.[2] "You have been given a singular gift," he proclaimed, "the gift to control your fertility. It presents a challenge: meet it and use the gift well."[3]

Those who come to a history of birth control shaped by the culture wars of the 1980s and the medical histories that focused on the eugenic elements of the movement may find Guttmacher's sanctification of contraception and fertility surprising. After all, in the 1980s, the religious right campaigned for abstinence-only education and against including birth control in school curricula and nurses' offices. Politicians supported by the religious right introduced policies that cut funding to women's health clinics, overtly targeting abortion but also making birth control less available. While statistics tell us that most sexually active Americans use contraception, when religious voices spoke out about birth control in the 1980s, it was mostly to restrict its access. For those who, shaped by this era, think religious organizations are on the opposite side of the cultural divide from reproductive health, Guttmacher's use of religious imagery in support of birth control is surprising. Why would the Jewish president of Planned Parenthood choose to frame himself as a preacher, an evangelist? Is he implying religious support for contraception, or is this simply a quip from a largely secular person invoking religion in a cheeky rebuttal to religious conservatives? Guttmacher may have been speaking metaphorically in the New York Times, but the religious implications of birth control were both real and numerous.

For example, the invention and Food and Drug Administration approval of oral contraception created public anxiety that the Pill would usher in an era of free love and the sexual revolution, in direct opposition to the norms of marriage and family. The sexual revolution, which the media of the time made much of, seemed like a result of the Pill and an affront to the Judeo-Christian values around family life, and it was broadly condemned as irresponsible by political pundits, clergy, and many other members of the Greatest Generation. How, then, could the use of contraception be lauded by someone who called himself a "preacher of social behavior" as a "gift" to be "use[d] well"? What, precisely, was socially responsible about contraception? Finally, for those who think of the birth control movement in general, and Planned Parenthood specifically, as hotbeds of racially based eugenics, why is Guttmacher telling the graduating class of Smith College, a group of predominantly white middle-class and affluent women, that they have the gift of controlling their fertility?

It is tempting to think of the history of contraception as a feminist history. When I began the research for God Bless the Pill, I did so because I was inspired by Elaine Tyler May's America and the Pill: A History of Promise, Peril, and Liberation. What, I wondered, would that story look like if one fully included religion in the narrative? I hoped and assumed that, as in May's title, the promise and liberation might outweigh the peril. I also saw in May's narration the assumption that religion was always conservative and opposed to birth control. When she writes about religious responses to the birth control pill, she focuses on the institutional Catholic Church's opposition to all contraception—an opposition that ultimately was decisively extended to oral contraception. She also highlights Evangelicals' opposition to the sexual liberalism and libertinism that they feared would emerge with widespread availability of oral contraception. May makes it clear that the history of birth control is more complicated than simply a tale of feminist victory. But the popular historical understanding remains that contraception became widely available and acceptable because women fought for it for feminist reasons: to control their own fertility, if not always their own bodies; and with the ability to control their own fertility, to enjoy sex and sexual liberation; to advance educationally and professionally; or, at the very least, to not be worn out with constant pregnancy and child-rearing or the worry thereof.

Because feminists would go on to make such good use of the contraception available to them, and to fight so hard to expand its access, it seems reasonable to assume that having that contraception in the first place was a result of their hard-won battles against patriarchal opposition, akin to the employment cases that Ruth Bader Ginsburg defended as a lawyer. In this version of the story, the religious right's backlash against family planning, which became a key piece of public discourse by the 1980s, makes sense. Religious people had always opposed the things that birth control made possible for women: consequence free sex, the ability to pursue educational and economic equality with men, and thus the ability to have roles beyond those of wife and mother.

What would happen, I wondered as I read *America and the Pill*, if one asked about liberal religion? I initially took this question to the Schlesinger Library, where I was delighted and bemused to find my own childhood minister, the Reverend Al Ciarcia of the Unitarian Universalist Church of Greater Bridgeport, on record publicly supporting birth control. He did so during the debates about the legalization of birth control for all married couples that surrounded the decision of *Griswold v. Connecticut*. I had known Ciarcia as an older man nearing retirement. He was kind to children, in that he always brought baked ziti to potlucks, but he was awkward with us, in that he never understood that I minded him pulling my braids. He had clashed with my mother, the church soprano and often the chair of the religious education committee, over both music and curriculum, leading me to think he must have been rather conservative. Apparently, at least in this case, I had been quite wrong.

My own childhood minister aside, *God Bless the Pill* demonstrates that it is a mistake to tell the story of contraception advocacy without liberal religious people. The support of liberal clergy turns out to have been an essential element of making birth control broadly accessible in the United States. Thinking about the twenty-first-century battles over reproductive health care, and about general health care for women and other disempowered gender groups, I deeply hope that exploring the history of how religious leaders were able to intervene to expand reproductive health care will offer my readers inspiration and perhaps untapped resources for the battles that are still to come.

That said, if the support of liberal clergy is one of the reasons that birth control became so readily available, at least for a while, these individuals were also part of the apparatus by which the birth control movement moved away from its radical and feminist origins in the early twentieth century. My impression of my childhood minister was that he was relatively conservative politically, but that was relative to his denomination, which is so liberal that it is no longer precisely Protestant. My childhood minister was perhaps liberal relative to the average American. But "liberal" does not, however, necessarily mean "feminist."

While feminists played some role in expanding access to contraception, many of the reasons birth control was both socially acceptable and widely available were profoundly traditional, designed to shore up a heteropatriarchal and consumer-oriented nuclear family. Exploring the worldview of the liberal religious actors in the birth control conversations at the middle of the century demonstrates that their understanding of the Judeo-Christian family was progressive—in its embrace, for example, of sex-positive theology and the ability of science to shore up the family—but profoundly traditional in its ideas of what family should look like. This liberal Judeo-Christian idea of the family was a plank in American rhetoric against the Cold War and profoundly connected to notions of whiteness and of religion. This meant that many aspects of family life received increased public prominence: Marital trouble between couples spelled trouble for the nation, and therefore marital counseling was a tool to strengthen the nation. The American mother as nurturing homemaker contrasted with the Soviet mother as worker, absent from her home and therefore unable to infuse it with warmth for her children.[4]

God Bless the Pill traces the logics of respectability that made contraception broadly available and argues that that respectability was largely tied to religion—from the public endorsement of contraception by clergy, to the explicitly theological elevation of marital sex and planned spacing of children, and the implicitly theological values of midcentury sociology. The good Judeo-Christian family turned out to have the same markers of healthy family life that were identified by sociologists and psychologists. This synergy was mutually reinforcing, as the religious endorsement gave weight to the findings of social scientists; and the research of sociologists and psychologists in turn made the values of religion seem modern and scientific. In exploring this dynamic, *God Bless the Pill* traces contraception moving from the hands of women into the hands of male authorities, both doctors and clergy, who worked as a team to ensure that medically prescribed methods were understood as scientific, and as godly when used appropriately in the context of marriage. In that context, contraception was a tool that could shore up the very idea of marriage. It allowed marriages to be sexually satisfying without being overly financially strained by too many children, allowed women to focus their energies on remaining sexually desirable spouses, connected couples to God through their sexuality, and allowed for the kind of resource-intensive, upwardly mobile child-rearing that became central to midcentury anticommunist ideology—ideology that was often explicitly or implicitly religious.

This book tells the story of a broad religious coalition of Protestant and Jewish clergy and laity—and some Catholic clergy and laity as well—who supported the use of contraception in marriage to create what the Christians called "godly families." These families used contraception as a tool. They could prayerfully decide how many children to have while guarding the physical, emotional, and economic health of their family—which centered on a sexually dynamic and loving marriage between a breadwinning father and a homemaking mother. Feminist uses of birth control—for educational, professional, or nonmarital sexual fulfillment—flew in the face of the rheto ric that had expanded contraception in order to support a particular kind of nuclear family. In this sense, the backlash against contraception—and the roles it allowed women to have outside their homes—had its roots in the same values that had made contraception available in the first place.

These American values had first been defined as central during World War II battles against fascism. But by the start of the Cold War, those values were also mobilized against communism. Rather than simply competing political or philosophical ideologies, these liberal American values were portrayed as the product of a Judeo-Christian society. Coined in the 1890s, the term "Judeo-Christian" was popularized by the National Council of Christians and Jews (NCCJ) at the behest of the United States government, in part as an attempt to counter use of the term "Christian" by antisemites at home and Christian fascists abroad.[5]

As historian Matthew S. Hedstrom puts it, the NCCJ devised an educational campaign to teach Americans that "Judeo-Christianity described not only an ancient reality but also a continuing cultural inheritance rooted in shared scriptures and common values. That heritage, they [council members] argued, had been essential to the historical development of American democracy and remained critical to its ongoing vitality."[6] While both contemporary scholars of American religion and many liberal contemporary clergy, particularly Jewish clergy, are rightly skeptical of the term, which both disguises the very real differences between even liberal Judaism and Christianity and masks diversity within Jewish and Christian traditions, it is impossible to overstate the importance of the term in the middle of the twentieth century. "Judeo-Christian" served to define American democratic values in terms that were both broad enough to envision a moderately religiously diverse United States that counted Catholics and Jews as full citizens, and restrictive enough to imbue those values with the timeless gravitas of religion.[7]

Cold War Religious Ideologies of the Family

Many of those democratic values played out in the arena of the American family. Given that most histories of the American family during the Cold War come out of feminist history, a discipline that has not traditionally spent much energy on the study of religion, it is not surprising that religion is largely absent from these studies.[8] Given the role of the Judeo-Christian model in the animating of American democratic values in the middle of the century, however, we must reexamine that feminist literature with an eye toward how explicit and implicit religious values shaped family life in the United States after World War II.

Elaine Tyler May opens her book *Homeward Bound: American Families in the Cold War Era* with a photograph of young newlyweds descending into a bomb shelter for their honeymoon. They would spend it in total isolation, surrounded by the consumer goods that would help them live out the two weeks of radiation fallout projected after an atomic bomb.[9] May features this couple, who appeared on the front cover of *Time* magazine, because their honeymoon stunt said much about how the post–World War II United States understood the American family. "This is a powerful image of the nuclear family in the nuclear age," she writes, "isolated, sexually charged, cushioned by abundance, and protected against impending doom by the wonders of modern technology."[10] This ideal family would move to the suburbs, perhaps through the GI Bill, where they would live in some isolation from their extended family networks. Their familial unit would be based on a strong marriage between a husband who was a provider and a wife who cared for herself so as to be a sexually desirable spouse, for their home as a consumer of the new fruits of domestically oriented capitalism, and for their children as a loving but not smothering mother.

This vision of marriage and the family shaped much of Cold War ideology. American propaganda presented the nuclear family as one of the strongest weapons Americans had against godless communism. The argument depended on the religiosity of that family—and, indeed, in the two decades after World War II, Americans went to church and synagogue in higher

numbers than at any other point in the century; so it was an era in which it
was unusually true that religion was central to the family unit. In addition
to its Judeo-Christian religiosity, the American nuclear family also demonstrated the "advantages" of capitalism over communism. American women
could focus on making their lives as wives and mothers in homes blessed
with washer-dryers, dishwashers, vacuum cleaners, and KitchenAid mixers.
In stark contrast, their Soviet counterparts were portrayed as apartment
dwellers who had to work two shifts in the factories in order to keep a roof
over their heads, whose children were raised in day care facilities without the
love of a mother. Cold War ideology saw both bachelors and homosexuals as
communist threats, as well as potentially implicated in sexual sin; American
democracy needed men who were strong, sexually satisfied providers, safe
from any sort of political deviance, and dedicated to the love and responsibility
they felt for wife, home, and children.

Children were automatically considered to be a key part of this family life,
the mode by which, in the words of the Christian marriage ceremony, husband
and wife became (quite literally) one flesh, such that marriage and family were
nearly synonymous. Parenthood was understood as a key to responsible citizenship and to a personally fulfilling life, particularly for women, who were
advised to treat motherhood as a profession to which they could bring their
education and the methods of scientific child-rearing to bear.[11] The ideology
that structured these families was strong. These were the families depicted
on the big and small screen, in settings such as *Leave It to Beaver* and *The Doris
Day Show*. They were the families extolled by Cold Warriors: marriage counselors, sociologists, politicians, clergy, and the pages of women's magazines.

While many families did not live lives in accordance with these ideologies,
among the white middle class, "individuals who chose personal paths that did
not include marriage and parenthood risked being perceived as perverted, immoral, unpatriotic, and pathological. Neighbors shunned them as if they were
dangerous; the government investigated them as security risks. Their chances
of living free of stigma or harassment were slim."[12] The expectation was that
good Americans lived in good nuclear families. Loving families were enabled
and promoted by democratic values, so the logic went; and those democratic
values were seamlessly supported by both Jewish and Christian teaching. *God
Bless the Pill* will point to the Judeo-Christian religious underpinnings of this
ideology of the family, demonstrating how much of it was supported by clergy,
and how that particular version of the family—upwardly mobile, with children
who were intensively parented by parents in sexually vibrant marriages—was
only possible because of their concurrent endorsement of birth control.

For much of the period that *God Bless the Pill* considers, the line between theology and social scientific disciplines like sociology and psychology was razor-thin, particularly for liberal and ecumenical Protestants and for Jews.[13] Both Catholics and conservative Evangelicals were more skeptical of the social sciences, particularly of psychology—with important exceptions that we will see in chapter 2. In this period and in this book, "theology" does not explicitly mean the "study or science which treats of God, His nature and attributes, and His relations with man and the universe." Rather, theology concerns how humanity should move through the world morally. Like theology, the social sciences were also interested in creating a better, more moral society—using their tools to promote "better living," the social science version of "better living through chemistry."

Not only were the goals of much midcentury social science and theological inquiry related, but the social sciences were interested in the realm of religion, and theologians were concerned with the findings of social science. For example, as R. Marie Griffith details in *Moral Combat*, Alfred Kinsey was concerned with religion in his research on sexuality; and religious leaders were attentive to the results of his work.[14] Similarly, Heather White's "How Heterosexuality Became Religious" in the edited volume *Heterosexual Histories* points to how religious leaders used psychological and sociological research on the family to locate heterosexual marriage at the heart of Judeo-Christian morality.[15] Throughout *God Bless the Pill*, liberal clergy use the tools of sociology, geography, demography, and psychology to argue for how communities should behave in the world. They support their moral pronouncements as much with the language of science as with the language of God; but in all cases, this language was put forward in service of morally shaping and improving their society.[16]

The Religious and Racial Politics of the Cold War Family

If these families drew from the white middle-class values that were understood to be rooted in Judeo-Christian tradition, their ability to move to the suburbs reinforced the idea that Protestants, Catholics, and Jews were largely the same when they were white. Specifically, government support helped low-income families move into the middle class as long as they were white, but African American and other non-white families were excluded from these forms of support by design. Catholics and Jews, long considered outsiders, were understood to be white in this system: They were able to move to the suburbs and received social support to do so. Their social acceptance was provisional—they might or might not be able to join the country club when they got to the suburbs. But Protestants, Catholics, and Jews increasingly lived together in suburbs marked by a white middle-class ethos of upwardly mobile, consumer-oriented middle-class families. These families and family structures were, in fact, a relatively new creation, reflecting a craving for stability born out of the stresses of the Great Depression, the Second World War, and the dawning nuclear age. But they were painted from the start as a return to a traditional family; and we continue to see the nuclear family as such today.

Whiteness was fundamental to the Cold War vision of the family, but it was rarely articulated, including in the theological frameworks that *God Bless the Pill* explores. Instead, the model for these families—what made them good, what made them "responsible"—was presumed to be universal. Indeed, much of *God Bless the Pill* will explore the implications of a new Christian theology called "responsible parenthood." The architects of these family structures, as we shall see, were not necessarily deliberately excluding families of color, so much as they were not thinking about them at all. They were not thinking about the particularities of life under systemic racism, or of other kinds of family structures that were not actually or automatically less healthy than the suburban nuclear family. Even when African American leaders such as Martin Luther King Jr. weighed in, they were likely to address structures that prevented African Americans from achieving the idealized family, rather than questioning whether the suburban nuclear family was empirically best.

The ideology or set of ideologies around contraception likewise had little to say about issues of race. But the clergy who advocated for contraceptive access, and who proposed the role that contraception could play in marriage, worked hard to set themselves apart from the eugenicists of the previous generation. While not all of them supported the civil rights movement, many were Freedom Riders or other kinds of liberal Protestants and Jews who were sympathetic to the cause. The kind of family that they centered and held up as ideal, however, was much more available to white people than it was to those of other races. The ideology of responsible parenthood was rooted in middle-class economic status. Middle-class status, or at least the promise of that status in the form of support for education and homeownership, was extended to many members of the white working class via the GI Bill. But the GI Bill did not offer those supports to most Black servicemen and servicewomen. Additionally, US law had long undermined the integrity of African American families, and the ability of African American men to earn enough to support their families. As a result, American Black culture included more matriarchal and extended family structures. Even when Black families were two-parent nuclear families, they were more likely than white families to include two wage-earning parents.[17] Using a racially coded white discourse, these clergymen focused on middle- and upper-class white families to the exclusion of both the poor and those of other races. And in doing so, they created an ideal that they perceived as universal.

In communities of color, this nuclear family structure, and the expansion of birth control for which its proponents advocated, received mixed responses. The possibilities of the small upwardly mobile family did appeal to certain civil rights leaders. Martin Luther King Jr., for instance, saw birth control as a tool that Black couples could use to control their family size, and therefore to lift their families out of poverty. He agreed with his white colleagues and counterparts about the need for population control on the global scale to combat the starvation and war that many feared would come from a rising population. That said, many communities of color were more skeptical of birth control than white people were, for reasons that were embedded in the deep historical connections among birth control, eugenics, and medical experimentation.

Birth Control and Eugenics: An Overview of Medical History

The modern history of birth control is inescapably intertwined with the history of eugenics. In the early twentieth century, eugenics was a respectable field of scientific inquiry, encompassing areas with which modern readers are comfortable, like prenatal care and early childhood nutrition, and areas that modern readers find repugnant, like trying to limit the reproduction of certain races who had been designated less "desirable." Eugenics dealt not only with inherited diseases, physical and mental, as well as diseases that were believed at the time to be inherited, but also with morality, which at the time was believed to be inheritable. In addition, the field included race science, in which traits like morality and intelligence were connected to certain races, and the races were arranged in a racial hierarchy. While there were disagreements about precisely what eugenics should encompass, its basic principles were understood as scientific fact and were embraced by most liberal and progressive thinkers, all of whom thought of themselves as men and women of science.

The birth control movement, by contrast, was much less respectable and well funded than the eugenics movement and was often seen as a cause of radicals and feminists. In an attempt to benefit from the respectability, social credibility, and funding of the eugenics movement, leaders of the birth control movement, including Margaret Sanger, tried to build relationships with its leaders. The birth control leaders had varying degrees of success, because even though many eugenicists were politically progressive, they did not want to be tainted by the perceived radicalism of birth control. Still, the many points of contact between the two movements mean that any history of birth control must address its links to eugenics.

To understand the histories of birth control and eugenics in the United States, and to understand why various American communities have reacted to contraception in a range of ways, one needs an overview of the history of obstetrics and gynecology. First, and perhaps most importantly, the history of obstetrics and gynecology is largely a history of white doctors and scientists experimenting on, dissecting, and otherwise exploiting the bodies of Black and brown women, leading to scientific advances from which the dual forces of sexism and racism prevented these women from benefiting. In the beginning of the twentieth century, the brutal history of gynecology was joined by a new emphasis on the "science" of eugenics, a field that drew support from medicine, public health, and social work, that found support from politicians and philanthropists.

Eugenics came in two forms. Positive eugenics took the form of encouraging "desirable people"—read as white, middle- or upper-class, married, educated, nondisabled—to have more children. Positive eugenics was encouraged by social reformers in the United States and Britain, but also in Germany's Third Reich, where "getting married and having children became a national duty for the 'racially fit.'"[18] Negative eugenics could take the form of tacitly or explicitly discouraging "undesirable" people—read as people with perceived or real genetic predispositions toward physical or mental illness, people with "socially deviant" lifestyles, the poor, immigrants, and people racialized as non-white, or as "lesser" whites—from having children; or it could take the result of state-sponsored birth control or forced or coerced sterilization campaigns. All of these movements have left their mark on twenty-first-century American conversations about reproductive health.

White women were often coerced into having children through restrictions on abortion and voluntary sterilization, so they tended to focus their reproductive health activism, called "reproductive rights," on the right not to have children. Women of color, by contrast, had to fight for the right to have children. They faced the very real threats of medical racism, ranging from denial of their pain and dismissal of their experiences, to lack of access to prenatal care, to forced or coerced sterilization, to being experimented on by medical authorities. At the same time, some men in communities of color, and some racial justice movements, condemned the desire of women of color to control their fertility; these men understood birth control as genocide. In 1994, Black women, with other women of color in alliance, founded the reproductive justice movement to respond to these realities. The movement centered on the right to have children, the right to not have children, and the right "to nurture the children we have in a safe and healthy environment."[19]

In addition, much early funding for birth control research came directly from funders with strong eugenic agendas. Often and particularly before World War II, these agendas represented a desire for healthier babies, a goal that someone like Margaret Sanger certainly shared, and for more white babies, a goal it seems unlikely that Sanger shared. The progressive movement, of which the eugenics movement was a part, was deeply interested in the state taking care of its citizens. For progressives, eugenics, like sanitation, or vaccination campaigns, was another way in which the state could do so. The state, however, was not necessarily interested in the internal desires of its citizens; its attitudes were both patriarchal and rooted in white supremacy.

There are many questions about how to think about the relationship between birth control activists and eugenics. I tend to follow both R. Marie Griffith and Melissa R. Klapper in arguing that most of the birth control activists coming out of white feminist traditions were not specifically hoping to make sure there were fewer babies of color. They were deeply invested in making sure that white women had the ability to control their own fertility; and they assumed that women of color would want the same thing. Women of color, of course, often did want the ability to control their own fertility, but for them, this also meant the freedom to have children. Because women of color, and communities of color, encountered plenty of campaigns based in negative eugenics, they were understandably skeptical, if not always of the technology of birth control, then of its purveyors.[20]

Because of her prominence in the history of the birth control movement, and because of contemporary debates about her reactions to eugenics, people often want to know how Margaret Sanger positioned herself with regard to eugenics. Sanger was deeply interested in giving women, particularly poor women, control over their fertility. She believed correctly that the ability to space out the birth of children would improve maternal and child health. She also believed that having fewer children overall would allow poor families to better focus their resources toward improving the quality of life of the family as a whole. These concerns were part of eugenics and allowed Sanger to make common cause with eugenicists, who were, as previously mentioned, broadly respected in the time period. It is less clear how Sanger understood race in her campaign for there to be fewer children overall.

Those who argued that Sanger did not racialize her mission to bring all women access to birth control point to the fact that when she opened a birth control clinic in Harlem, she hired a Black doctor and had support from community leaders such as W. E. B. Du Bois.[21] Sanger's Negro Project seems to have been founded because Black women were being denied access to New York City health services. But was her goal to give these women agency or to make sure that there were fewer Black babies?[22] Those who argued that Sanger was a proponent of race-based eugenics point to her own writings and to those of W. E. B. Du Bois, who wrote, "The mass of ignorant Negros still breed carelessly and disastrously, so that the increase among Negros, even more than among whites, is from a portion of the population least intelligent and fit, and the least able to rear children properly."[23] Some argue that hiring a Black doctor to run her Harlem clinic and gaining support from people like Martin Luther King Jr. are evidence that Sanger was not racist.[24] Others argue that Sanger hired a Black doctor for his "tractability," saying that his success would depend on his training by white medical professionals. The doctor, in this interpretation, was there to gain the trust of the African American population, but not to affect policy at all.[25]

Additionally, while eugenics certainly had racial dimensions, it also had genetic dimensions. Eugenicists believed that their field would ideally shape the reproductive decisions of white middle- and upper-class couples as well. The American Institute of Family Relations (AIFR) wanted white middle-class couples to become "eugenically literate and reproductively ambitious."[26] Unlike Sanger, who wanted birth control for the "poor" and "diseased," but also so that "respectable" women could enjoy marital relations without fear of pregnancy, organizations like the AIFR proposed more children from the white middle class, presuming that they were otherwise fit.[27] That said, the couples these associations counseled would learn about any prospective hereditary problems in their family trees, and learn to avoid reproducing if they threatened to pass on any mental or physical disease. Eugenics, then, was about race, but not only about race.

What seems safe to say is that Sanger was an extremely complicated figure who favored the self-determination of women, wanted them to be free to enjoy sex, wanted every child to be a wanted child, and wanted to do everything possible to ensure that children would be born healthy.[28] Having worked as a public health nurse, she was particularly aware of the need for birth control among poor communities, and those communities were disproportionally made up of immigrants and people of color. Sanger was also an elitist who did not see the ways that structural racism leads people to what she saw as ignorant or degenerate behavior. While she had African American allies, they were often people who owed much to the politics of respectability. The historical record does not clearly demonstrate whether she was explicitly interested in making sure there were fewer Black babies, or whether she was interested in improving the lot of the poor, a goal that she believed meant fewer babies overall in both Black and white communities. Either way, Sanger was in no way free from the racism of her day. Metaphorically speaking, she was also usually happy to get into bed with eugenicists if she thought they would help her open clinics, whether or not she subscribed to their specific agendas.[29]

That said, Sanger did have some sharp disagreements with eugenicists. While she supported mandatory sterilization for people who she believed lacked mental or moral capacity, she opposed sterilization on the basis of race or class. In her publications, she featured essays by eugenicists, but in doing so, she was largely sharing prominent voices of the day who were writing on birth control. While she absolutely gave voice to those ideas, eugenicists also

Margaret Sanger, birth control activist. From the Margaret Sanger Papers, courtesy of the Library of Congress, Prints and Photographs Division, LC-USZ62-105456.

were extremely wary of Margaret Sanger and did not necessarily want her present at their conferences. They did not want their work to be associated with Sanger's birth control movement because, as is central to my argument in this book, birth control first had to shift to become respectable, and in the heyday of eugenics, that shift had not yet occurred.

Indeed, Sanger courted eugenicists partially because she wanted to make contraception acceptable. But Sanger differed sharply from eugenicists in her beliefs about how fertility should be controlled. Sanger founded the birth control movement because she wanted reproductive control in the hands of women—rather than in the hands of men, perhaps specifically in the hands of their husbands. She sacrificed some control to doctors in order to make contraception respectable, but she was not interested in placing that authority in the state. Meanwhile, eugenicists objected to exactly the agency that birth control placed in the hands of women—who could, once home, take pills or insert a diaphragm, or not. That was why eugenicists generally supported sterilization instead of contraception, and often were happy to put this authority in the state.

During and after the Second World War, the eugenic programs of the Third Reich caused many American progressives to lose faith in the ideals of eugenics, at least in their most extreme forms. While white liberals, including religious liberals, still retained their trust in science and the government, Protestant clergy supporting birth control specifically used the religious language of free will to guard against the dangers of compulsory eugenics. This is not to say that programs with eugenic histories did not continue to shape the American landscape. Rather, whiteness continued to infuse even the most liberal (white) conversations about reproductive health. The people framing and controlling these conversations, however, often understood themselves as working against "bad" eugenics, by which they meant compulsory eugenics. At the same time, they assumed that everyone would share the goals of healthier babies and upwardly mobile families, and they believed that contraception and the family structures of the white middle class were the ways to achieve those goals.

While eugenicists were skeptical of birth control, both because it was not respectable and because it largely placed reproductive agency in the hands of women, Sanger did manage to convince some of them to lend her movement their clout, clout that came in the form of money for clinics and respectability. The linkage between eugenics and birth control would not trouble white women who used it, whether for reasons tied to their ideologies of the family or to their own liberation, sexual or otherwise. Yet it posed a real challenge for communities of color, particularly women, who found themselves navigating their own desire for reproductive agency with communal fears that birth control was essentially a form of genocide.

Within a generation, the ambivalence of the African American community toward birth control would sometimes shift to become opposition. In 1962, the Urban League, which had cooperated with Sanger and the Birth Control Clinical Research Bureau to open the Harlem clinic, withdrew its support for contraception.[30] Even more dramatically, in 1967 the Black Power Conference in Newark, New Jersey, proclaimed that birth control was "Black genocide." Later that year, a crowd of Black protesters chanted "genocide" as they burned down a birth control clinic in Cleveland.[31] By 1972, according to the *American Journal of Public Health*, 40 percent of African Americans believed that birth control clinics were part of a drive to eliminate the Black population, a distrust that blurred the lines between abortion and contraceptive access and coerced sterilization.[32] When asked specifically about birth control itself, rather than about clinics, which were often run by white people, Black women supported contraception at a rate of about 80 percent and used it at a rate of about 75 percent. At least for Black women, then, the issue was distrust of clinics rather than disapproval of contraception.[33]

This dynamic highlights the dilemma that often faced Black women as they navigated patriarchy within Black communities, where birth control could be used to increase the possibility for sexual pleasure and personal agency, and also as a tool of oppression. This contrast also highlights the ways in which Black feminists have found themselves at odds with several groups. They battled with Black men who often not only feared the eugenic aspects of contraception, but also, like white men, noticed and appreciated the ways contraception could erode patriarchal structures in the community. Further, Black feminists battled with white feminists who were likely to support contraceptive agency in their own lives but to support contraceptive coercion in the lives of Black women.

What we can see here is a very real set of questions. To what extent were birth control clinics set up in Black neighborhoods to give Black women access to birth control a civil rights issue; and to what extent were they set up there for negative eugenic reasons? This dynamic, the question of expanding access or promoting negative eugenics, has animated how both activist and scholarly worlds have understood the birth control movement. At times, activist groups have come up with creative solutions to ensure that Black women can have access to contraception without relinquishing control to white power structures. For instance, when the Black Panthers reversed their position on birth control, they began to frame it, along with abortion, as an important part of women's liberation; but they still firmly opposed sterilization, abortion, and contraception when coerced. The answers are complicated: White feminists often wanted to be in alliance with women of color but were unwilling to listen to them or to examine their own racism. The birth control movement and the eugenics movement were distinct, and while they overlapped in many places, they also had moments of sharp tension.

Conflating birth control and eugenics has several risks. First, it is simply incorrect to equate all white birth control activists with eugenicists, and when we do that, we flatten out much of what was racially complicated and problematic about their work. This book, in many ways, is an attempt to explore birth control activists who were deliberately distancing themselves from eugenicists, but whose vision of the family was still deeply tied to white supremacist and patriarchal notions of the family. These birth control advocates put forward a culturally specific notion of the family that they saw as universal. They therefore failed to understand how communities of color were structurally undercut as they tried to reach this ideal and were pathologized for realities outside their control. These activists also did not see that those communities had created other family structures that were different but not, by definition, lesser. I write with the hope that in seeing how these men—and they were largely men—could set themselves against race-based eugenics while still not interrogating how they were perpetuating racist structures, readers will examine their own assumptions and limits.

In addition, when we equate birth control technologies with eugenics, rather than seeing them as tools often developed in exploitative contexts that do not have to be exploitative, we give weapons to those who would like to roll back not only the problematic aspects of birth control, but also its liberatory aspects. Anti-choice organizations put up signs in predominantly Black neighborhoods that frame abortion as genocide. These groups are often not invested in undercutting structural racism; they are simply mobilizing the fears born out of structural racism to undercut the rights of women. They also have in mind a particular vision of the ideal family—nuclear, white, and middle-class—and are actively involved in other political activity that undercuts not only the liberation of women, but the liberation of people and communities of color in the United States.

Birth Control and Regulation

The contemporary history of birth control is a history of regulation. This had not been the case in many other historical moments, including in the American colonies, and in the United States up through the middle of the nineteenth century. In the pages that follow, we will explore the contemporary regulation of birth control, and we will explore the purposes that are served by that regulation. Contraception will become scientific so that it can be regulated by men of medicine. It will become moral so that its use can be guided by clergy. It will be a tool through which society can regulate families, upward mobility, and the global population—through which there is the hope of controlling both famine and war. It will become a weapon in the fight against communism.

All of these topics appear in the primary source material for this book. What is often absent from that material, however, is the fact that birth control can regulate these aspects of life and society by regulating women's bodies. Over the course of the twentieth century, many new forms of birth control would be developed and popularized: the diaphragm and the cervical cap, the birth control pill, the intrauterine device, contraceptive implants, and the morning-after pill. None of the major contraceptive advances of the twentieth century feature male bodies. The condom has a longer history dating at least to ancient Egypt, where men wore linen sheaths, and perhaps more effectively to ancient Rome, where they created sheaths out of bladders.[34] Each of the twentieth century's birth control technologies, however, worked by acting on the body of a woman, and while they were tools with immense potential for political freedom, they also created a new site for the regulation of women's bodies.

For thought leaders in the middle of the twentieth century, it was through regulation of women's bodies that society could achieve its big goals: conquer famine, end war, win the Cold War. To put it in religious terms, this regulation allowed man and the women he regulated to fulfill the biblical commandment to be good stewards of the earth, making sure not to overly tax its resources with too many people. It was also by making a woman's body sexually desirable and controlling her reproduction that she and her husband could have a satisfying sex life, one that would secure their homes from communist threats and ensure a healthy and stable home for their children, ensuring their upward mobility.

This, too, had a Judeo-Christian valence. In this era, Protestants and some Catholics spoke compellingly about marriage as the relationship on earth that allowed couples to best emulate Christ. They increasingly emphasized, rather than downplayed, the importance of the sexual element of marriage, and coupled this new emphasis with a theology of "responsible parenthood," a term chapter 2 will explore in depth. Responsible parenthood contended that it was fundamental to Christian marriage for a couple to prayerfully decide how many children they should bring into the world without straining their own or society's resources. Birth control ushered in a new moral arena for Christian marriage. Jews, meanwhile, came to publicly assert the modern qualities of their ancient religion by pointing out that Jewish texts had long pointed to both the value of sex in marriage, and the permissibility of birth control as a tool to guard maternal and infant health. Birth control, in this framing, was and had always been an inherently Jewish value.

One of the ironies of this history is that, while all of these things are done through the regulation of women's bodies, the actual women—their hopes, their dreams, and even their bodies—are remarkably absent from the discourses around contraception. In this way, women become an absent referent.[35] This very absence is, of course, part of what allows their bodies to be posed as the answer to so many social and familial ills. Because of the absence of women's voices in much of the archival material that I use, I have turned to popular culture and literature to attempt to peer into the voices and experiences of women. I have hoped that these printed materials will give us insight into how women's perspectives were imagined in the public discourse at the time.

In discussing this project over the course of my research, many women have shared their birth control stories with me. I have heard stories about women who lost control of spring-loaded diaphragms while attempting to insert them in dorm bathrooms, such that the diaphragm skidded across the floor for all the women in the bathroom to see. I have heard about women who chose to use the diaphragm because they wanted to do something "more natural" than the artificial hormones of the birth control pill, only to realize that the diaphragm meant smelly, poisonous spermicidal jelly. Women who lived through the early years of the Pill have told me that it made them feel liberated; perhaps more of these women have said that birth control did not make them feel liberated. Rather, it made it harder to say no to sex, and became yet another way in which all of the labor of the relationship fell to them. In other words, I have heard stories of birth control as a tool of feminist and sexual liberation, and birth control as a tool of the heteropatriarchy. Ultimately, I decided that including the accounts of women's affective experiences with religion and contraception would make this book unwieldy and would tell a slightly different story from this one. I hope that I, or someone else, will one day write that book.

God Bless the Pill details this history of the role of religions in the shaping of contraceptive ideology and practice across four chapters. Chapter 1 thinks about how religious leaders moved birth control into the mainstream in the years immediately after World War II. Chapter 2 examines how advances in birth control technology, particularly the FDA approval of the birth control pill in 1960, created "responsible parenthood," a new venue of moral action for American couples, particularly Protestant ones; and it addresses Catholic and Jewish responses to those new moral arenas. Chapter 3 looks outward at how responsible parenthood shaped the American imagination of what the developing world might want or need. Chapter 4 analyzes the backlash that arose against contraception in the 1970s and 1980s; it explains why, after several decades of expansion of contraceptive rights under a religious coalition, religious groups increasingly became opposed to contraception.

A Note on Terms

In writing a history of contraception in the twentieth century, it is hard to know what terms to use to describe the actors. I write in a moment when we are more attuned than ever in recent memory to the reality that cis women are not the only people with the capacity for pregnancy and that not all women are able to become pregnant. As an activist and an advocate for reproductive health care, I support the use of language that highlights the diversity of bodies and gender identities that need care around supporting or preventing pregnancy. As an historian keyed into the rhetoric of the long twentieth century, I have opted to use the term "women." I do this because the story about contraception in the twentieth century is a story about the regulation of bodies in relation to a heterosexual and patriarchal family structure. The regulation of bodies that might bear children was about the regulation of women—as objects of male sexual desire, potentially as bodies with their own heterosexual desire, only to be acknowledged and nurtured in the context of marriage, and as wives and mothers, under a patriarchy. The discourses that I am analyzing are about people who were called and understood themselves to be "women"—or rather, as noted above, discourses that are bizarrely about everything other than women. Using the words "woman" and "women" underscores the worldview in which this history operates, and to do otherwise would likely obscure it. For that reason, I tend to use the language of women, as would have been used by my historical actors. I invite my readers, however, to keep in mind the implications of these discourses for the full range of people with the capacity for pregnancy.

The Diaphragm Debates

The history of the diaphragm dramatizes how religion regulates sexuality. This regulation is not only about the "conservative" kind of religion that represses sex and sexuality. It is also about a collection of liberal theological arguments that shape how people understand what is proper with respect to sexuality and conception. In the mid-twentieth-century United States, religious perspectives on contraception included not only Catholic theological proscriptions, but also Christian and Jewish arguments about how contraception could be a good—even godly—part of sexuality if properly regulated.

Taken together, these religious voices show how clearly the disciplinary technology of the diaphragm was only acceptable within the context of marriage. The diaphragm was one of the first contraceptive technologies that required a fitting in a medical office, and it quickly became clear that contraception would be more morally and religiously acceptable if it was regulated by the medical establishment. This meant that many early regulatory questions and debates about morality focused on the diaphragm: Who was entitled to the diaphragm? What sort of process did women need to undergo to get access to the diaphragm? And what did having a diaphragm say about them? As the public conversation demonstrates, the answer to these questions of access and meaning depended heavily on the social positioning of the specific women in question. These conversations demonstrate that the diaphragm and its acceptability were firmly linked to marriage, such that liberal clergy could present contraception as functionally a marital and medical right that should not be limited by class. That said, the less affluent the married woman, the more she would be subjected to medical scrutiny in her desire for contraception.

While clergy were preoccupied with getting married women access to contraception regardless of their economic status, popular fiction addressed the question of what contraception meant in the lives of unmarried women. Fiction demonstrates that the linkage between birth control and marriage proved to be so strong that the decision to acquire a diaphragm could take on a veneer of commitment more significant even than the decision to have sex itself. These fictional depictions, as well as the public record of political debate over diaphragms, make clear that the diaphragm was used by unmarried women as well—but not without potential penalty. Examining popular accounts of single women using contraception gives us insight into some of the stigma and significance that the diaphragm took on in the cultural conversation of the late 1950s. Accessed through the medical establishment, the diaphragm had become an acceptable tool for improving marriage and health. It also became a talisman of marriage for the unmarried, all the while shadowed by shame and coercion.

The diaphragm was not the only form of contraception available in the first half of the twentieth century, but it was one of the only forms of contraception that required medical supervision—a reality that created a double bind.[1] The fact that doctors acted as gatekeepers to the diaphragm made the diaphragm respectable. Other contraception might be pornographic, but the diaphragm was scientific. The fact that doctors supported the diaphragm made it possible for clergy to support it, at least for married couples, thus increasing its respectability. On the other hand, this respectability excluded the unmarried, and accessibility was not to be taken for granted for lower-income or non-white women. For these groups, the rhetoric around and scrutiny embedded in contraception increased feelings of shame and made access difficult, regardless of how contraception was framed for married women, and particularly middle-class white women, who could access it through private doctors.

Among religious voices in favor of contraception, particularly in these early debates, there was often agreement between Protestants and Jews, though they tended to place their emphasis in different places. For example, Rev. George Stierwald, assistant rector at St. James Protestant Episcopal Church and president of the East Manhattan Ministerial Association, declared from his pulpit in 1958, "Birth control is Christian." Stierwald spoke as part of a campaign, conducted largely by the Protestant and Jewish clergy of New York, in support of doctors who hoped to be able to prescribe contraception in public hospitals. Protestants like Stierwald argued decisively for sex as a moral good in marriage, regardless of its role in procreation. As Stierwald proclaimed, "The sex act is one of the greatest treasures of marriage, irrespective of its purpose of pregnancy. Therefore, parents who in Christian conscience wish to plan their family may use contraceptive methods or devices in their sex relation and secure the other great spiritual benefits without involving conception."[2] This sort of marital sex positivity was largely a new thing to hear from the Protestant pulpit.

For Jewish colleagues, the benefits of marital sexuality had been expressed for somewhat longer. The Jewish conversation around contraception was often framed in terms of members of a minority religious tradition protecting their ability to practice their own religion without governmental regulation. But leaders also understood that Jewish thought itself was likely to hold little sway with the public. As a result, Jewish leaders tended to lean into the rhetoric of public good. Long before Steirwald's comments, in 1915, Sidney Goldstein, associate rabbi at the Free Synagogue, framed birth control as a moral issue. He based his argument on a stated interest in the "health, morals, and general welfare" of the public, the moral good of voluntary motherhood, and the argument that birth control would not lead to sexual immorality. He did not make his argument based in Jewish law.[3] But while each group leaned harder into one or another aspect of the argument, Protestants and Jews generally agreed: Marital sex was good regardless of procreation. Birth control made that kind of sex possible, and it was a scientifically valid aspect of contemporary medical care. To deny doctors the right to follow medical best practices, or women and families the medical advances made possible by science, would be a violation of rights. By declaring contraception a religious good, these clergymen were both making a moral statement and staking out access to contraception as an issue of separation of church and state.

Clergymen were free to declare access to contraception a moral good because they could link it to another source of authority increasingly gaining in status: science. Clergy built alliances with the physicians trained in these scientific forms of contraception. By advocating for birth control as part of medical best practice, Clergy could advance goals of marital stability through sex, middle-class child-rearing practices, and separation of church and state. Doctors could gain respectability and moral authority from the support of clergy.[4] These (usually male) doctors were vocally supportive of contraception for married couples, a stance that they articulated in terms of the positive role of sex in marriage, the need to control population growth, and the rights of doctors and patients to offer medical advice and make medical decisions based on their own religious rights.

Placing contraception in the realm of both science and regulation, however, opened it up to politics—and in the United States, religion has a complicated relationship with politics, particularly when political issues touch on sexuality and therefore morality. There were debates about birth control in which religion took an active part, but they did not look like the conservative religious rhetoric of today. These were debates about contraception, including whether it was a medical best practice, whether the objections of the Catholic Church mattered, and which Protestant and Jewish opinions had traction. But even when clergy and science worked together to make access to the diaphragm respectable, they caused other consequences that foreshadow ongoing debates about birth control.

The medical and clerical surveillance that made the diaphragm respectable also opened up the possibility of shame, especially for unmarried women. They had to be willing to have sex, to plan for sex, to talk about sex, and to acknowledge sex in front of authority figures, in the face of a rhetoric that framed them as "naughty girls." In addition, when one had to see a doctor to access birth control, one needed funds—unless one could go to a public hospital. But the medical practices of public hospitals, which depended on taxpayer dollars, were subject to much more public scrutiny than their far more expensive private counterparts. Poor women, then, even respectably married mothers, had to expose themselves and their sex lives to scrutiny, often by more than one doctor, in order to access the diaphragm. Just who would feel this coercion and shame is a question that will be explored extensively in later chapters; but here we see that such feelings are, on some level, rooted in the intertwined and co-constituting nature of science and religion.[5]

The History and the Technology of the Diaphragm

Like so much in the history of contraception, the diaphragm in its modern form came to the United States largely through the efforts of the nurse and contraceptive activist Margaret Sanger.[6] Sanger's 1925 claim that that Holland-Rantos, a company funded by her husband, was the first company to manufacture the "spring type" diaphragm, was exaggerated. But Sanger was largely responsible for making the diaphragm respectable. She destigmatized the technology by medicalizing it, bringing it into the (largely male) realm of doctors and medical science, and out of the informal networks of women—the midwives, mothers, and older sisters who had long been the carriers of birth control knowledge.[7]

It was not a foregone conclusion that medicalizing birth control would destigmatize it. For instance, medicalization did not remove the stigma of AIDS, and it has inconsistently affected public attitudes toward addiction and mental health. Medicalization, however, did reshape birth control, likely for several reasons. First and foremost, in removing birth control from the realm of women and giving it instead to the realm of medicine, gatekeeping increased. Doctors were very effective gatekeepers, and medicalization meant that birth control could only be accessed by people having sex in the socially approved context of marriage. This move also shifted contraception from the arena of home remedies to science. Contraception was incorporated into medicine at a moment in which society was particularly invested in the potential of science to create modernization. This act of moral gatekeeping placed doctors in the position of doing a kind of theological work—ensuring that contraception was not allowed to undermine the social standards for sexual behavior.

The fight for medicalization was not an easy one. Before 1915, Sanger's activism had focused on women helping other women to access contraceptives and contraceptive information. This informal network took place in a range of settings, and often without the intervention of doctors. Throughout the nineteenth century, pessaries, devices that fit into the vagina for contraceptive and other purposes, had been available commercially in the United States. But the 1873 Comstock Act classified birth control as obscenity. That move made contraception disrespectable contraband, a move that effectively blocked birth control from being part of public health campaigns, though use of contraception continued, particularly among women with access to private physicians.[8] The move from obscenity to approved medical practice made it much more possible to discuss contraception in terms of public health, but also had very concrete ramifications: As we shall see, Sanger's birth control clinics were closed down by police until she got doctors on staff, and it was only when the US Court of Appeals reclassified pessaries as medical equipment rather than obscenity that they could be easily and legally shipped through the mail. If this process of medicalization removed much of the moral stigma of contraception for married women, it did so by adding a degree of moral control and replaced the surveillance of obscenity police with the surveillance of doctors.

In 1915, Sanger traveled to Holland, in part to work with Aletta Jacobs, a doctor and birth control activist. Unfortunately, because Aletta Jacobs believed so strongly that only doctors should prescribe diaphragms, she would not meet with or train Sanger.[9] Instead, Sanger studied with one of her colleagues, Dr. J. Rutgers, from whom she learned the details of how to fit a diaphragm. Sanger later wrote of the experience: "From Dr. Rutgers I learned much of the complexities of the technique of contraception. . . . Under his tutelage, I began to realize the importance of individual instruction for each woman if the method advised was to benefit her. Fortunately, my knowledge of anatomy and physiology stood me in good stead for learning this quickly. To my surprise, I found over fifteen different kinds of devices in use as contraceptives, and fourteen sizes of the diaphragm, or Mensingar pessary, adopted and generally recommended."[10] Jacobs held the firm opinion "that it was not for 'laymen' to interfere in this work; it was a doctor's subject, and only professional men and women should take it up," and the experience of training with Rutgers led Sanger to believe that contraceptive technology was best left in the hands of doctors.[11]

While many professions make distinctions between professionals and amateurs, frequently referred to as "laymen," the root of the "lay" metaphor is religious. It is worth lingering for a moment on that metaphor, because here Jacobs's comment serves to link doctors with the clergy. Just as the examining room becomes like the confessional (or the ministerial or rabbinic study) as a place of potential shame, judgment, or acceptance, so the doctor becomes clergyman, a term that I am purposefully gendering. Although, as Dr. Aletta Jacobs demonstrates, women were among the ranks of both clergy and medical doctors, they were few and far between. It was in this space that women would have to submit both their bodies and their rationale for wanting birth control to examination by medical gatekeepers. These doctors, just like clergy, were charged with making sure that women had "moral" and "responsible" reasons for desiring contraception. This association with clergy, however subconscious it might have been for Jacobs and for Margaret Sanger, was important, as we shall see in the case of the alliance between doctors and clergy that would arise in the much-watched New York City diaphragm debates of 1958.

By the time of those debates, the form of the diaphragm had changed and developed significantly. In the 1950s, the version that was most commonly available in the United States was the spring diaphragm.[12] It was a latex or rubber shield or dome that was inserted into the vagina and held in place over the opening of the cervix by a coated spring, the front of which rested behind the pubic bone. Before the diaphragm was inserted, it was filled with spermicide. After sex, the diaphragm remained in place until the spermicide had enough time to kill all of the sperm present in the semen.

The diaphragm required a fitting by a medical professional because using the wrong size could be uncomfortable or ineffective. While the other most common forms of cervical cap did not need fitting and were simple to insert, the diaphragm required measurements of body parts that women had often not seen themselves and as much as forty-five minutes of instruction before they could take the object home and use it. The spring diaphragm, as opposed to other available forms of contraception, therefore required a kind of professional contact, rendering it a form of contraception associated with the male medical world and therefore with science, respectability, and authority—including the authority of the (equally male) clergy.

Sanger's decision to push for a method of contraception that would remain in medical hands had two ramifications: It became medical, and it became respectable, both of which are extremely important for understanding the acceptability and accessibility of the diaphragm. Historian of contraception Andrea Tone notes that Sanger wrote to Clarence Gamble—doctor, birth control advocate, and eugenicist—that her "greatest achievement" was "to keep the movement strictly and sanely under medical auspices."[13] Tone argues that it was this achievement that made (this form of) contraception respectable. Sanger's own experience demonstrated that medical oversight was central to making contraception widely available. As a nurse, she had been trained by Dr. Rutgers to fit women for contraception. But her clinic, opened in 1916, was forcibly closed the same year. A court decision allowed her to reopen in 1918, with "medical supervision," which was to say, a doctor.[14] This decision represented a major step in rendering contraception legal.[15]

But the full legality of contraception was not clinched until December 7, 1936, when the US Court of Appeals for the Second Circuit ruled in Sanger's favor in United States v. One Package of Japanese Pessaries. In 1932, US Customs had confiscated a package of 120 rubber pessaries sent to Sanger by Dr. Sakae Koyama of Osaka, Japan, with the idea that she would test them through her Birth Control Clinical Research Bureau. The case, which was tried by Sanger's attorney Morris Ernst while she was in India, addressed all objects banned by the Comstock Act of 1873. The Comstock Act, Judge Augustus Hand argued, banned material that was to be used for "immoral purposes." It did not ban specific objects—therefore, if the objects were not intended for immoral purposes, they were acceptable. "[Congress's] design, in our opinion, was not," Hand wrote, "to prevent the importation, sale, or carriage by mail of things which might intelligently be employed by conscientious and competent physicians for the purpose of saving life or promoting the wellbeing of their patients."[16]

As Ernst, whose practice focused on civil liberties law, noted, "Nowhere in its opinion did the Court specifically state under what circumstances a doctor was free to prescribe a contraceptive."[17] As far as he was concerned, "the inference was clear that the medical profession was to be sole judge of the propriety of a prescription in a given case, and that as long as a physician exercised his discretion in good faith the legality of his action was not to be questioned."[18] *United States v. One Package of Japanese Pessaries* effectively ended the Comstock Act's restrictions on contraception—as long as contraception itself could not be seen as immoral. The case was also a significant step in defanging the Comstock Act altogether, such that by the late 1950s the influential law was no longer a dominant part of the New York landscape.[19] But the difference between not being pornographic and being respectable was still huge. Medicalizing contraception was central to it becoming the latter. ´

Sanger's fight for birth control and birth control activists to be seen as respectable was vitally important because, throughout the first half of the century, they were seen as anything but. As demographers and eugenicists established their scientific bona fides in the 1930s and 1940s, they actively distanced themselves from the birth control movement, which they saw as overly feminine, with a discourse written chiefly in sentimental terms. They excluded birth control advocates from their scientific conversations in part by depicting these largely women-led movements as "troublesome amateurs and propagandists."[20] Involving doctors and clergy in advocating for birth control moved it away from these women-led networks, and brought birth control more clearly into the realm of demography and social engineering.[21] The respectability lent by the involvement of male doctors also proved necessary in moving contraception into the mainstream.

But this newfound respectability came at a cost. The diaphragm's connection to the medical profession made it more difficult for women, particularly poor women, to access, in part because of the shortage of public clinics and in part because of cost, which in the 1930s ran between four and six dollars for the device and a single tube of contraceptive jelly.[22] The exam and additional spermicide added to the cost. As a result, there was a major class gap between those who could use the diaphragm and those who could not. By the 1940s, the diaphragm was the form of contraception most recommended by doctors.[23] And yet, a 1947 survey showed that while the diaphragm was used by 27 percent of middle-class couples, only 2.7 percent of lower-class couples did so.[24] Birth control advocates continued to push for easily accessible contraception, which they saw as an issue of equity. Wealthy women could and already did access contraception through private doctors. Medical professionals and clergy wanted all women to have that level of access.

The key to expanding access to birth control was increased respectability. By the late 1950s, when New York City debated making the diaphragm available in public hospitals, most of the effects of the Comstock Act had been repealed throughout most of the United States.[25] The diaphragm was fully legal in New York, where it was, if not precisely uncontroversial, at least understood to be part of a scientifically valid and legitimate practice of reproductive medicine.

It is important to recognize that Margaret Sanger and the Protestant and Jewish clergy who supported making contraception available were for the most part not invested in positive and negative eugenics, in attempting to foist reproductive technology on poor women so as to prevent them from reproducing while trying to convince middle class and wealthy women to have many children. But as we will see in the next chapter, their desire to frame contraceptive use as an arena of moral agency was problematic in ways tangentially related to eugenics. The desire on behalf of doctors and clergy for equity in birth control access was still rooted in particular values around population control, marriage, and families. Medical and religious leaders wanted contraception to be managed. They wanted it to be available, yes, but only to married women. Married women, it was assumed, would use contraception to plan their pregnancies. Those planned pregnancies, it was likewise assumed, would encourage the creation of particular kinds of middle-class homes. This class-bound regulatory project would rest, as we shall see, unevenly: on the (public) discourse of men and the (private) bodily labor of women.

Religious Responses to Contraception

As Margaret Sanger fought to make birth control accessible, often aligning herself with the respectability of doctors, Protestants and Jews were also beginning to encourage the use of contraception, at least within particular contexts. Although mainline and liberal Protestant denominations had issued statements on ideal Christian family life since the early decades of the twentieth century, before 1930, only one Christian religious body in Europe or North America appears to have formally sanctioned birth control: the New York East Conference of the Methodist Episcopal Church.[26]

Episcopalians had condemned contraception on at least two occasions in the early twentieth century. At the 1908 Lambeth Conference of the Anglican Communion, it was decided with minimal debate that "the Conference regards with alarm the growing practice of the artificial restriction of the family, and earnestly calls upon all Christian people to discountenance the use of all artificial means of restriction as demoralizing to character and hostile to national welfare."[27] Episcopalians echoed this sentiment in 1920, stating: "We utter an emphatic warning against the use of unnatural means for the avoidance of conception, together with the grave dangers—physical, moral and religious—thereby incurred, and against the evils with which the extension of such use threatens the race." Yet they also acknowledged that there might be exceptions, which they called "abnormal cases," and this time, the decision required considerable debate.[28] At least initially, twentieth-century Protestant denominations reacted to contraception on a continuum from skeptical to disapproving.

But within a decade, the Protestant consensus on contraception was starting to shift, even among the Episcopalians who, in the Lambeth Conference's 1930 statement on contraception, shifted their position to what might be best described as limited permission. They noted that "where there is clearly felt moral obligation to limit or avoid parenthood," couples must use "Christian principles" to decide on the best method of birth control.[29] The bishops expressed a preference for "complete abstinence from intercourse" as the "primary and obvious method . . . in a life of discipline and self-control lived in the power of the Holy Spirit." Despite this strong preference for abstinence, they acknowledged that "in those cases where there is such a clearly felt moral obligation to limit or avoid parenthood, and where there is a morally sound reason for avoiding complete abstinence, the Conference agrees that other methods may be used, provided that this is done in the light of the same Christian principles."[30] This provisional acceptance of birth control did not mean that all reasons for using birth control were legitimate. The conference ended its statement with "its strong condemnation of the use of any methods of conception control from motives of selfishness, luxury, or mere convenience."[31] The Episcopalians had come around on birth control, but in very limited ways.

While the Lambeth acceptance of birth control was far from a ringing endorsement, it did seem to open a floodgate among Protestants and, as we shall see, prompted backlash from the Catholic Church. In 1931, the Committee on Marriage and Home of the United States Federal Council of Churches declared "the careful and restrained use of contraceptives by married people" to be "valid and moral" if used to "safeguard the health of the mother and child" and protect "the livelihood and stability of the family."[32] No direct action came from this statement, but it prompted much public debate, and it represented a shift from a commonly held Protestant condemnation of contraception. That same year, the Congregational Christian General Council declared that it favored "the principle of voluntary childbearing, believing that it sacramentalizes the physical union and safeguards the well-being of family and society." The use of the word "sacramentalize," only a year after Lambeth, strikes a very different tone from the Anglican Communion's grudging acceptance of contraception, and it points to the start of a Christian conversation that sees birth control as an active good in Christian family life.

Soon, the Philadelphia Yearly Meeting of Friends (the Quakers) "stressed the importance of approved contraception for freedom and spontaneity in the sex relation, often injured by fear of pregnancy, and for family welfare and health through the spacing of children."[33] In 1946, the General Convention of the Protestant Episcopal Church drew connections between "the proper conveyance of medical information" and "more wholesome family life, wherein parenthood may be undertaken with due respect for the health of mothers and the welfare of their children."[34] In 1947, the Evangelical and Reformed General Synod affirmed "in the interest of a more stable family . . . the right of married persons to all appropriate medical aid in the wisest planning of their families."[35] The Protestant churches' support for birth control was becoming increasingly clear. That support was contingent on contraception being used in the context of family life and, when it was necessary, according to the best medical advice.

By 1958, even the bishops of the Lambeth Conference had changed their tune and issued a statement that no longer declared birth control to be avoided unless absolutely necessary. They still saw the decision to use contraception as weighty, writing that "it must be emphasized once again that family planning ought to be the result of thoughtful and prayerful decision."[36] Given that, however, "Christian husbands and wives need feel no hesitation in offering their decision humbly to God with a clear conscience."[37] Unconcerned with the means of contraception that a couple might use, saying that these decisions were "matters of clinical and aesthetic choice," the clerics noted that "scientific studies can rightly help, and do, in assessing the usefulness of any particular means; and Christians have every right to use the gifts of science for proper ends."[38] To do this, the Anglican bishops asserted, was responsible parenthood "built on obedience to all the duties of marriage, requiring a wise stewardship of the resources and abilities of the family as well as a thoughtful consideration of the varying population needs and problems of society and the claims of future generations."[39] Within the space of fifty years, then, contraception had moved from something that was either unacknowledged or condemned by much of the Protestant mainstream to something that was actively endorsed as an arena for prayerful and responsible decision-making.

Sociologist Melissa J. Wilde has argued that the shift these denominations made regarding birth control was almost completely motivated by eugenic concerns, pointing out that their periodicals were almost exclusively preoccupied with getting contraception into the hands of the poor. That meant, at first, promoting birth control to poor European immigrants—who were generally classified as "lesser" whites in the eugenic logic of the late nineteenth and early twentieth centuries—and eventually to non-white populations.[40] But the story is more complicated than that. While Wilde is correct that most denominations did not come to their support for birth control for feminist reasons, and while certainly many of the attitudes expressed by their leaders were deeply paternalistic, Wilde overstates their dedication to both positive and negative eugenic programs. The clergy themselves, as we shall see in the next chapter, specifically decried state-sponsored eugenics. Indeed, their own child-rearing and marriage manuals do not mention contraception, but generally suggest an expectation of approximately 3 children. This makes sense, as the average national birthrate for white women was 3.56 children in 1900 and 2.51 children in 1930, down from more than 6 children on average a century before.[41] White middle-class women had long been using birth control to limit their family size. What was distinctive about the early decades of the twentieth century was that these women's clergy had begun to endorse and even promote that behavior.[42]

Traditionally, Jewish culture placed a very strong emphasis on family life and framed motherhood as the central aspect of women's lives. As a result, one might reasonably expect that many Jewish immigrants experienced tension between these traditional values and their desire to assimilate into an American middle class characterized by a relatively small family size. Sanger's first clinic was located in Brownsville, a neighborhood in New York City that was largely Jewish at the time. But, as historian Melissa R. Klapper writes, most Jewish women "saw birth control not as a rejection of motherhood, but as an improvement upon it."[43] In their eyes, the birth control movement "endowed childbearing with a voluntary, positive spirit with obvious ancillary benefits in terms of health, marital relations, and social mobility."[44] Klapper goes on to note that secular Jewish women were not concerned with the opinions of their male clergy. But even the more "tradition-minded American Jewish women" found support from their clergy, who generally supported contraception if it improved the "lives and well-being of mothers."[45]

Early on in Margaret Sanger's birth control work, she gained support from some progressive rabbis. Sanger reached out to Stephen Wise of New York's Free Synagogue. She also won over Edward Israel of Har Sinai in Baltimore, who testified in favor of birth control at legislative hearings, and encouraged the rabbinical arm of the Reform movement, the Central Conference of American Rabbis, to endorse birth control. Both men used their influence as clergy in testifying to legislators in support of birth control bills in public hearings and in private letters. That said, they initially did so on moral, rather than religious, grounds.[46] Rather than argue publicly that Judaism supported contraception, figures like Sidney Goldstein tended to draw from arguments about population control and improving "health, morals, and general welfare of the public."[47] He also argued strenuously that birth control would not lead women into immorality, and that a low birthrate was a sign of being a highly evolved species.[48] Some of Goldstein's arguments are troubling to us today because of their eugenic cast. But in his early twentieth-century moment, arguing for birth control because it would improve public health was in accord with the commonly accepted scientific understandings of the day, and with the idea that birth control was moral precisely because it would improve public health.

This is not to say that religion was absent from birth control debates. In a 1925 letter to S. Adolphus Knopf, a contraception advocate and eugenicist who was concerned about the implications of women with tuberculosis bearing children, Stephen Wise wrote that although "the teachings of Jewish religion" did not "sanction" birth control, the modern rabbi could argue for contraception on the grounds that "the religion of Israel holds human life to be sacred."[49] In 1936, Rabbi Moses D. Abels helped Margaret Sanger's assistant Florence Rose build an argument for birth control based on Talmudic citations; he simultaneously explained, however, that the Brooklyn Association of Rabbis would not endorse birth control because there were also many Talmudic citations that did not support it. In 1927, Professor Jacob Lauterbach, a Talmud professor at Cincinnati's Hebrew Union College, wrote a paper that established the acceptability of birth control according to rabbinic sources, a paper that would ultimately inform the pro-birth-control positions of the Reform and Conservative movements alike.[50] Jewish leaders acknowledged that not all religious interpretations of Jewish law supported the moral permissibility of birth control, but by the early 1940s, some rabbis nonetheless made their support of contraception official.

The National Clergymen's Advisory Committee of
the Planned Parenthood Federation of America

On February 17, 1943, at the Town Hall Club in Times Square, the Planned Parenthood Federation of America (PPFA) held a dinner to organize its first National Clergymen's Advisory Committee.[51] Planned Parenthood's National Committee on Federal Legislation for Birth Control had reached out to clergy in 1936. That year, the committee members got sixteen clergymen to sign a statement countering attacks by Cardinal Hayes of the Archdiocese of New York; and some clergy had helped with the national educational outreach. The National Committee itself, however, had disbanded in 1936, and there had been no outreach to clergymen since then.

Initially, in 1943, clergy were the recipients of Planned Parenthood outreach rather than being part of the outreach team themselves.[52] According to a letter that Sanger's assistant Florence Rose wrote to Dr. Dwight Bradley, executive director of the Council for Social Action of the Congregational Christian Churches, the hope was that such a committee would "develop among ministers a wider understanding and support of its program, as well as to aid it in offsetting organized opposition on moral and religious grounds."[53] Rose noted that Dr. Bradley had already indicated to "Mrs. Sanger" a willingness to join the project, and included a list of other clergy who had also expressed a "willingness to serve." It was an illustrious list of twenty-two, including such figures as the Reverend Dr. Harry Emerson Fosdick of Riverside Church, perhaps the leading Protestant voice of his era; the Reverend Dr. Robbins W. Barstow, the president of the Hartford Theological Seminary who would, in 1945, go on to be the first executive of the Commission for the World Council Service and, in 1950, a founding staff member of the National Council of Churches; Dr. Algernon Black, leader of the Ethical Culture Society; and prominent clergy from a range of cities including New York, Washington, DC, and Cleveland.[54]

The meeting was attended by four members of PPFA and seven New York City clergy, including specialists in family life: L. Foster Wood, secretary of the Commission on Marriage and the Home for the Federal Council of Churches; Dr. Sidney Goldstein, chairman of the Jewish Institute on Marriage and the Family; William Melish, chairman of the Department of Christian Social Service of the [Episcopal] Diocese of Long Island; and denominational leadership, including Theodore Savage, executive secretary of the Presbytery of New York, and Samuel Cohen, executive secretary of the United Synagogues of America. Also in attendance was a visitor from Massachusetts, the Reverend

Cornelius Trowbridge of Church of the Redeemer in Chestnut Hill, Massachusetts, a suburb of Boston. The group was small but composed of clergy with notable power within their respective hierarchies.

At the meeting, D. Kenneth Rose, national director of the Planned Parenthood Federation, updated the clergy on the advances they had made around acceptance of birth control in medical and public health communities. He then noted that they faced three primary impediments to further progress: "(1) the need for greater public education to interpret and clarify present day medical, legal and public health aspects of Planned Parenthood; (2) the need for more adequate sex instruction to replace attitudes which still regard any subject concerned with sex as inherently indecent or immoral; and (3) Catholic opposition."[55] Rose expressed certainty that the first two challenges could be addressed with "long-range educational efforts," but he framed the Catholic opposition as an immediate problem, about which he invited discussion.

The conversation that ensued did much to set the tone that the National Clergymen's Committee would take over the next two decades. The Reverend Mr. Trowbridge explained that in deeply Catholic Massachusetts, Catholic opposition largely took the form of intimidation of the press and radio, such that "misrepresentation made it practically impossible to get the true facts before the public."[56] Based on his experience, Trowbridge did not think that the best way to approach ministers was to ask them to support public health and oppose their Roman Catholic colleagues. Rather, he argued for "enlisting the interests of clergymen . . . on the basis of their moral responsibility in preserving the family and the home."[57] His assumption was that the committee would get more allies by framing their agenda in positive terms around morality and family life, and that those allies would help combat the Catholic opposition that would naturally arise in response to their public stance.

Rabbi Dr. Sidney Goldstein took a slightly different approach in the meeting, arguing that it was the duty of "ministers" to take a stand that "since birth control is a recognized public health procedure, it is undemocratic for any State or City Health Department to withhold such basic health information."[58] He argued that, rather than be on the defensive with the Catholic opposition, they should force the issue of birth control as a public health service and then, when "Catholic opposition became evident, do everything possible to expose such opposition as a denial of the people's civil liberties as well as a denial of a basic public health service."[59] Goldstein was arguing that Catholics threatened the separation of church and state. Catholic opposition to contraception should not shape public health services through municipal agencies, because to do so was to deny "the people" their rights—a people that presumably included Protestants and Jews, and also any Catholics who did not want to take the stand advocated by the Catholic Church.

The difference of opinion between Trowbridge and Goldstein demonstrates the two primary approaches that would shape the debate over the next fifteen years. Protestants took a moral stance, framing birth control as a way that clergy could help people access the technology they needed to make moral and healthy choices for their families. Jews framed the issue of birth control access in terms of the right to choose the most appropriate and scientifically advanced medical treatment. Both of these perspectives also played out in the remainder of that day's meeting. The committee planned educational outreach to seminaries and religious publications to emphasize the role of birth control in the stability of the home; but they also planned for a basic statement regarding Catholic opposition, should the need arise.

Over the next decade or so, the National Clergymen's Committee vacillated between offensive and defensive stances against the Catholic Church, framed more or less explicitly in terms of religious freedom. There were apparently moments when the committee did try to communicate directly with Catholic organizations with whom they had the shared goal of "family betterment." At least in 1946, when Planned Parenthood sent such material to Catholic Charities, this outreach did not go well. Miss Mary E. Whitehead, the supervisor of the organization's Family Department, was "not at all pleased with the resolutions" that she received from the National Clergymen's Committee, and wrote to its executive director, Guy Emery Shipler, that his ideas were "by no means directed toward the same objectives as my own work." She did not simply mean that she disagreed with his methods. She saw real danger in contraception, writing to him, "I can never agree with you that you are promoting family betterment, in my honest opinion you are fostering a cancerous condition which will do great damage to family life and to America."[60] She closed her letter by informing Shipler that she would destroy any further material that he sent.

The correspondence between Whitehead and Shipler demonstrated that while Planned Parenthood did exhibit anti-Catholic sentiment in its understanding of Catholicism as a major source of opposition to birth control, the organizational leadership was not necessarily wrong about the position of the Catholic Church. As the 1958 New York City battle over diaphragms in public hospitals would demonstrate, this kind of institutional Catholic opposition expressed by Shipler was very real and could create very real barriers to contraception access.

Responses from the Black Churches

Almost from the beginning of the birth control movement, there were fears from some Black voices that contraception would hurt Black communities, concerns that were deeply rooted in a long history of white control over Black reproduction, and of white medical experimentation on Black people. Other people, particularly in leadership positions, tried to position freely chosen birth control as helpful for the betterment of the material conditions of Black life in the United States.[61] These responses to contraception came from social scientists and religious leaders alike.

In the July 1945 issue of the *Negro Digest*, sociologist and Morehouse College professor E. Franklin Frazier wrote an article combating the idea promoted by "self-appointed guardians of the Negro race" that birth control was bad for Black communities.[62] Frazier was the author of *The Negro Family in the United States*, and he would go on to publish *The Negro Church in America* and become the first Black president of the American Sociological Association. He had encountered the logic of Black leaders arguing that because the Black death rate was so high, Black communities needed a similarly high birthrate.[63] But he took objection to these "prophets," who "declare[d] 'our strength lies in numbers, our only salvation!'"[64] To be clear, Frazier did not think that these voices were completely wrong. He agreed that there was far too much death in Black communities due to "disease, poor living conditions, and lack of medical care."[65] In fact, he pointed out that "for every white mother who died in childbirth, there are two Negro mothers who fail to survive," and that "negro babies die at one and a half times the rate of white infants."[66] Forty thousand Black babies, he claimed, were either stillborn or did not reach their first birthday.[67]

This horrific loss of life, Frazier argued, underscored the need to use birth control. He offered an anecdote by way of example: Once, in rural North Carolina, he met a "Negro peasant woman" who had given birth to thirteen children, "as many as the Lord saw fit to send."[68] "Recognizing that life is a rugged business, she fed them solid food in the first week of life to 'toughen their stomachs,'" Frazier stated.[69] Some of her babies were stillborn, and others died in infancy, such that only three survived. Clearly, Frazier argued, this woman would have been better off if she had only had three children or perhaps six, whom she could have spaced out using family planning so as to improve their health and hers. The net number of children would have been the same or higher, and she would have endured much less suffering and loss. For Frazier, then, the "survival and progress of the Negro race depends not upon how many babies are born, but on how many live to become strong, healthy, useful adults."[70] He was not interested in the birthrate so much as in the number of children who lived to adulthood.

That said, Frazier's use of the term "useful" here might suggest a value on some lives or life choices over others, and that interpretation would be fair. He went on to explain that Black thriving depended "on the number of well-trained clear thinking leaders it can develop, not on masses of cheap, unlettered labor to be exploited and cast aside because there are 'so many where that came from.'" His vision of a successful Black community also had to do with stewarding community resources so as to "uplift" the race through increased social mobility and modernization. Birth control was, in Frazier's view, a tool that could better allow Black parents and the African American community to engage in the kind of resource-intensive parenting that had begun in earnest right in this moment, at the close of the Second World War. Like so many other proponents of racial uplift, Frazier was addressing real problems, but the framework and solutions he provided were ultimately based in a model that potentially disempowered the very people he sought to help.[71]

There were some leaders in the Black Protestant community who shared the views reflected in the white mainline. In December 1957, a woman wrote to an advice column that was answered by the Reverend Dr. Martin Luther King in the pages of Ebony magazine. The woman was pregnant, but she said she and her husband already had seven children, and "our four-room apartment is bursting at the seams and living space in Harlem is at a premium."[72] She explained that while she had suggested birth control to her husband, he responded that "when God thinks we have enough children, He will put a stop to it. . . . He says that birth control is sinful."[73] In responding to the letter, King told the woman, "I do not think it is correct to argue that birth control is sinful."[74] He argued that it was not a "religious act to allow nature to have its way in the sex life."[75] Rather, the "natural order" was something to be "guided and controlled," and birth control allowed "rational control" rather than a "resort to chance."[76] For King, as for other clergy of the time, birth control turned reproduction into a site of decision-making, and therefore a site of rational decision-making and moral agency.

King's explanation for why this rational control was necessary offers some insight into why he found birth control necessary, and also demonstrates how theology was informed by the sociology of the time. King was extremely worried about urban living conditions for poor African American communities, a concern that was reflected in this letter. "Changes in social and economic conditions make smaller families desirable, if not necessary. As you suggest,

"FOR THE NEGRO INTELLIGENT GUIDES TO FAMILY PLANNING ARE A PROFOUNDLY IMPORTANT INGREDIENT IN HIS QUEST FOR SECURITY AND A DECENT LIFE" MARTIN LUTHER KING, JR.

Poster for the Planned Parenthood—world population (US). Courtesy of the Library of Congress, Prints and Photographs Division, LC-USZ62-107188.

the limited quarters available in our large cities and the high cost of living preclude such large families as were common a century or so ago," he wrote.[77] Birth control was a tool through which Black families could navigate urban life in poverty and perhaps move the family into the middle class. He also expressed concern for maternal health, if in somewhat coded words, writing that "women must be considered as more than 'breeding machines.'"[78]

The ratio of Black to white maternal mortality rose steadily through the middle of the twentieth century. In 1940 it was 2.4 times higher, in 1950 it was 3.6 times higher, and in 1960 it was 4.1 times higher.[79] King's concern for women facing excessive pregnancies must be understood in the context of this increasing death ratio. Maternal death threatened not only Black women but also, he feared, the stability of the Black family, because it meant that children were growing up in single-parent homes, with stepparents, or with extended families.

King's logic expressed concern for maternal health, reflected the particular concern of a community with high maternal death, and was very much in keeping with American clergy's broader concerns for family stability. But it is important to make a distinction between King's logic on birth control here and feminist concerns for women's agency more broadly. In the same column, he observed that "it is true that the primary obligation of the woman is that of motherhood."[80] For King, the goal of birth control was not to be avoiding motherhood in order to meet other goals. Rather, he stated that "an intelligent mother wants it to be a responsible motherhood—a motherhood to which she has given her consent, not a motherhood due to impulse and to chance."[81] Birth control allowed mothers to marshal the tools of science to be the best mothers possible, and to choose the mode of their motherhood. But in King's vision, while birth control allows women to perfect their maternity, it should not enable them to have purposes outside of motherhood.

The New York City Diaphragm Debates

What I have chosen to call the New York City diaphragm debates became a media phenomenon in the early spring of 1958, leading up to July 16, 1958, when the Jewish Dr. Louis Hellman was denied permission to fit a Protestant woman for a diaphragm in the public Kings County Hospital. The young woman, who remains unnamed in the historical record, was diabetic, and she had already had three pregnancies with two cesarean deliveries.[82] As Hellman would tell the *New York Times*, if she could not receive a "contraceptive device," he would have to sterilize her, as "another pregnancy would endanger her life and the life of the child."[83] There had long been an unwritten policy that the New York City public hospitals did not prescribe or stock any form of contraception. But under pressure from medical societies and other prominent voices, the hospital commissioner, Morris Jacobs, seemed to be wavering in this stance. The question of contraception in public hospitals had been active for several months. Hellman and his patient provided a test case that sparked a campaign spearheaded by religious leaders to make birth control, particularly the diaphragm, available in public hospitals serving the city's low-income women.[84]

Embedded in the debates were, again, parallels between the authority of the doctors and that of the clergy. Earlier that spring, the New York Academy of Medicine questioned Jacobs on whether public hospitals would provide birth control for their patients. On April 11, 1958, he responded: "The care and treatment of patients are the responsibility of the Medical Board. There shall be no interference in proper and accepted therapeutic practices nor intervention in ethical relationships between patient and physician." The relationship between doctor and patient, then, came to echo the relationship between clergy and congregant. The state structured the legal form of the relationship, allowing doctors and clergy a confidential space in which to conduct ethical decision-making, but determining what ethical debates might occur in that private space.[85] When asked for clarification, Jacobs refused to say whether his statement covered contraceptive counseling.[86] Hellman was one of several doctors who told the New York Times that if Jacobs would not say whether they were allowed to prescribe contraception that they deemed ethically and medically appropriate, they would find out by testing him.

Doctors also noted that even if the policy allowed contraceptive counseling, it was not particularly helpful if they could not write prescriptions that could be filled at public hospitals. In May 1958, this was a major question. As the New York Times pointed out, "The purchase of contraceptive supplies with city funds would undoubtedly arouse the opposition of the Roman Catholic Church, whose members constitute a large proportion of the city's taxpayers."[87] The Times was correct to point to the objections of the institutional Church. As of December 31, 1930, the papal encyclical Casti Connubii had prohibited Catholics from using any form of artificial birth control, including the diaphragm. The Catholic leadership of New York underscored this prohibition in 1958, when Monsignor Thomas Flynn, information director for the diocese, told the Times, "The Catholic Church holds that 'any unnatural or artificial method of birth prevention is an immoral practice.'"[88] He went on to observe, "We would certainly be entitled to voice our objections if the city embarked on a program we considered immoral," and he added that the Church "would consider it immoral if the city embarked upon a birth control program."[89] The formal objections of the Catholic Church to birth control in general, and to a city-funded birth control program in particular, were clear.

The question of what the 48 percent of New York City taxpayers who were Catholic would have thought about birth control in the public hospitals, and the use of their tax dollars to pay for it, is less clear. As historian Leslie Woodcock Tentler notes, by the mid-1960s, "probably half of all Catholic wives of childbearing age were, by then, making use of contraception, many with an apparently easy conscience."[90] The fact that approximately half of all married Catholics would be using birth control within a decade suggests that Catholic taxpayers would not have been uniform in their opinions in the late 1950s.

Indeed, during the controversy itself, even some Catholics who disapproved of birth control believed that devices like diaphragms should be available in public hospitals.[91] As "bachelor girl" Terry Edwards, a legal secretary and secretary of the Writer's Guild, told the New York Amsterdam News: "I am against all birth control, as I agree with the Roman Catholic Church groups who find use of artificial contraception immoral. But, since the State of New York has authorized physicians to prescribe and advise contraception, I must disagree with Dr. Jacobs as I feel that this should pertain not only to private agencies, but to city hospitals as well."[92] In other words, many Catholics would prove to be interested in using birth control, even if they were doing so in defiance of official Church teachings. Additionally, even among Catholics who agreed with the Church that birth control was immoral, there were those who felt that, given that it was legal in New York, it should be available in public hospitals. Fears of Catholic objections, however, were cited by the press as the reason that there were no "contraceptive devices" in the hospital storerooms.

The absence of actual contraception from public hospitals, whether or not it was explicitly forbidden for doctors to counsel or prescribe contraception to patients, added another layer of medical surveillance to the process by which women accessed diaphragms and other legal devices. One doctor described this procedure: When he prescribed a contraceptive device, the pharmacy referred the order to the hospital director. The director, in turn, could "[refer] it downtown" to the hospital commissioner's office.[93] Hospital commissioner Morris Jacobs, however, as the *Times* explained, reiterated that there was no formal ban on birth control at the hospitals, but he again refused to say whether he or anyone else would approve those referred prescriptions.[94] So it was unclear whether women would be able to have their public hospital prescriptions filled without going to private clinics that required money. As the public-hospital debate unfolded, it would become clear that if you did not have money, you would be subjected to immense scrutiny—and the more steps there were in the process, the more chances there were to insert scrutiny.

This byzantine process and the prospect of private clinics' involvement in it put poor women in precisely the situation that birth control advocates had been trying to avoid: reinstating financial barriers to access contraception. As Dr. William Vogt, the national director of the Planned Parenthood Federation of America, pointed out, the absence of diaphragms in the public hospitals was thus hugely problematic. He told the *Times* that, even if doctors were allowed to prescribe them, "no program of contraceptive services can be meaningful unless the agency offering it stocks contraceptive materials and supplies for its patients."[95] In other words, even if doctors in public hospitals could write prescriptions for diaphragms, those prescriptions were meaningless unless the hospitals could also provide the contraceptives themselves.

If the debate about writing prescriptions surfaced questions about what advice doctors could give, the question of taxes made the diaphragm itself the subject of contention. Jacobs hoped to reach a compromise position by creating a distinction between the *advice* given to the woman, who could not be forced into using a contraceptive that she did not want, and the *diaphragms*, which, if they were to be stocked in public hospitals, would have to be paid for and supported by an infrastructure made up, in part, of people who did not approve of contraception. He hoped to create space in the hospital policy for doctors in public hospitals to advise non-Catholic patients on contraception, patients who could then be referred to private hospitals to actually receive the fittings and fill the prescriptions for the physical devices. This would allow Protestant and Jewish doctors to provide contraceptive services to Protestant and Jewish patients, since the majority of the leadership in those traditions considered contraception morally acceptable, and sometimes even a moral good. At the same time, Jacobs's plan ensured that tax dollars from Catholics would not be used for the contraceptive devices that were deemed immoral by both the Church and a "large proportion of Catholics in the city."[96]

Jacobs likely hoped that this solution would answer the concerns of his medical colleagues without displeasing his boss, Mayor Robert F. Wagner, who had publicly declared that "he was, as a practicing Catholic, personally opposed to birth control in public hospitals."[97] But as the *Times* pointed out, Jacobs's compromise did not take into account the reality that patients in municipal hospitals were often unable to afford private care. His plan also did not address a question that had preoccupied the press: whether Catholic public hospital staff who disapproved of contraception would still be required by the city to offer contraception advice to Protestant and Jewish patients. If not, would public hospital patients be able to select doctors based in part on religion? The debate clearly, and almost certainly erroneously, assumed that the majority of Catholic doctors would be unwilling to prescribe contraception, and the majority of Catholic patients would not want it. There was no room for the possibility of medical professionals and patients who both considered themselves to be Catholic and would be happy to prescribe or interested in using contraception. Likewise, it was not imagined that people might see their doctors across religious lines, that a Jewish woman might want her Catholic physician to provide contraception.

The delineation of public hospital doctors by religious affiliation also raised the question of control. Doctors were expected to surveil women's bodies and decide whether their reasons for contraception were medically or morally necessary. They were also supposed implicitly to enforce religious teachings and moral codes. Underpinning the assumption that doctor and patient would share a religion was the hope that a doctor could be trusted to enforce religious teachings. Those arguing for contraception in public hospitals were careful not to argue that Catholic doctors should be obligated to prescribe contraception, or that Catholic women should be permitted to use it, but rather that Protestant and Jewish doctors and patients should be allowed to follow the teaching of their own traditions. The debate was an attempt to navigate all of the competing religious needs in play in a way that respected the differences between the formal teachings of Protestants, Jews, and Catholics, in a city where Catholics made up almost half of the population. Assuming that the doctor and patient would share a tradition allowed the doctor and his moral code to serve as a gatekeeper for his patient. This approach did not, however, take in the reality of many public hospital clinics, where a patient got the doctor on duty that day. While this situation would not have posed a problem for Catholic women who did not want contraception, a public hospital would not necessarily have allowed a Protestant, Jewish, or Catholic woman who wanted contraception to select a doctor who was willing, at least in theory, to provide it.

In this formulation, the doctor-clergy alliance represented a formidable alliance of control. It made birth control respectable and available for women, but only if those women were married and only if the doctor approved of their choices. Many people asked how to balance the interests of doctors, the different clergy, and taxpayers. Left unasked was why the women who sought contraception were not being placed at the center of the debate or the decision-making. In all the questions raised around the diaphragm in public hospitals, almost never was the answer that the woman, whose body would bear the consequences of its use, misuse, or absence, should be in control of how she squared the teachings of her traditions with her use of contraception. These questions, of course, were particularly important because public hospitals were for poor and middle-class women. Wealthy women could and did select private doctors who would meet their contraceptive needs.[98]

All this debate played out in the months before the Jewish Dr. Louis Hellman attempted to fit his Protestant patient for a diaphragm on July 16, 1958. In the weeks beforehand, Hellman had followed all the required protocols. He requested permission from the Kings County Hospital executive committee. This chain of approval underscores the element of surveillance braided into debates about the diaphragm—Hellman's patient could not simply ask him for contraception because she wanted to end her childbearing or space it out. Rather, he had to convince a committee that she needed contraception to protect her health. The committee needed to rule on the request—potentially calling Hellman's medical judgment into question, but also foreclosing requests for contraception that were not medically urgent. On July 1, the committee granted permission for the patient in this case.[99] This was unusual, but not unprecedented, and still in line with Jacobs's declaration. Though not standard policy, Kings County Hospital had previously allowed the prescription of therapeutic birth control in cases where there was a medical reason to delay childbearing, but where the couple in question wanted to preserve the option of children in the future.[100]

But at 9:30 in the morning on the day of the fitting, Hellman's supervisor, Dr. Henry Gollance, informed him that Jacobs had forbidden him to proceed, though he did not offer an explanation as to why. Hellman requested that Jacobs put the order in writing. Gollance said that he would telephone Jacobs. Hellman returned to his own office to wait. At 10:15, Gollance called Hellman and said that the ban stood, but that Jacobs would not put it in writing.[101] Why Jacobs would not put the denial in writing remains unclear. Hellman did not fit his patient for a "contraceptive device" that day. One can only speculate that he did not defy the order because he had a bigger plan in mind: the press.

Because this was a deliberate test of a publicly debated policy, Hellman responded to the denial by calling the *New York Times*. The next morning, the paper reported on the situation. As Edith Asbury would later point out, Hellman's "calculated move was the culmination of a campaign spearheaded through the Academy of Medicine to lift the unwritten but definite ban on contraceptive counseling in city hospitals."[102] Very quickly, several medical authorities weighed in. Dr. Alan Guttmacher, then both the director of obstetrics and gynecology at Mount Sinai Hospital and the chairman of the medical committee of the Planned Parenthood Federation of America, told the *Times* that he was "shocked and disgusted" by Jacobs's actions. As he saw it, Jacobs's inaction "dooms patients at the city hospitals to inferior medical care in this all-important area of preventative medicine."[103] Guttmacher, along with his colleagues at the New York Academy of Medicine, made it clear that Jacobs was deviating from best medical practices. Leading physicians affirmed that birth control was not medically controversial, lending weight to the argument that Jacobs was letting his medical decisions be swayed by outside pressures, especially from Catholics.

Outpacing the medical response was the almost immediate religious response. On July 23, a week after Dr. Jacobs forbade Dr. Hellman to provide his patient with a diaphragm, the *New York Herald Tribune* reported that the chairman of the Department of Christian Social Relations for the Protestant Council of the City of New York had telegraphed Jacobs requesting an immediate meeting to communicate the council's disapproval of the ban. Jacobs, however, had declined to meet with him. Note the dates here. The patient was denied her contraceptive fitting on the sixteenth. The story broke in the *New York Times* the next day, the seventeenth. By the time the paper for the twenty-third was typeset, the council had already reached out to Jacobs and been rebuffed.[104]

That extremely tight turnaround time suggests that council members did not need a great deal of internal debate before they announced their position. These were groups who had debated their attitudes toward birth control already. They had moved from seeing it as obscene at the turn of the twentieth century to, one by one, denomination by denomination, issuing statements that allowed for contraception and even framed it as necessary or good. By the time the New York debate took place, they were prepared. The following Sunday, the Reverend Dr. Hampton Adams, minister of the Park Avenue Christian Church, used his 11:00 a.m. sermon to declare that "the health, economic stability, morality, and intelligence of future generations of mankind require that methods of birth control be known and the practice sanctioned."[105] Adams was staking out moral territory. This was not about couples simply wanting consequence-free sex. Although birth control allowed sex that had nonprocreative positive consequences, it also allowed for the creation of physically, economically, and morally healthy and happy homes, which, in turn, created a healthier, happier society, immediately and in the future.

The Unitarians articulated the substance of the Protestant argument. Eleven Unitarian ministers wrote to the Board of Hospitals, asking them to overrule Jacobs because the denial of contraception was "unwise and a denial of the rights of full medical treatment." According to the Unitarians, Jacobs was making a "moral" decision that rightly belonged to the individual patients.[106] Mainline Protestants increasingly understood the use of contraception in marriage as a potential moral good, in part because they valued the idea that a couple would prayerfully decide when to become parents, and to how many children. In this way, the use of contraception allowed a new arena of religious moral decision-making in which the state essentially had, in their view, no right to intervene, either by forcing people to use contraception, or, in this case, by limiting access to contraception for those dependent on public hospitals. In this scenario, birth control was liberating for married couples because it gave them more power to shape the number of children in their families. But with that agency came a host of obligations and moral considerations about vocation and responsibility to society.[107]

While the clergy of many wealthy Protestant pulpits actively supported the fight to get public hospitals to provide contraception, the stakes were higher for clergy whose congregants depended on public hospitals for their medical care. Parenting manuals from many Protestant denominations made the assumption that their readership would have small families of two to four children. Birthrates among the upper classes tended to reflect these trends, with predictable implications for maternal health and labor-intensive parenting. But these advantages, which, as we shall see in the next chapter, were framed as being of great social import, were out of reach for those who could not afford contraception.

The clergy serving working-class congregations used moral language, criticizing the city for denying accepted medical therapy to their parishioners. For instance, the Group Ministry of the East Harlem Protestant Parish found the municipal hospitals' decision to withhold contraception and education about it from impoverished families to be "immoral." Many residents of East Harlem could only afford public hospitals, so the public hospital ban barred them from access entirely.[108] These clergy also may well have been thinking about the economic implications of limiting birth: Perhaps fewer mouths would mean more ability to move out of poverty. In addition, the Interdenominational Ministers' Alliance in Brooklyn, with some 150 members who pastored some 175,000 of Brooklyn's Protestants, including Dr. Hellman's patient, announced on August 15, "The use of medically approved contraceptive devices, practiced in Christian conscience, fulfills rather than violates the will of God."[109] For many of these ministers' parishioners, it did not matter that contraception was legal if it was not available at public hospitals. The unwritten ban created an equity issue, one that limited the ability of low-income Christians to make what their clergy determined to be a godly choice.

If Protestant clergy articulated birth control as an arena of Christian moral agency, Jewish leaders, ranging from the very liberal to the Orthodox, again framed the issue in terms of protecting their rights as a minority religious tradition. The Orthodox Rabbinical Alliance explained to the press that Orthodox Judaism permitted contraception only when it was practiced by a married woman, for health reasons, after consultation with both medical and religious authorities. Even with all of those conditions, the alliance objected to Jacobs's policy. The group's members saw it as inappropriately tying the hospital's policy to the tenets of one faith, Catholicism, thus jeopardizing divisions between church and state.[110] On the other side of the Jewish theological spectrum, Rabbi Edward F. Klein of the Stephen Wise Free Synagogue on August 23 called Dr. Jacobs's ban "an infringement on Civil Rights—the civil rights of the patient, the civil rights of the Protestant and Jewish communities."[111] For American Jews, who were acutely aware of themselves as a religious minority in New York City and the country more broadly, it was particularly worrisome to feel that the tenets of one faith would drive public policy, even if that other faith was Catholicism, also historically an outsider tradition in the United States. The fact that Jewish law explicitly permitted forms of contraception meant that a policy rooted or even perceived to be rooted in Catholic teaching explicitly favored one religion over another.

Ultimately, on September 17, 1958, after an unremitting campaign by New York clergy, women's groups, and various medical associations, the Board of Hospitals reversed its position and allowed the therapeutic prescription of contraception in public hospitals. Jacobs made it clear that contraception would only be offered for medical reasons, not for sociological or emotional reasons, which he deemed nonmedical. Hospital staff who objected to contraception on religious grounds would not be forced to provide it. More than one doctor would have to agree that it was medically necessary for a patient to receive it. The woman would then be given the opportunity to speak to a clergyman ("man" used deliberately) of her choice. The hospital board also indicated that it was more likely that a woman would be able to get access to contraception if she had previously been pregnant and her pregnancy had endangered her life, because it was reasonable to assume that subsequent pregnancies would do so as well.[112] Not only did women have to have medical reasons, those medical reasons essentially had to be life-threatening, foreshadowing later "life of the mother" exceptions to abortion policy.

In this final policy, perhaps better than anywhere else, we see how contraception was disciplinary, and that its potential to change society lay in the hands of those that controlled access. Because those in control were interested in maternal health as it contributed to family stability far more than they were interested in women's self-determination, and because they were interested in political compromise, if not with the institutional Catholic Church, then with powerful Catholic politicians who were in line with the Church, the policies reflected those priorities and compromises. In a private clinic, one could simply purchase contraception. But if one depended on public hospitals, one could not have contraception for anything shy of medical necessity, usually life-threatening reasons; for many women would mean that they had already risked their lives through a difficult and potentially unplanned pregnancy. Such a woman had to present herself, and her private decisions and medical fears, to multiple—and most often male—doctors. The involvement of clergy, even though it was not mandatory, implied that she might need moral consultation in her decision.

The largely male layers of authority here exposed even the married woman seeking contraception to potential shame, judgment, and external control. This compromise, therefore, did not offer the full range of contraception for which the clergy called. The decision did not give couples using public hospitals the kind of access to contraception that the mainline theology of responsible parenthood required.[113] They did not have the moral autonomy that many of the denominations, Harry Emerson Fosdick, and the National Council of Churches said was necessary. Nor were they allowed contraception for the full range of reasons that the clergy deemed morally good, which included limiting their impact on the planet, scaling the number of children in the family to their emotional and financial resources, or enjoying the spiritual benefits of marital sex apart from the possibility of procreation. Therefore, even as they permitted contraception in some cases, the New York City municipal hospital system ended up being far more closely aligned with official Catholic teachings than with the Protestant mainline, or with almost all of Judaism.

These public debates framed the moral management of contraception in the largely male terms of medical and religious authority and extensively addressed the discourse of population control. This is the biopolitics of contraception on the global scale, and it is framed in these public and male discourses as vital and moral work. In the experiences of women, however, there is another form of labor present. Women talk about the very physical work of the diaphragm. We do not know whether the male clergy, talking from pulpits and in the press about contraception, had encountered the diaphragm; they did not, in their formal, official, and public roles, speak about the intimate details of diaphragms. We can assume that some of them had seen and used them: Many were married, and the diaphragm was a very common form of contraception. Many of their wives may have used diaphragms. They may have seen diaphragms on their wives' night tables, or experienced interruptions when their wives got out of bed to insert diaphragms. They may even have inserted them into their wives' bodies. We do not know, because they did not talk about such things in public.

Women, however, did the majority of the labor. They made the doctor's appointments. Their bodies were examined, their bodies were fitted with devices. Women were the ones whose motives and sex lives were scrutinized; their husbands' choices were mostly represented through their voices. They were the ones whose bodies and labor bore the results of diaphragm failure, out of whose bodies goop oozed after sex. They were the ones who dealt with embarrassment if diaphragms skittered out from under bathroom stalls, who decided whether to put in a diaphragm in anticipation of sex, or interrupt sex to insert the diaphragm—and had to remain sexy regardless of the choice that they made.

The Diaphragm Debates in Popular Culture

Only a year after the diaphragm became available in New York's public hospitals, it also broke into American popular culture. Although clergy were still preoccupied with getting married women access to contraception regardless of economic status, popular fiction addressed the question of what contraception meant in the lives of unmarried women. While newspaper sources traced out the terms of a public debate around the diaphragm, fictional accounts allowed for another angle on the construction of the diaphragm in the cultural imagination. As such, they provide us with a window into popular attitudes and cultural norms of the moment. In these accounts, we see that unmarried women were also interested in contraception, and that, at least for some, the diaphragm gave nonmarital sex an overlay of commitment reminiscent of marriage.

In 1954, four years before the Protestant and Jewish clergy of New York City would shame public hospitals into providing diaphragms, Mary McCarthy published a short story called "Dottie Makes an Honest Woman of Herself" in the *Paris Review*. In 1958, the year of the diaphragm debates, Philip Roth would publish another iconic mid-twentieth-century depiction of a diaphragm in *Goodbye, Columbus*, also in the *Paris Review*. Both stories had lives outside of the literary magazine. *Goodbye, Columbus* was combined with a collection of short stories published in 1959 and won the National Book Award in 1960. "Dottie Makes an Honest Woman of Herself" was incorporated into McCarthy's novel *The Group*, published in 1963, which occupied the number one spot on the *New York Times* bestseller list for five months that year. By the end of 1964, almost 300,000 copies had sold.[114] Both novels depict the diaphragm as an emotionally complicated piece of technology, with moral and interpersonal implications that outstrip the act of sex itself, through the specter of surveillance brought on by acquiring and using a diaphragm. In this sense, the fictional accounts answer a question the public debates didn't ask: Who controls contraception decisions? Within a decade, both of these books were also turned into major motion pictures, offering further insight into contraception's integration into popular culture.

These cultural depictions of the diaphragm, contrasted with a historical depiction of a battle over contraceptive access, suggest that the clergy's support of contraception did not actually do as much to alter the moral territory of the mid-twentieth century as they had hoped, or as the rhetoric of the sexual revolution might suggest. Protestant and Jewish clergy argued that marital sex was right and good and that, almost as a direct result, so was contraceptive technology. Such technology allowed people to have marital sex without endangering the health of the wife, who was, for clergy, also always a prospective mother. It also made it possible for *married* couples to practice "responsible parenthood," which is to say, to have only the children whom they could care for economically, physically, and emotionally, according to the standards of the rapidly expanding middle class. Moreover, birth control allowed these middle-class families to avoid contributing to population explosion, and to pursue vocations outside of, or in addition to, parenthood.[115]

In 1958, the clergy who advocated for birth control were not discussing the possibility that unmarried women would take advantage of it. Rather, they took something more akin to the stance of Dr. John Rock, one of the doctors who developed the Pill. He argued that "nice girls" remained virgins until marriage precisely because they were "good," not because they feared pregnancy, and that therefore access to contraception would not change their behavior. "Naughty girls," meanwhile, would have sex anyway, so letting them have contraception simply spared society the problem of morally loose mothers.[116] Clergy were able to sidestep the question of contraception for single women, always talking only about the morality of contraception in marriage. At least at this moment, clerics did not openly discuss the contraceptive needs of unmarried people, and certainly did not advocate for them. Clergy's ability to avoid the issue of birth control for unmarried women was predicated instead on the surveillance of the doctor as gatekeeper, and the belief that responsible doctors would not provide contraception to these patients. That was not, however, precisely how women's health clinics worked, as the worlds of the novels would show.

Yet in their novels, Philip Roth and Mary McCarthy both portray "nice" girls from good homes who do end up having sex before marriage, more or less without thought of contraception. In these fictional accounts, going to a doctor to get contraception is every bit as morally problematic, if not more so, than actually having sex, in part because it brings surveillance into the equation. Both authors link the ring of the diaphragm to a wedding ring. The act of acquiring birth control makes the women feel more, not less, committed to the men in their lives. Nonetheless, in both stories, it is the contraception that, in the end, dissolves the relationship.

McCarthy's short story was a popular success, but that success also came with pushback. Ireland, Italy, and Australia banned the book because of the "clinical detail" with which it told of "women's secrets."[117] Among the secrets that McCarthy chronicles are Dottie Renshaw's loss of virginity and fitting for a diaphragm. Dottie, a recent Vassar graduate, meets the unsubtly named Dick at the wedding of one of her more liberal friends. Two days later, she goes home with him for the first time, and he deflowers her on a towel in his bed. While McCarthy's description of their sexual encounter and Dottie's thoughts afterward are explicit, the story, and later novel, were more commonly noted for the discussion of birth control that followed this scene.[118]

The next morning, as he throws her out of the apartment, Dick commands Dottie, "Get yourself a pessary . . . a female contraceptive, a plug. You get it from a female doctor. Ask your friend Kay." While Dottie is struck by Dick's lack of love for her, her conversation with her friend Kay and Kay's husband temporarily changes Dottie's mind. They explain to her that the demand for a diaphragm suggests that Dick plans on sleeping with Dottie regularly. Their logic is that "no man of honor would expect a woman to put up the doctor's fee, plus the price of the pessary and the jelly and the douche bag unless he planned to sleep with her for long enough for her to cover her investment."[119] Instead, a "man out for a casual affair found it simpler to buy Trojans by the dozen."[120] Though condoms decreased his pleasure, they did not tie him to the girl. The married couple help Dottie see commitment in Dick's command. He might otherwise sleep with her and discard her, but if he has asked her to get a diaphragm, Kay's husband assures Dottie, Dick will expect to keep the diaphragm in his apartment. Dottie believes Kay's husband that Dick is making a commitment.

Dick immediately and clearly tells Dottie that he does not love her, cannot afford to take her out, and will only see her when she comes to his room for sex. Even so, as she sits in the women's health clinic waiting for the fitting, the importance of the diaphragm becomes even clearer in her mind: "Dottie's heart was humming happily as she sat, three days later, beside Kate Petersen, in the woman doctor's office suite. Actions spoke louder than words and, whatever Dick might say, the fact remained that he had sent her here, to be wedded, as it were, by proxy, with the 'ring' or diaphragm pessary that the woman doctor dispensed."[121] Dottie's hair is freshly waved, she has had a facial, and she is confident because she has knowledge. She had gone to a birth control clinic and been assured that the diaphragm had "the backing of the whole US medical profession; it had been found by Margaret Sanger in Holland and was now for the first time being imported in quantity into the USA."[122] It was appealing because it "combined the maximum of protection with the minimum of inconvenience and could be used by any woman of average or better intelligence, following the instructions of a qualified physician."[123] McCarthy went on to describe the physical process of the fitting twice—once theoretically, as Dottie understood it from her conversation with the birth control bureau, and then again when she experienced the exam, fitting, and lesson in insertion, during which she lost her grip on the spring-loaded diaphragm and it "shot across the room."[124]

In addition, the diaphragm implied trust: The man was trusting the woman with the contraception and therefore trusting her not to trick him into marriage. If she was unmarried, he was committing to storing the diaphragm for her, which was a "sacred trust" "precluding" him from bringing other women home. Indeed, "a man entrusted with this important equipment was bonded . . . like a bank employee; when he did stray, he was likely to do it in her place or in a hotel room or even a taxi—some place not consecrated with by the sacral reminders."[125] Should their relationship end, it was very difficult to dispose of the "hygienic relics."[126] They were too private to be thrown away for the cleaning woman to find. And being rubber and metal, they could not be burned. Being personally fitted, they could not be returned by mail or given to another lover. Getting rid of a diaphragm was like "getting rid of a body."[127]

Here, you can see the idea that the diaphragm, personalized and costly, made the relationship public. A man had to be faithful because any other lovers would see his partner's contraceptive equipment in the house, tucked away in the private spaces of bathroom or bedside table. The unmarried couple could not casually end the relationship once the woman owned a diaphragm, because they could not easily dispose of the diaphragm for fear of it being seen. Because of this burden of trust and commitment, it is possible to interpret the diaphragm as making the extramarital relationship *more* moral, not less. The diaphragm, then, goes from being an instrument of immorality to a "sacral reminder" and a "hygienic relic," the ring in the pessary gesturing to an engagement ring on a finger.[128] In McCarthy's story, although Dottie has engaged in premarital sex, it is through the trip to get the diaphragm that she "Makes an Honest Woman of Herself."

To the reader, it is clear from the beginning of this tale, in both its short story and novel form, that Dick is a cad and Dottie is being had, both literally and figuratively. Only Kay's interpretations and her husband's endorsement of Dick's character give credit to the idea of the diaphragm as symbol of good intentions. In the context of McCarthy's novel, however, it becomes clear that Kay's judgment and her husband's character are both lacking.

Either way, it is the pessary, rather than the sex act itself, that is the source of reassurance and, as it develops in the novel, the reason why Dottie ultimately decides not to see Dick again. She decides that he should not have asked her to go through the process of the fitting, and that his request does not, in fact, represent commitment but rather callousness. She abandons her diaphragm, jelly, and douche bag under a bench in the park and elects to marry someone else. Dottie has seen that Dick did not mean to make a commitment, that she misread him, and that without him she cannot continue to own such a damning piece of equipment. Like disposing of an engagement ring, the diaphragm must go, and so she abandons both the diaphragm and the affair.

In Philip Roth's 1958 novel *Goodbye, Columbus*, it is also the process of getting a diaphragm, rather than the first sexual encounter, that becomes an opportunity to reflect on the relationship and the commitment it entails. Getting a diaphragm demonstrates for the women in both fictional accounts that they are not the "naughty" girls of John Rock's imagination. If Dottie is certain of this fact, Brenda still fears being naughty. Roth's novel features a narrator, Neil, who lives with his aunt and uncle in a working-class Jewish suburb of Newark in the late 1950s and works in a low-paying library job, and Brenda, a Radcliffe student home for the summer. The novella is overtly about class tensions within Jewish communities, but the relationship itself rises and falls on Brenda's diaphragm.

The two begin sleeping together with no apparent concern about whether they love each other. But after some weeks, while Neil is a houseguest in the home of Brenda's parents, he asks her to get a diaphragm. At first, she demurs, assuring him that they are "careful." When he presses, she homes in on the materiality of the diaphragm: "You want me to own one . . . like a walking stick or a pith helmet."[129] He explains that he wants her "to own one for . . . for the sake of pleasure," his pleasure, he specifies. They argue, calling each other silly and selfish. Brenda was happy to sleep with Neil but does not want a diaphragm because she does not "feel old enough for all that equipment." The diaphragm, she says, is "such a conscious thing to do," and therefore, she argues, it would change her. He suggests that it would change them; and it is clear to the reader that he sees that change as positive, she as negative. He tells her to go to "the Margaret Sanger," as the birth control clinic is called, and this familiarity prompts Brenda to ask Neil whether he has done this before. He explains that he has "read Mary McCarthy."[130] Roth's reference to McCarthy indicates the popular success of the book—she could be casually referenced, and the reader would recognize her as a source of information, an "authority" on the diaphragm.

Brenda objects to the fact that Neil has given her the choice either to go through the embarrassment of being fitted for a diaphragm as an unmarried woman, or to lie to a doctor about her marital status. She shows no shame or moral qualms about the sex itself, but she does agonize over taking the deliberate steps to acquire a diaphragm. The sex can remain private, but the process of getting a diaphragm opens her up to moral control. There are questions, including about her marital status; there is scrutiny of her body; there is the possibility of judgment. And indeed, while we do not hear of judgment at the doctor's office, Brenda does, in the end, encounter judgment. Ultimately, perhaps to confirm her love for Neil, Brenda calls the Margaret Sanger. Though Neil assured her, from his reading of McCarthy, that the clinic staff would not ask whether she was married, they do indeed ask; and she hangs up. Neil tells Brenda that instead they can go to a doctor. She objects to the idea of "some dirty little office," and he assures her that instead they will go to "the most posh gynecologist in New York."[131] Even though she has capitulated to Neil on the subject of the diaphragm, Brenda still has doubts: "Neil, I shouldn't have called the Margaret Sanger—it's not right."[132] Her comment that it is "not right" is tied to the idea of a clinic, perhaps because she sees it as dirty and lower-class, but also because the staff had asked whether she was married. The idea that the medical authorities of the clinic can peer into the morality of her choices via her marital status unnerves her far more than having sex out of wedlock.

Brenda wants Neil to accompany her to the gynecologist, but he points out that even a husband would not go to the office with her. He does, however, accompany her into Manhattan from New Jersey, and, though he wants to stay at a bar in the Port Authority Bus Terminal, she persuades him to walk her to the office. While Brenda goes in to get her diaphragm, a process that remains mysterious for Neil and therefore the reader, he waits for her inside St. Patrick's Cathedral. Though, as a Jew, he cannot bring himself to kneel, he does lean forward onto a pew in front of him, hands clasped and eyes closed:

> I wondered if I looked like a Catholic, and in my wonderment, I began to make a little speech to myself. Can I call the self-conscious words I spoke prayer? At any rate, I called my audience God. God, I said, I am twenty-three years old. I want to make the best of things. Now the doctor is about to wed Brenda to me, and I am not entirely certain this is all for the best. What is it I love, Lord? Why have I chosen? Who is Brenda. . . . I was getting no answers, but I went on. If we meet you at all, God, it's that we are carnal, and acquisitive, and thereby partake of You. I am carnal, and I know You approve, I just know it. But how carnal can I get? I am acquisitive. Where do I turn now in my acquisitiveness?[133]

Neil had pushed Brenda to get the diaphragm, but in this moment, while she is being fitted, he does more soul-searching than at any other moment in the novella. Neil and Brenda had not wedded themselves to each other when they first began to have sex; rather, the doctor, acting as a sort of officiant, weds them with the diaphragm. Therefore, despite his own pursuit of pleasure, it is this moment, rather than having sex, that prompts Neil's soul-searching. Here Roth echoes McCarthy, where Dottie equates her diaphragm with a wedding ring, but in this novel the sentiment comes from the male narrator.

Given the fact that this Jewish man has his most introspective moments, in which he communes with God, while sitting in a Catholic church while his (also Jewish) girlfriend violates the teachings of the Church, and while he contemplates the nature of their carnal love, is Roth perhaps pushing back against the Church? In this historical moment, the concept of a "tri-faith America" made up of Protestants, Catholics, and Jews was coming into being. But it was becoming increasingly clear, through moments like the New York City battle over contraception, that the Catholic Church had far more power in that triumvirate than did Jews.[134] In this moment, Roth symbolically undercuts that power, even as he tacitly acknowledges it, by placing the pivotal scene in the cathedral. Even those in Catholic space are not necessarily pulled by the dictates of the Church.

In the end, however, the diaphragm and the scandal that it creates breaks the young couple up, rather than wedding them to each other. Even though Neil plans to visit Brenda at college, she leaves her diaphragm at home when she returns to school, and her mother finds it. The shame and anger that results causes more strain than the relationship can take. Though Brenda is more troubled by the diaphragm than by the fact that she is sleeping with Neil, we do not know which most bothers her parents. What we do know is that for the unmarried woman, sex was a problem socially if there was evidence; and the diaphragm provided that evidence.

Within a decade, both of these novels had become major motion pictures. United Artists released *The Group* in 1966, and the film offers a mid-1960s imagining of the 1930s. Three moments from the film seem particularly relevant here. As in the novel, the group of college friends first come together after graduation for Kay's wedding to struggling playwright Harald. The women see the newlyweds off for a honeymoon at Coney Island, then discuss over lunch the speed at which the two got married. Perhaps, one woman speculates, Kay and Harald "had" to get married, to which another friend, shocked, responds, "Oh no. Kay knew all about what to do." The shock is not about the implication that Kay and Harald have had premarital sex but about the suggestion that Kate would not have been able to protect her (unmarried) self against pregnancy.

This is striking, since *Eisenstadt v. Baird* did not provide unmarried women with legally protected access to contraception until 1972. It is also striking because Kay, one of the least affluent members of the group, is more dependent on women's clinics than her classmates might have been. Her friends' assumption, however, also turns out to be false—Kay is not pregnant at her wedding, but she is also not using contraception. Recall that in the short story and novel, Kay and Harald are Dottie's resources for learning about contraception—though Kay herself is not using a diaphragm. In the film, it is Dottie who tells Kay about the diaphragm. Dottie does ask Kay for advice, and it turns out that Kay is not only ignorant of contraception but aghast that Dottie has gotten information about it. Kay observes that she should have done so herself but did not have the nerve to do so until she was married. Last, in the short story and novel, Dottie is able to imagine that Dick is implying a marriage-like relationship with his instructions to get a diaphragm. In the film, no such imagining is possible. He tells her that he likes her but will not "like her more" with a diaphragm. In the film, Kay does not suggest to Dottie that Dick asking her to see a "lady doctor" means that he is committing; Kay tells Dottie that he is using her.

Goodbye Columbus, released by Paramount Pictures in 1969, also differs from its book, in part because it includes a lengthy and explicit debate about the diaphragm versus the Pill. Between the 1958 book and the 1969 movie, the Food and Drug Administration had approved the birth control pill, which did more to separate sex and reproduction than any other mode of contraception. Theoretically, it also gave women much more control over their fertility, as they took full responsibility for its use. As Brenda points out, however, the Pill came with many side effects.

In other ways, however, the films both made more explicit a reality about the diaphragm that was evident but not emphasized in the books: The new liberated single woman might have access to contraception, and it might theoretically put her in charge of her sex life. But in both stories, the women were pressured—not into the sex, but into the use of the contraception. They were given the sole burden of birth control in the context of shared pleasure. But in neither case did that responsibility result in the emotional reciprocation for which both Dottie and Brenda had hoped. In addition, while clergy approval might have successfully made contraception respectable within the context of a marriage, for women using contraception outside marriage, contraception could serve as semipublic evidence of sex—sex that was premeditated and potentially a source of shame.

Conclusion

In the late 1950s, the diaphragm was legal in New York State and in much of the rest of the United States. But that does not mean that it was uncontroversial. The political and cultural scene of the mid- to late 1950s demonstrates that the diaphragm was a contested technology. It was held up as both a moral good to be used in Christian marriage and a source of shame for unmarried women who might seek one out. The diaphragm was a right that should be available to all women, regardless of income. Indeed, it was a violation of individual medical and religious rights for the Catholic Church's objection to the diaphragm to prevent women from accessing it, particularly if those women were Protestant or Jewish.

The diaphragm was, for many, respectable and scientific, depending as it did on a fitting by a doctor in a medical clinic. That scientific respectability allowed clergy to argue that birth control was Christian as long as it was used prayerfully and within marriage. Religious leaders were able to endorse the diaphragm in part because they knew that hospitals and doctors would regulate it, would keep the diaphragm within the bounds of marriage and respectability. But the cost of that regulation was that low-income women could not have contraception unless it was deemed medically necessary by a hospital board—an unreasonably high bar to clear.

The diaphragm, then, was subject to layers of control. Couples were supposed to use their religious resources, Protestant theologies and Jewish law, to decide whether and when to bear children. Their reproductive lives could be moral if appropriately restrained or immoral if not. Those religious frameworks provided an element of control and also the possibility for external judgment if one's own decisions did not appear to reflect the values of one's community. Additionally, as the response of the Orthodox rabbis demonstrates, there were religious groups who wished to exert control over when and how members of their community might use birth control. The Orthodox rabbis would theoretically have disapproved of Catholics who ignored the Church teachings on contraception, not of the Church for prohibiting it. Their complaint was simply a separation-of-church-and-state issue. They believed that rabbis should participate in disciplining Jews according to Jewish law, Protestant ministers according to Protestant theology, and Catholic priests according to the teachings of the Church—and that the state should support all of those religions equally. Religion, then, was a functional layer of control.

The medical establishment added further layers of control around the distribution of the diaphragm. First, and regardless of whether one went to a doctor in a private or public setting, the doctor controlled a woman's access to the diaphragm. She needed a physician to prescribe the device, fit the device, and teach her to use it. Even today, women in the United States need medical support to get both the diaphragm and the birth control pill, which are available over the counter in some other parts of the world. Though women doctors were more represented in gynecology than in other specialties, this meant that a woman often needed to approach a man, with both the authority of his gender and his medical training, to access contraception; and he could deny her. He could decide that she lacked a good reason to want contraception, or that he simply would not provide contraception to, for instance, unmarried women. It is almost impossible to overemphasize the importance of this shift from how birth control had previously been accessed through networks of women or from lay midwives.[135]

Second, in public hospitals, the medical boards provided yet another layer of oversight. Assuming a woman's doctor agreed to fit her, the medical board demanded a medical reason to delay or prevent childbearing, not an emotional or economic one. These levels of medical authority sometimes worked against the religious authority. A couple might prayerfully decide not to have a child for an economic or vocational reason, only to be denied contraception by the medical board for the lack of a medical reason. Even so, the knowledge that doctors served as gatekeepers increased the clergy's comfort with contraception as a scientifically grounded and respectable option.

Both religion and medicine could paint contraception as respectable because they tied it to marriage. In all of the debates about diaphragms and public hospitals, there was barely any mention of contraception outside marriage. Contraception was a moral good within marriage. The fact that it would be restricted accordingly by hospital boards was such a given that the "problem" of unwed motherhood barely appeared in the debate. Birth control, however, was definitely on the radar of unmarried couples and clearly part of the cultural milieu, as the fiction of Mary McCarthy and Philip Roth demonstrates.

Accustomed as we are to conservative backlash against contraception, it is perhaps not particularly surprising to see both McCarthy, a feminist, and Roth, something of an antifeminist, depicting the diaphragm as a source of shame for unmarried women. That shame represents the third form of social control. Whether these novels reflected the experiences of actual women we cannot know. But both stories reflect a world that assumed premarital sex was something that nice girls would do, with relatively nice men and perhaps with less nice men, and about which they would feel little shame. Within that world, the diaphragm was, for both authors, indicative of moral weight. It represented a commitment and trust far beyond what was suggested by the sex itself, even a metaphoric marriage. The diaphragm also had the potential to represent the shame of nonmarital sex by introducing surveillance into the relationship. Doctors became part of the equation with their invasive questions, including questions about marriage.

It is surprising that the sense of shame threaded through the novels was not reflected in the attitudes of mainline Protestant and Jewish clergy of New York. Protestant and Jewish clergy were loud and vocal supporters of contraception, attempting to frame its use as a potential moral good permitted—and even at times encouraged—in their traditions. They were able to do so, however, specifically because the apparatus of control was not *dismantled* but rather *transferred* from theology and clergy to science and doctors. As a result, surveillance remained a central part of the process, and along with it the social policing of sexuality—both of married couples and, as the novels portray, of single women.

In fact, the clergy could proclaim the value of contraception on the assumption that it would only be available within marriage, specifically because they were depending on the control of doctors who would ask young women whether they were married. That authority may not have been absolute; clearly McCarthy and Roth suggest a world in which unmarried women had access to doctors who would write such prescriptions. But in the public clinics, at least three levels of control—religious, medical, and social—coexisted.

These modes of control functioned unevenly, in part because there was no religious consensus about what it meant to use contraception. The Catholic Church formally forbade its use, but historical sources and historiography tell us that many individual Catholics either chose to use birth control or, at the very least, believed that it should be available to non-Catholics at public hospitals. Protestants saw contraception as an important tool in marriage, helping couples plan their families and benefit from the spiritual elements of their sexual relationships. Jewish law allowed contraception under certain circumstances, and although the various Jewish movements had differing positions, all of them wanted the diaphragm to be broadly available so that couples could make decisions under the advisement of their clergy.

The point here is that even though contraception was allowed in several different arenas during this period, it was also highly contested. Even among those who wanted birth control to be legal and available, there was not agreement about when it should be used and by whom. Debates about contraception began before the New York City public-hospital debates in 1958, and they continued long afterward. But this moment demonstrates that there was a multifaceted public debate of what was ostensibly a deeply private matter—the privacy of which was actually central to its moral framing.

Family Planning for the American Family

In 1966, singer, songwriter, activist, and folk hero Pete Seeger released an album called *Dangerous Songs!?* It included songs about freethinking ("Zei Gedanken sind frie"), abolition ("John Brown's Body"), capital punishment ("Walking Down Death Row"), and draft dodging ("The Draft Dodger's Rag"). Alongside these was a song called "The Pill." Written by the Scottish singer-songwriter Matt McGuinn, it tells the story of a woman who married her man, Willie, and planned to fill her house with children. When she went to her priest for help and advice, he chastised her for only having six children to show for her seven years of marriage. By the close of the song, the narrator, who has been singing in the chorus that she is "pining for the pill," observes that at forty, she has twenty-two children, and she is hoping that the Vatican will approve the Pill before her husband comes home from work—even though she knows Willie would welcome more children. In introducing the song, Seeger notes that McGuinn means no offense to Catholics. From his standpoint, at least the Vatican was having debates about the Pill. The Scottish Presbytery was, according to McGuinn via Seeger, most definitely not.

Embedded in the song are many of the midcentury hopes for contraception and the family, hopes shared by Protestant clergy, many Catholic faithful (including some Catholic clergy), and Jewish leadership. The Pill provided a mode of contraception that could keep families manageable. One would not, as the woman in the song worried, run out of names, because one could limit the number of children to the number that could be cared for and supported in the resource-intensive mode of an increasingly consumer-oriented and college-educated community. One could even do this while enjoying a fulfilling sex life. This was a version of birth control that created a strong family unit. The song points to the burden of childbearing on women, and the Pill's promise of protection against the ravages of constant pregnancy. Yet in the world of this song, the Pill's most radical implication was the relief that it would provide for women and families, and the potential that such relief would be available even to Catholics. The song does not touch on the broader feminist potential of the Pill for women in terms of the new possibilities it opened up, in or out of marriage. Rather, it focuses on the potential of the Pill to transform family life.

This chapter thinks about how the birth control pill—the first readily available contraceptive in the US market to separate the act of contraception from the act of sexual intercourse—created a new venue for moral action: the managing of marriage and family life. As the previous chapter shows, many religious Americans, including ministers and rabbis, had supported readily accessible contraception as an important part of married life. With the advent of the birth control pill, Jews, Protestants, and even some Catholics found themselves once again attempting to craft cohesive theologies of birth control, theologies that strongly advocated the use of contraception so long as it was in its proper place to support and strengthen the American family. For Christians, this theology was built on the relatively new Protestant ideal of a sexually satisfying marriage with a newly articulated theology of responsible parenthood. Jews, by contrast, turned to Jewish law, arguing that contraception had been permitted even during the time of the Talmud, a claim used to make even the most observant Judaism look "modern" and "American."

The advent of the Pill allowed theologians and laity to articulate a new kind of sexually fulfilling marriage. This kind of marriage would bring a couple closer to God, solidify their relationship in the face of external stressors, and allow them to carefully, prayerfully plan the birth of each child. While these theologians wanted couples to be able to plan and limit the number of children they had, they still saw children as central to marriage. The birth control pill, then, was a way of regulating women's bodies in order to regulate the family.

These religious leaders understood this regulation to be necessary in part because, if Planned Parenthood's 1954 annual meeting articulated what historian Elaine Tyler May refers to as the "promise" of the Pill, plenty of people also believed that the Pill created "peril."[1] One of the primary challenges facing Pill boosters was the question of how to maximize the former while minimizing the latter. The fact that some liberal theologians saw moral possibility in the birth control pill is well borne out in the historical record. But history tends to better remember the moral panic over sexual libertinism that the invention of oral contraceptive pills engendered. While the idea of a sexual revolution was popular with the news media at the time, and in the cultural memory since, historians of sexuality do not identify a sexual revolution as a truly unprecedented phenomenon of the '60s. The term "sexual revolution," which has received sweeping cultural attention, links together as a cohesive social shift a number of social factors including later marriage ages, increased premarital sex and birth control options, a culture of openness about sexual pleasure, and the sexual freedom represented by the Summer of Love.

But in *Intimate Matters: A History of Sexuality in America*, the now-classic first full-length study of sexuality in the United Sates, John D'Emilio and Estelle B. Freedman demonstrate that many of the behaviors associated with the sexual revolution had long existed in American life. Beth Bailey's *Sex in the Heartland* points out that many of these social trends—such as the Summer of Love and increased availability of contraception for married couples—had little to do with one another. It was the application of the term "revolution" that both linked otherwise unrelated practices and framed them as a threat to the existing social order in the popular imagination. Historians do not dispute the reality of these trends and practices. Rather, they argue that while the middle of the twentieth century saw a shift in how Americans understood and lived their sexual lives, those changes were often the result of larger and longer trends, rather than part of a sudden change.[2] That said, at the time, there was notable attention to perceived changing norms and behaviors, and many social commentators worried about the impact of the Pill on the sexual practices of the nation. Advocates for the Pill, including Dr. John Rock, one of its developers and primary spokesmen, argued that "nice girls" would not seek out the Pill; and "naughty girls" would have sex anyway, so society might as well mitigate the effects.[3]

But skeptics abounded. In 1966, *U.S. News and World Report* asked, "What is the pill doing to the moral patterns of the nation?"[4] The article quoted a wide range of community leaders, including clergy and educators, who believed that by severing sex from reproduction, the Pill was changing sexual morality in the United States for the worse. John Alexander, general director of the Evangelical InterVarsity Christian Fellowship, worried, "I think it is certain that the pill will tear down the barriers for more than a few young people hitherto restrained by fear of pregnancy. . . . I am very much afraid that sexual anarchy could develop."[5] Members of the Protestant mainline voiced concerns about sexual permissiveness as well. In 1966, the General Assembly of the Presbyterian Church (USA) worried that the birth control pill could lead to "confusion about the meaning of sex."[6] If the Pill were to become widely available outside marriage, some religious leaders and university and civic authorities fretted, it would erode the moral boundaries that confined sex to marriage.[7]

The focus on the Pill as a tool for marriage underscores a key aspect of the midcentury religious support for contraception—contraception was good if, and only if, it was in service of a particular kind of sexuality: heterosexual and married. Heterosexual marriages, in turn, served as the basis for a particular kind of family: a family with middle-class status, upwardly mobile aspirations, a breadwinner father and a homemaker mother, and a nice suburban home with all the modern conveniences. As articulated in the introduction, this kind of family was seen as America's primary bulwark against communism.

Laws about contraception are made on a state-by-state basis. By 1965, only Connecticut and Massachusetts forbade contraception to married couples, a decision that was reversed by the Supreme Court Case *Griswold v. Connecticut*. *Griswold* ended the State of Connecticut's ban on birth control for married couples by establishing the "heterosexual act of intercourse in marital bedrooms as protected by a zone of privacy into which courts must not peer and with which they must not interfere."[8] With this decision, heterosexual marriage was given rights that were not given to other forms of sexual conduct. It did not apply to all sex in private between consenting adults; nonmarital sex was not granted similar privacies. Not only was the court perfectly comfortable policing privately occurring homosexual sex, but the justices were not granting this right to privacy to all heterosexual couples either. Single people would not have the right to contraception until the Supreme Court case *Eisenstadt v. Baird* seven years later. Indeed, in 1965, marital sex did not even necessarily imply consensual sex; or rather, all marital sex was understood to be consensual by the very reality of marriage. It would be almost thirty years before marital rape became illegal in all fifty states.

Ironically, as scholars such as Lauren Berlant, Janet Jakobsen, and Ann Pellegrini point out, the very enshrining of heterosexual marriage as private yet fundamental to citizenship brings that private life very much into the public eye as a central and defining ideology.[9] The language in *Griswold* linked marriage and marital privacy with religion—not by endorsing a particular tradition, but rather by noting that marriage is "older than the Bill of Rights— older than our political parties, older than our school system. Marriage is a coming together for better or for worse, hopefully enduring, and intimate to the degree of being sacred. It is an association that promotes a way of life, not causes; a harmony in living, not political faiths; a bilateral loyalty, not commercial or social projects. Yet it is an association for as noble a purpose as any involved in our prior decisions."[10]

Since the *Griswold v. Connecticut* case was predominantly concerned with the rights of married couples to have access to birth control, in this case, marriage quite directly related to sexual intercourse. By claiming that intimate and harmonious marriage was older than any of the apparatus of the American state, the court attempted to naturalize it—to place it, by virtue of its age and sacrality, above many of the man-made institutions that the court could regulate. Furthermore, while the court did not frame sex in terms of romantic love, it remained clear that sex was not simply sex: It was connected ideologically to concepts such as "intima[cy] to the degree of being sacred," and "an association for as noble a purpose as any involved in our prior decisions." In the American political and popular imagination, then, marital sex was framed as both natural and intimate, which allowed it to exist beyond the gaze of the law. However, just as marital sex was too private and intimate to be under the purview of the law, it became even more important that it be mediated by religion, a mode of regulation often imagined to be every bit as private and intimate as marriage.

This Supreme Court decision had an ahistorical and almost fictitious quality. Heterosexual marriage under patriarchy was clearly both commercial and social, and it was hardly bilateral. Banks, for example, were legally allowed to discriminate against women in issuing credit cards. What's more, the idea of a heterosexual marriage marked by privacy and intimacy was actually a very recent development. Think, for instance, of the public beddings of monarchs in England, whose laws provide a basis for much of American law, or of marriages arranged between near strangers for political or economic dynastic reasons. In the American political context, think about the economic necessity of marriage in the early colonies or on frontier farms.

In such contexts, a gendered division of labor meant that marriage was often a business arrangement as much as or more than it was a romantic one. Families often lived in one room, such that the marital bedroom hardly offered a zone of privacy. The modern American concept of the home, and of the role of women within it, developed in part through late nineteenth- and early twentieth-century welfare policies that structured social support around ideologies of motherhood and the "family wage" earned by a husband, a historically specific product of the Industrial Revolution that cast women primarily as mothers and the home primarily as private.[11] I am historically nitpicking here in service of a greater point, which is to say that, as is often the case with Supreme Court decisions, that *Griswold v. Connecticut* did not de- scribe historical realities so much as it spoke them into being. In this case, the *Griswold* decision elevated the midcentury's intense focus on heteronormative marriage as a primary religious bond and offered it a kind of protection not granted to other sexual relationships.

Race was largely absent from the discourse about how contraception could help build strong Christian and Jewish families, except to note that race-based eugenics was unacceptable. That said, the families that the clergy imagined were white. Or, at least, they were middle-class and upwardly mobile in ways that were made structurally possible for white families through generational wealth and government support such as the GI Bill and made structurally unlikely for Black families, who did not receive the same sources of support. Black families and other families of color were also actively undermined by a white supremacist society upheld in various regions and eras by Jim Crow laws, underfunded educational systems, redlining, and race-based policing, among many other factors. As is so often the case, when nothing is said about race, the imagined ideal family was both presumed to be white—with all the cultural particularity and privilege thereof—and the ideology of these families was presumed to be universal.

Although the architects of the Protestant theology of responsible parent- hood explicitly wrote against the eugenics of a previous generation, and they likely carefully avoided racially charged language, they had designed respon- sible parenthood around the realities of a white middle class. Thus they also created an ideology that would ultimately code white family practices and advantages as "responsible." This coding served to undermine other forms of American families, and to punish racially minoritized and economically marginalized communities for not being able to overcome the structural forces that prevented them from achieving responsible parenthood. As we think toward the moral debates around the Pill's release, it is essential to understand that this kind of contestation and racial coding was also present alongside the Pill from its very earliest development.

The Development of the Birth Control Pill

The birth control pill was developed throughout the 1950s, largely through the instigation of Margaret Sanger and Katherine McCormick. A philanthropist and an activist for both suffrage and birth control, McCormick almost exclusively funded the research required to develop the Pill. While Sanger had built alliances with eugenicists and others who were interested in family planning as modes of social control, she and McCormick continued to believe that the holy grail of birth control would be something that women could use without the consent or even the knowledge of the men in their lives. In the twenty-first century, the fact that women bear the full responsibility for most forms of contraception—both the emotional and physical labor of using it and the blame when it fails—often causes struggle and frustration. In Sanger's and McCormick's time, giving women a means of conception that only they could fully control was a way of protecting women.

McCormick first funded Gregory Pincus, an independent researcher whose initial work on fertility had caused a scandal at Harvard by working to make a world where "women would be self-sufficient; man's value zero." He was dismissed as a result.[12] Pincus and Hudson Hoagland of Clarkson University founded the Worcester Foundation for Experimental Biology, where most of the early research on contraception would take place. Pincus's research focused on animal testing, and when the time came to begin human trials, the collaborators (Sanger, McCormick, and Pincus) recruited John Rock, a Harvard Medical School professor and the director of the Brookline Reproductive Study Center in Massachusetts, to oversee the testing on humans. Rock was initially included in the project because he was legally and logistically well positioned to conduct tests on people. But his presence would ultimately prove useful from a public relations standpoint as well: As a Catholic and a social conservative who disapproved of birth control for nonmedical reasons, he was an ideal front man for the birth control pill, helping to establish it as something that would support the traditional family, rather than usher in an era of feminist rebellion.

It was at this moment, the moment of testing on humans, that the actual ethical implications of birth control research become murky. From a factual standpoint, human-subject research took the following trajectory. Rock ran initial trials on sixty volunteer subjects who were either local nurses or women being treated for infertility, the theory being that the Pill would suppress their ovarian function, and then when they went off the Pill, they might produce an excess of eggs. The trials were complicated, in part because the monitoring for data collection was extensive. That reality, combined with women's hesitation toward being research subjects, caused the researchers to enter into one of the most clearly ethically troubling pieces of the study. Pincus used fifteen psychiatric inmates at the Worcester State Hospital to test the Pill—women who could not refuse to be part of the study, and who were trying neither to achieve nor to avoid pregnancy. Both scholarly and popular histories of the birth control pill tend to agree that Rock's initial tests were ethical and Pincus's subsequent tests were not.

Rock and Pincus's final human trials of the contraceptive pill are where ethical debates tend to occur. After their tests based in the United States, they decided to conduct large-scale trials in Puerto Rico. They recruited two women to run the studies: Dr. Adaline Satterthwaite, a physician at Ryder Memorial Hospital, and Dr. Edris Rice-Wray, professor at Puerto Rico Medical School, director of the Public Health Department's Field Training Center for Nurses, and medical director of the Puerto Rican Family Planning Association. And this is where interpretations differ. Clearly, many women participated in the trials. Equally clearly, they were given doses of progesterone that were much higher than those in birth control pills on the market today, and many women suffered severe side effects.

At the time, the study received major pushback from officials, the press, Catholic priests, and men who thought contraception undermined their authority as husbands. In spearheading the pushback against contraception, Catholic authorities framed their objections in racialized terms: White doctors were experimenting on and therefore exploiting brown women, turning them into research subjects without concern for the risks of the tests. In addition, Catholic authorities accused the researchers of conducting trials in Puerto Rico precisely because the population was poor, vulnerable, and not white. They said much less about the reality that the majority of the participants in the study were Catholics who had signed up to do so despite the Church's condemnations of contraception. In the end, both Rice-Wray and Satterthwaite lost their positions. In this phase of testing, white doctors and feminists from the United States most certainly ran a major trial of oral contraceptives on a majority-brown, majority-poor population. How should we understand this reality?

One could take a charitable approach and argue that the researchers chose Puerto Rico because, unlike in Massachusetts, there were no laws there restricting contraception, and because the island was very densely populated and "impoverished women living in crowded, disease-ridden conditions were desperate for birth control."[13] Women were not coerced into participating in the tests; rather, there were waiting lists to be part of the clinical trials. This point of view argues that, although we know in hindsight that the researchers exposed women to dangerously high doses of hormones, they did not know at the time that those doses would be harmful, or whether lower doses would be effective. In this telling, because the researchers were very concerned about the health effects of contraceptive pills, the women's well-being was closely monitored, and the women received better medical care than was normally available to them. Women were also free to leave the study if they found the side effects unmanageable. In addition, researchers were not legally obligated to notify test subjects if a medicine was experimental until 1962: In short, these researchers followed or exceeded all of the standards of the day for human-subject research. In this framing, much of the pushback came from the Catholic Church, which opposed contraception as "unnatural," and because it undermined the Catholic vision of the Christian family; thus the Church's ethical objections to the study were essentially a red herring designed to block research.[14]

Intersectional feminist critics of the Puerto Rican contraceptive trials point out that by the time the testing began, the United States had long been very concerned about overpopulation in Puerto Rico, and that both Drs. Rice-Wray and Satterthwaite were employed by programs funded out of these concerns. Some argue that the women who participated in the study were not adequately informed of the risks or were in other ways coerced. Others suggest that unnecessary risks were taken or that Puerto Rico was chosen precisely because Puerto Ricans were neither US citizens protected by American laws, nor foreign citizens protected by their own government. These voices argue that, by doing the tests in Puerto Rico, Pincus, Rock, Rice-Wray, and Satterthwaite were able to cut corners that they would not have been able to cut at home.

Perhaps the most useful take on the development of the Pill in Puerto Rico comes from Laura Briggs, who reminds her readers that the forces that led to the Puerto Rican drug trials were themselves made up of a range of actors with a range of motivations. All of the players certainly believed that overpopulation presented a real and pressing threat, and Puerto Rico was a place where they believed that overpopulation was already doing great harm to the local communities.[15] According to Briggs, three pharmaceutical companies had patents on hormonal birth control, but two of them decided that human testing was too dangerous. It seems likely that Searle, the company that teamed up with the doctors, activists, and philanthropists, thought that testing in Puerto Rico was a good idea in part because, if there were ill effects from the tests, the women would have less power to make legal or public relations problems for the company.[16] Briggs also notes that while Pincus invested in Searle, made quite a bit of money off the birth control pill, and sometimes played a bit fast and loose with the results of the studies, which upset his collaborators, Rock did not invest in Searle because he thought it was inappropriate to make money off his patients in such a way. She further observes that all historical records suggest that Rock was an extremely kind man who cared a great deal about the welfare of his patients and was deeply concerned about side effects.[17]

Additionally, Briggs argues that, while "the trials—and the pill generally—have also been criticized as an example of male and masculinist science being callous about women's bodies. . . . It bears underlining that the people most directly involved with these trials were women and feminists."[18] There is plenty of evidence that Satterthwaite, for instance, was much more concerned than Pincus about the side effects that women experienced, and she refused to back down in her protection of their patients. Briggs also notes that the two white North American women doctors worked closely with Puerto Rican women, notably two nurses, Mercedes Quiñones and Iris Rodriguez, and a social worker, Noemi Rodriguez.[19] While their voices are not preserved in the archive, "they were well educated professionals who had come to birth control work because they believed in the cause."[20] While it remains true that many women experienced very severe side effects—50 percent of the women involved in the study dropped out, and the majority cited these symptoms as the reason—all signs point to most of the researchers being very concerned about subjects' reactions. What's more, as evidenced by both the dropout rate from the study and the fact that once word of the side effects got around in the community it was hard to get volunteers, there is little reason to think that people were compelled to participate against their will.

Briggs's work demonstrates that the development of the Pill, including the large-scale trials in Puerto Rico, was certainly a product of its moment motivated by fears about overpopulation, the racial, class, and postcolonial implications of which will be further unpacked in chapter 3. The scientists working to develop the Pill were also perhaps overly trusting in the solutions provided by modernity and science. That said, Briggs draws a distinction between research that is the product of colonial powers and genocide and research that is deliberately trying to perpetuate colonialism and genocide. Arguing that it is an oversimplification to see the development of the Pill as simply men exerting their agency on the bodies of women, or the white West filling its needs through the exploitation of brown women, she suggests instead that a complicated network of motivations and agencies brought about the birth control pill. Once the Pill was developed and released, its developers needed to make sure that it did not create a moral panic. Public religious conversations led to the development of a Protestant theology of responsible parenthood.

The Protestant Theology of Responsible Parenthood

Responsible parenthood framed birth control as a tool in a morally lived marriage, instead of seeing contraception as a morally neutral but respectable choice that one might make out of medical or perhaps economic necessity.[21] The concept appeared in various Protestant committees and publications throughout the 1950s, but it was Richard M. Fagley who articulated a pan-Protestant theology called "responsible parenthood" in the 1960 book *The Population Explosion and Christian Responsibility*. Fagley was a Congregationalist minister who served as the representative of the Commission of the Churches on International Affairs at the United Nations, a commission sponsored by the World Council of Churches and the International Missionary Council. From his position as a leader in a global ecumenical movement, he believed that he could speak to how birth control, if used properly, could serve as a moral, Christian response to the challenges that Fosdick and Rock had seen in the post–World War II world: the need to have happy, healthy, stable families, and the threat that the world's population would outstrip its food supply.

Fagley's theology proved popular enough that within a year of *The Population Explosion and Christian Responsibility*'s publication, the National Council of Churches (NCC) endorsed responsible parenthood in a vote of 83–0, with four abstentions. The group's mission, as described in its 1961 statement on responsible parenthood, was "in part 'to do for the churches such cooperative work as they authorize the Council to carry on in their behalf.'"[22] The organization also recognized "that any member church may disassociate itself from an action of the Council."[23] In the 1950s and early 1960s, the NCC served as the leading Christian ecumenical organization, reaching beyond the Protestant mainline to include Evangelical, Orthodox, and peace churches, though its often left-leaning political views aligned it most closely with its mainline members. The NCC's resolutions did not compel member denominations to adopt its viewpoints as policy; but the adoption of responsible parenthood was published in its magazine, the *Christian Century*.

It is through responsible parenthood's presence in the *Christian Century* that we can see just how seriously the Protestant mainline took the new theological approach. The *Christian Century* was and remains the most prominent

publication of the Protestant mainline, seeing itself as the Protestant equivalent of the Catholic *Commonweal* or the religiously unaffiliated *New Republic*. Its
centrality to postwar liberal Protestant conversations can hardly be overstated.
Newsweek called the periodical "the most important organ of Protestant opinion today" in 1947, and *Time* referred to it as "Protestantism's most vigorous
voice."[24] Multiple iterations of the responsible parenthood conversation
were featured in the *Christian Century*, and while these opinions reflected the
mainline religious elites, through the magazine these conversations could
also be found in homes, churches, and public libraries affiliated with liberal
and moderate expressions of Protestantism.

Responsible parenthood was an idea with reach, and as Fagley's title
suggests, it was framed as a partial solution to the problem of a growing
population. Religious concern with the perceived burgeoning population had
both domestic and global ramifications, and they were intertwined. While
the next chapter will more directly address what the population panic meant
on the global stage, this chapter will consider what responsible parenthood
meant for the American Christians who would read about the concept in, for
instance, the pages of the *Christian Century*. These Christians were a population that was, by and large, white, middle-class, and, in the postwar years,
upwardly mobile.

Responsible parenthood suggested that science had changed the composition of the modern family and the global population, and therefore it was
in science that a solution could also be found. Medical science had reduced
death rates, which meant that people lived longer, and, more importantly, that
more children lived to adulthood and were able to reproduce. These combined
factors meant that the number of people whom the planet needed to support
was growing at a rate that was potentially beyond what was sustainable.[25]
If, however, advances in medical science had created the problem, medical
knowledge was still, according to Fagley, "a liberating gift from God, to be
used to the glory of God, in accordance with his will for men." Fagley maintained that this knowledge "affects deeply the size of the family and the rate
of population growth and has therefore created a new area for responsible
decision."[26]

By linking birth control technology to other widely accepted medical advances, advances that lowered the infant mortality rate, Fagley attempted to
undercut the Catholic Church's arguments that birth control was unnatural
and immoral. The innovation of responsible parenthood was to extend this
logic to the more contested idea of birth control. The move was echoed even
by some of the movement's Catholic supporters, including Father John A.

O'Brien, a theologian at Notre Dame University. For Fagley, to reproduce without a conscience was not merely ignorant or irresponsible, it was perhaps even "un-Christian." In this way, responsible parenthood harnessed the technological advances of medical science in the service of a particular vision of morality, as well as Christian marriage and family life.

Given these two realities—scientifically developed contraception and a rising population—what, then, should the Christian family look like? The theology of responsible parenthood, as put forth by the NCC, argued that (1) "parenthood is a divinely ordained purpose of marriage for the embodiment and completion of the 'one flesh' union, for the care and nurture of children, for building the home as a true community of persons, and for the peopling of the earth (Gen. 1:28). It is participation in God's continuing creation, which calls for awe, gratitude, and a sense of high responsibility"; (2) mutual love and companionship were also ordained parts of marriage, including sex, and "most of our churches hold such expression right and necessary within the marriage bond, independently of procreation"; and (3) "vocation, or the service of the couple in society, is another high purpose through which 'the two become one.'" While vocation was understood to include children and family life, the National Council of Churches claimed that vocation also "can assert a separate or even conflicting claim on conscience." Just as, for Catholic religious, vocation included celibacy, for some couples it could include family limitation.[27] These points fulfilled a formal acknowledgment that marital nonprocreative sex had value, and, moreover, that potentially constant reproduction was not the default reality of married life. While the operating assumption was that people would and should still have children, the NCC believed Protestant spouses could exert their moral agency about how many children they could raise in a way that would be financially sustainable, and spiritually and emotionally nourishing for all concerned.

In deciding when to have children and how many, married couples needed to consider four points. First, they were to consider the right of the child to be wanted, loved, cared for, educated, and "trained in the discipline and instruction of the Lord." Couples who planned their families appropriately would be able to give children a home with a mother who did not work, who could apply the best resources of scientific child-rearing to their upbringing, being warm but not smothering. They could also ensure that they could provide for their children, live in the new postwar suburban developments, and provide them with college educations so that their sons could enter the professions and their daughters could provide culturally rich, scientifically managed homes for the next generation.

Second, the couple was to consider the prospect of health for the future child "if medical and eugenic evidence seemed negatively conclusive," which is to say, if doctors suspected a future child would have a disability of some sort, parents were encouraged to take such factors into account before having children. Third, couples were supposed to consider the mental and physical health of the "mother-wife," and the need to safeguard it by spacing children.[28] It is important to note that this concern for the mental and physical health of women was not, as evidenced from the term "mother-wife," particularly for their own sakes. Rather, a mentally and physically fit woman would be better able to fulfill her responsibilities as a mother and a helpmeet. The goal was less her bodily autonomy and personal dreams and more safeguarding her health to protect the stability of her family. Last, the couple was to take into account the broader social situation, "when rapid population growth places dangerous pressures on the means of livelihood and endangers social order."[29]

As troubling as these viewpoints might seem to the modern reader from the standpoint of disability rights and contemporary women's rights, to the largely white, able-bodied male leaders of the NCC, these principles served as a universal good that represented progress. Loving, sexually satisfying marriages provided a basis for stable and nurturing families, whose use of contraceptive technology allowed parents to minimize suffering from illness, injury, or financial strain, and gave them the capacity to care more fully for the planet by limiting the number of children they brought into the world. The model of responsible parenthood came out of a white middle-class model for what family life looked like, but part of the attempt of the theology was to universalize such a model.

Race and Responsible Parenthood

Some voices within the civil rights movement noticed and objected to the application of white values to Black families. When faced with the Moynihan Report in 1965, for instance, civil rights leader Floyd McKissick responded, "My major criticism of the report . . . is that it assumes that middle class American values are the correct values for everyone in America. . . . Moynihan thinks that everyone should have a family structure like his own. Moynihan also emphasizes the negative aspects of the Negroes and then seems to say that it's the individual's fault when it's the damn system that really needs changing." While McKissick had structural critiques of the Moynihan Report in that he believed that it blamed Black people for not being able to overcome the hurdles posed by structural racism, he also objected to the privileging of white family structures.

Other voices, however, saw possibilities for Black advancement in at least some aspects of responsible parenthood, hoping that limiting reproduction could improve the lot of African Americans more broadly.[30] The Reverend Dr. Martin Luther King worried that structural racism prevented Black families from having "healthy" families, very much on the model supported by the Moynihan Report, instead of seeing it as racism to expect Black people to model their lives on white families. King did worry about some of the policy implications of the Moynihan Report, and its potential for creating policies that blamed Black people, in particular Black men, for dynamics created by structural racism. But he shared the report's concern that a prevalence of matriarchal families, at least in a patriarchal society, would hurt Black communities. He was also profoundly worried about the impact of urban life and urban poverty on Black families.[31]

For all his critiques of capitalism, King's vision of the ideal family shared much with that of his white mainline clergy colleagues. He wanted Black people to have the same opportunities as white people to create nuclear families based on a solid and loving heterosexual marriage including a strong husband and father. He believed that contraception offered Black families a tool that would help them achieve that family structure. That was why King framed the family planning movement and the Planned Parenthood Federation of America as "natural allies" with the civil rights movement—because, as he stated, they sought to "inject any form of planning in our society that enriches life and guarantees the right to exist in freedom and dignity."[32] King's arguments also demonstrate how neatly certain theological constructs of family life dovetailed with the sociological research that examined and diagnosed perceived problems with Black urban life.

In 1965, Planned Parenthood awarded Martin Luther King Jr. the Margaret Sanger Award, the organization's highest award and one that is given for "leadership, excellence, and outstanding contributions to the reproductive health and rights movement."[33] Coretta Scott King, accepting the award on her husband's behalf, was quoted as saying, "I am proud tonight to say a word on behalf of your mentor, and the person who symbolizes the ideals of this organization, Margaret Sanger. Because of her dedication, her deep convictions, and her suffering for what she believed in, I would like to say that I am proud to be a woman tonight."[34] While Coretta Scott King's words perhaps offered a hint of feminism, the remarks that her husband sent focused primarily on how history might remember Sanger, and how family planning could help Black communities by strengthening families and promoting the human dignity of African Americans.[35]

When King accepted the Margaret Sanger Award, Black nationalist groups had already begun to frame birth control as an attack on African American communities (see chapter 3). Many Black nationalists, particularly men, were highly critical of birth control and birth control movements. They criticized the scientists who developed and the physicians who prescribed birth control pills, arguing that they rushed to market without adequate attention to the side effects of the medication. Even more sharply, they argued that birth control campaigns were motivated by a desire on the part of white society to commit genocide against African Americans. By demonstrating that Black couples who could access the Pill actively sought it out, King attempted to counter this narrative.

It was with that broader context in mind that King framed Sanger's early birth control work in terms of resonance with the civil rights movement. "There is a striking kinship between our movement and Margaret Sanger's early efforts," King wrote in his comments to the Planned Parenthood Federation of America.[36] He continued, "She, like we, saw the horrifying conditions of ghetto life. Like we, she knew that all of society is poisoned by cancerous slums. Like we, she was a direct actionist—a nonviolent resistor. She was willing to accept scorn and abuse until the truth she saw was revealed to the millions."[37] King lauded Sanger's willingness to go "into the slums and set up a birth control clinic."[38] He pointed out that this willingness cost her, as "for this deed she went to jail because she was violating an unjust law." Using religious language to validate Sanger's actions, he argued that in violating the law of the land, she was "obeying a higher law to preserve human life under humane conditions. Margaret Sanger had to commit what was then a crime in order to enrich humanity."[39] Rather than painting Sanger as a eugenicist with attitudes that harmed African American families, he suggested instead that "our struggle for equality by non-violent direct action" owed much to Margaret Sanger, and claimed, "Negroes have no mere academic nor ordinary interest in family planning. They have a special and urgent concern."[40] It was not, King argued, that Sanger was targeting Black families inappropriately—it was that she understood the unique tragedy facing the Black family.

King located what he framed as the "special and unique concern" that Black families had in family planning in a number of social factors, all tied to systemic racism. First, he noted that the Great Migration had taken families out of rural settings and into cities, and that that move had ramifications for what kind of family size made sense: "The size of family that may have been appropriate and tolerable on a manually cultivated farm was carried over to the jammed streets of the ghetto." If children had been able to help with farm labor in the country, in the city, where there was little space and fewer jobs, more children were simply more mouths to feed. Families who had "carried with them the folkways of the countryside" would find themselves adapting to the new conditions of urban life with difficulty, largely because of "the absence of institutions to acclimate them to their new environment."[41] King credited Margaret Sanger as being one of the only people "who offered an important institutional remedy," but because she was "unfortunately ignored by social and political leaders in this period . . . Negro folkways in family size persisted."[42]

According to King, the combination of a lack of social support for new migrants and the systemic racism that they encountered in cities resulted in "high rates of illegitimacy and fragile family relationships."[43] King, like many Americans operating in a post–World War II Judeo-Christian model, lifted up the moral values of the nuclear family, and argued that any tools that could improve family life for Black communities deserved consideration. He saw family planning as such a tool, one that would allow African Americans to shape their families in line with both American and the newly developed Christian ideals of responsible parenthood. "There are mountainous obstacles still separating Negroes from a normal existence," he told the Planned Parenthood audience. "Yet one element in stabilizing his life," King added, "would be an understanding of and easy access to the means to develop a family related in size to his community environment and to the income potential he can command."[44] In these comments, one can hear King's concerns about weak family structures that echo through the sociological literature, and an argument that those structures are not weak because of inherent failures of Black families but because of the social conditions in which structural racism and poverty forced them to live. His remarks also reflect the hope that contraception and the theology of responsible parenthood could improve those conditions by offering married couples the agency to prayerfully plan their families with an eye toward stewardship of their children, economic resources, and communities.

King was careful to avoid the suggestion that Black communities were uniquely in need of help: He rooted their struggles, including struggles in family size, in poverty. According to King, large family size was not a problem unique to Black families; rather, he said, "like all poor, Negro and white, they have many unwanted children."[45] King wanted to underscore that extra children were not simply an inconvenience or a surprise. Instead, these children were unwanted, a burden. He observed, "This is a cruel evil they [Black families] urgently need to control. There is scarcely anything more tragic in human life than a child who is not wanted. That which should be a blessing becomes a curse for parent and child." In this language, redolent with subtly Christian references, extra children are a tragedy, made perhaps even more devastating by the fact that unwanted children are also avoidable. For King, it remained central to underscore that these circumstances were not, somehow, innate to Black people or communities. "There is nothing inherent in the Negro mentality which creates this condition," he explained. In fact, he added, "when Negroes have been able to ascend economically, statistics reveal they plan their families with even greater care than whites. Negroes of higher economic and educational status actually have fewer children than white families in the same circumstances."[46] King's observation that Black couples with the resources to access birth control did and should do so served to undercut white assumptions that Black parents did not accept the scientific, modern advantages of birth control; it also undercut some Black nationalist arguments that birth control was not good for Black families.

The Catholic Father of Oral Contraception

This remarkable new moral avenue of responsible parenthood developed not only over and against Catholic opposition to birth control, but as part of an ongoing—if surprising—conversation within the Catholic Church about the morality of birth control. Granted, as we saw in the previous chapter on the diaphragm, the institutional Church did not endorse contraception; and American Catholic leadership at times intervened in public debates to attempt to limit contraceptive access. Catholic objection to birth control, however, was far from universal: Many lay Catholics were very interested in contraception, and many parish priests—and even some high-level theologians—supported their desires.[47] This support for the Pill came from two particularly important kinds of authority: theologians and other religious leaders within the Catholic Church, and the primary front man for the Pill, physician and Catholic John Rock.

John Rock, the Harvard Medical School professor, researcher, and physician who had, along with Gregory Pincus, developed the birth control pill, was also the doctor primarily responsible for promoting it. This choice was made in part because of his professional reputation. As historian Andrea Tone explains, he was understood to be the best obstetrician in New England.[48] Importantly, Rock was also a devout Catholic with five children, and he attended daily Mass, had a crucifix above the desk in his office, and had long supported contraception despite the position of the Church. In 1931, he had publicly advocated for the repeal of Massachusetts's contraceptive bans on the grounds that birth control was at times medically necessary. In 1943, writing in a national medical journal, Rock claimed, "The intelligent American couple is committed to contraception as a means of limiting the number of children to that which can be reared in each family according to the American standard of education and health."[49] This meant, in part, making sure that a couple could afford to raise children in the resource-intensive style of the midcentury, which increasingly included an expectation of college. But it also meant avoiding giving birth to children whose "known inheritable factors . . . preclude the likelihood of health and happiness of the offspring, or which promise to make of the child an unwarrantable burden on society."[50]

Last, Rock was concerned for maternal health. "No wife should be expected to bear children unless she can do so without serious threat to her own health

"Every baby wanted and loved." Courtesy of the Library of Congress, Prints and Photographs Division, LC-USZ62-113629.

and reason," he asserted.[51] Rock's concerns demonstrate the complicated nexus of motivations underscoring the midcentury birth control movement. His comments reflect support for upward mobility, medical if not racial eugenics, and a concern for maternal health, including mental health; but they did not necessarily indicate an awareness of or interest in women having an identity beyond that of wife and mother.

As radical as these practices were, it would be a mistake to see Rock as particularly socially liberal—which in some ways made him the perfect PR man for the Pill. Even as he advocated for birth control, he did not think that contraception should be used by unmarried women. Rock also did not think that married couples should use it lightly, writing that they should not use it for "no good reason." Each couple should have as many children as they could "properly rear and as society can properly engross." Rock was motivated by social concerns around the health of families and around population control, but he did not think that couples should reject parenthood or reject a number of children for whom they could responsibly care. But while not a social liberal, the doctor was adamantly in favor of making legalized, medically prescribed contraception available for married couples who looked to implement responsible parenthood.

Rock was also sympathetic to couples overwhelmed by the number of children they had already produced, and by the choice of risking more children or attempting to live together in celibacy—he came, through his practice, to see contraception as potentially good for the health of marriages. For these reasons, he trained his students at Harvard to fit women for diaphragms throughout the 1940s and 1950s, despite the fact that his own church had specifically banned barrier methods of contraception.

Though Rock was willing to provide barrier methods of contraception, part of the appeal of the birth control pill to him was that it would be acceptable to the Catholic Church, or so he believed. This belief was based on the fact that while Pius XI's 1930 encyclical *Casti Connubii* had prohibited artificial contraception, calling it an intrinsic evil, by the mid-twentieth century, the Church had acknowledged and even tacitly condoned the idea that Catholics might wish to limit their family size. Indeed, there was much conversation in Catholic circles about how to best employ what was popularly, and at the time not pejoratively, called the "rhythm method." From Catholic doctors and from Church-provided premarital instruction, couples could receive information about managing fertility through periodic abstinence. Rhythm was popular precisely because it was seen as scientific and reliable.[52]

Catholic Morality and Family Limitation

Although some church leaders still hurried to place limits around the rhythm method, it was abundantly clear that Catholic women used it for all kinds of reasons beyond those restrictions. According to Father N Orville Griese in his 1944 The "Rhythm" in Marriage and Christian Morality, the use of the rhythm method was only acceptable for extreme reasons, including maternal health, extreme poverty, and well-founded fears of stillbirth or congenital health problems. Though Griese put strict limits on when it was moral to use the rhythm method, and Pius XI seemed to endorse his views, statistics suggest that many more Catholics used the rhythm method without being in such dire straits. Tentler notes that the use of rhythm increased dramatically in the United States during the 1940s and early 1950s, and that national fertility surveys suggest that many of those users were well-educated Catholic wives. A survey in 1955 demonstrated that 80 percent of Catholic wives with some college education were using or had used rhythm.[53] Clearly, at least in the United States, Catholics were using the rhythm method far more often than serious medical or economic reasons might dictate.

In some ways, Pius XI seemed to acknowledge these societal desires. In his November 26, 1951, address to the Italian Union of Large Families, he noted, "Nevertheless, the Church can comprehend with empathy the real difficulties of conjugal life nowadays. We affirmed the legitimacy and at the time the limits—in reality fairly wide—of a regulation of offspring, which contrarily to 'birth planning' is compatible with the law of God."[54] Though Pius XI was clearly speaking against using birth control simply for consequence-free sex, his comment made a distinction between "birth planning," or the practices forbidden by Casti Connubii, and "legitimate" modes of regulating (read: limiting) offspring. This is an admittedly fine line, and one that caused Rock to think that the Vatican might be moving in a direction sympathetic to the birth control pill. Writing in Good Housekeeping magazine the year after the Food and Drug Administration had approved the Envoid oral contraceptive for use in the United States, Rock quoted Pope Pius XI in a similar speech to the Union of Italian Catholic Midwives on October 26, 1951, and the Very Reverend Monsignor George Kelly, noting that there were sometimes justifications for family planning. Their justifications were very much in line with Rock's, focusing on the "medical, eugenical, economic, or social order."[55]

Perhaps more importantly, for those who, like Rock, assumed that the birth control pill would be acceptable to the Catholic Church, Pius XI suggested that believers might turn to science for assistance: "We could actually hope

"Nice weasling on the pill!" Courtesy of the Library of Congress, Prints and Photographs Division, Carolyn and Erwin Swann Collection (SWANN no. 642, signed by Mischa Richter).

(but we leave the final judgment to the medical science) that such [science] could give that licit method a sufficiently sound basis, and the latest information seemed to confirm such hope."[56] The logic here was that because the Church had allowed couples to limit their family size by taking advantage of the parts of a woman's menstrual cycle when she was naturally least likely to conceive, and because the Pill used naturally occurring hormones to regulate a woman's cycle, it seemed like it might potentially be a form of birth control acceptable to Catholics.[57]

Rock was correct to note that the Pill would open up conversations about contraception in the Catholic Church. After the FDA approved the birth control pill, conversations about contraception were actively debated in the Christian Family Movement (CFM) and in other Catholic circles. An article by Father Walter Imbiorski, director of the Chicago Cana Conference, published in the CFM conference newsletter, raised many questions: If contraception were truly against natural law, why did only Catholics recognize it as such? Could one allow contraception in marriage while simultaneously coming up with compelling arguments against premarital sex? Was sex necessary to a healthy marriage, or could a couple have a good, happy, close, and celibate marriage if they did not want to have more children? Would contraception improve marriage? Should people think carefully about how many children they could raise well?[58]

These debates about contraception were not simply a matter for theological conversation. In the mid-1960s, more or less in tandem with the Second Ecumenical Council of the Vatican, more commonly known as the Second Vatican Council or Vatican II, the Catholic Church convened the Papal Commission on Birth Control. Officially the Pontifical Commission for the Study of Population, Family, and Births, the group was itself the brainchild of Cardinal Leo Joseph Suenens. Prior to becoming a cardinal, as the archbishop of Malinese-Brussels, Belgium, Suenens had become particularly interested in the question of birth control. In his attempt to reconcile the Church's position on contraception with both medical advances and his understanding of the experiences of the laity, particularly women, he held a series of conferences at the University of Louvain in the years before Vatican II to consider the issue from medical, economic, theological, and sociological perspectives.

When the newly appointed cardinal found himself one of the primary organizers of Vatican II, he feared that birth control would not receive sufficient attention, given all the other issues on the table; so in 1963 he proposed a separate commission on his pet project.[59] In an interview, Suenens explained that he hoped that the commission would be able to provide "an intelligent position on responsible parenthood and at least try to reform the old idea, 'the more children the better.'"[60] It is unclear what motivated John XXIII to actually appoint a commission on birth control. Scholars and journalists have offered a variety of views, including that the group was formed because "complicated Vatican politics" had kept "family limitation and global population growth" off the table at Vatican II.[61] Alternately, some argued that John XXIII was motivated to approve the commission less because he shared Suenens's views, and more because a series of conferences looming in the next year would address questions of population control. The Papal Commission on Birth Control would ensure that the Vatican had a response should those conferences call for "family limitation."[62] Most optimistically, one author suggested that the pope was concerned about "the birth control question as it impinged on the lives of good Catholics."[63]

Regardless of why it was formed, the Papal Commission on Birth Control met five times over a period of several years, adding more delegates at each meeting. Initially restricted to six members who were demographers, sociologists, and physicians, by its final meeting in 1966 the commission had grown to seventy-two members. At that time, delegates included priests, theologians, laity, and three married couples.[64] Scholars of Catholicism vary in their interpretations of the papal commission and on whether its existence and work indicated a genuine willingness on the part of the Church to change its stance on contraception. But what is certainly the case is that the group, which served an advisory role, did endorse a change in the Catholic Church's position on contraception. The Church kept the commission's findings quiet for a year. Then, when the pope issued *Humanae Vitae* in 1968, which asserted that abortion was forbidden and also "excluded [from Catholic life] . . . any action which either before, at the moment of, or after sexual intercourse, is specifically intended to prevent procreation—whether as an end or as a means," he went against the delegates' recommendations.[65] While I address *Humane Vitae* in a later chapter, what is manifestly clear from the Papal Commission on Birth Control's recommendation is that it was completely possible for an international collection of high-ranking Catholics, the vast majority of whom were celibate priests, to endorse the use of contraception, at least the use of the birth control pill, largely for reasons connected to the theology of responsible parenthood.

Bringing Responsible Parenthood to Clergy and Congregations

What did this responsible parenthood look like in the lives and experiences of American families? And what did this vision of family and parenthood mean for the question of population explosion that became so central in the middle of the twentieth century? How does understanding the role of religion in these stories change how we see them? The answer depends more on whose voices we privilege. In this case, the distinction that matters is less "Catholic versus Protestant" and more "clergy versus laity" or, perhaps even more importantly, "predominantly male voices versus predominantly female voices." The official Protestant statements on responsible parenthood—the *Majority Report of the Birth Control Commission* and formal National Council of Churches educational campaigns about responsible parenthood—show real interest in using new scientific developments to regulate marriage and family life for a variety of purposes. But the understanding that these technologies were actually regulating women's bodies in order to do so is absent from their theologies, as are the emotional, practical, and embodied realities of family life.

Average couples might well have encountered theologies of responsible parenthood through their clergy. William Genné, director of family ministries for the NCC from 1957 to 1975, conducted outreach and training based on the principles of the NCC statement. In 1961, Genné and his wife and professional collaborator, Elizabeth, participated in a conference sponsored by the Canadian and National (USA) Councils of Churches which was attended by more than five hundred administrators and opinion shapers from thirty-three denominations across fifty-seven states and provinces. The conference had a five-pronged mission: (1) to face "the confusions, the ambiguities, and the failures of our Christian attitudes and behavior in the realm of sex and family life today," (2) "to bring the resources of science" to bear on that discussion, (3) "to set [those] discussions within the framework of biblical thought," (4) "to allow ample time for thorough discussion," and (5) "to bring positive proposals to the churches for their future policies and programs."[66] The conference, then, sought to bring the resources of science and religion together to create a new, Christian understanding of family life.

The NCC's statement of responsible parenthood was axiomatic for attendees. Participants opened each day with a reading from scripture, participated in three-hour-long work groups, and formulated "positive proposals" to the participating churches, which would then structure their own policies and outreach programs around sex and family life.[67] The conference covered a range of topics, such as "factors in the formation of marriage," "contemporary sexual behavior," and "facts and issues in family planning." Family planning was treated as central to the conversation, on a par with the nature of marriage and Christian responses to sexual behaviors like infidelity. William and

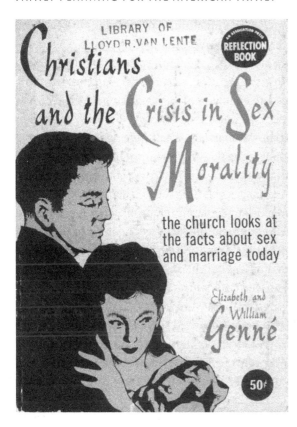

Cover of *Christians and the Crisis in Sex Morality*, by Elizabeth and William Genné. Courtesy of the National Board of the YMCA.

Elizabeth Genné published highlights from the conference in *Christians and the Crisis in Sex Morality*, a "faithful reflection of the spirit of the North American Conference on Church and Family."[68]

At the conference, Protestant conversations about contraceptive use veered into discussions about sex education. The Gennés compiled information showing that the use of medical birth control among Protestants rose in tandem with level of education, arguing that low income and a low level of education were the strongest detriments to contraceptive use. The authors pointed to reports about the prevalence of unwanted children in low-income families. In addition, they drew from research that warned of young people who were raised in contexts where adults demonstrated limited control over their own reproduction, and who would, in turn, make intemperate choices in their own reproduction and produce children for whom they could not care.[69] These reports understood working-class, and often non-white, families as in particular need of birth control and sex education. The Gennés argued that Christians who had "managed to learn how to combine, in [their] thinking hearts and spirits and actions, all the functions and meanings of sex" were best equipped to teach youth about healthy sexuality.[70]

To undertake the teaching of sexuality and family planning within a Christian context, the NCC, through the Gennés, began to develop and distribute a program through churches and chaplains. This program held that couples should be encouraged to wait two years after marriage before having their first child, so as to ensure that the marriage was stable and that they were ready for parenthood. To counter the fear that the presence of birth control might result in declining moral standards, the NCC's sex education programs emphasized to young people that sex was a privilege reserved for marriage. These ideas were disseminated through a variety of means. The Gennés called for ministers to remind their congregations of the obligation to plan their families, and encouraged congregations to offer information and support to congregants. Also, Protestant hospital chaplains were instructed to make sure that all non-Catholic patients had contraceptive information available to them on a par with that for other medical services. Moreover, the Gennés advised that Protestant chaplains in the armed services should aid military wives in obtaining contraceptive services.[71] Protestant missionary services, they believed, should include contraceptive services in their offerings to "suppressed minority migrants and American Indian groups."[72] As director of family ministry, William Genné traveled to churches and other community groups, particularly in the Northeast, giving them tools to implement these agenda items.

Responsible Parenthood in Christian Family Life

In many cases, women—as actual people living in actual bodies—are stunningly absent from this discourse. The voices of real couples writing about their lives are also largely absent from the historical record. That said, in his role as the Catholic celebrity doctor responsible for the birth control pill, John Rock received both hate mail and fan mail that offer some insight into how the American public understood the Pill. Often, the critical letters were from Catholics who referenced Rock's own Catholicism. A typical response came from a woman who chastised Rock for his association with Planned Parenthood. She argued, "As a Catholic—how could you believe that you have a right over life [and] death? God alone has this right [and] by cooperating with an organization that recommends murder through Birth Control you advocate murdering of babies God wills in the world."[73] Letters like this, though, were in a distinct minority. Most correspondents commented on the

Pill as a tool of social good, or on its impact in their own lives. Sometimes religion was mentioned, but only in briefly, as in the case of one woman who wrote a substantial letter asking Rock for medical advice, noting in passing that she and her husband found their family of four children to be sufficient, and stating, "The moral issue has never been a factor here, though we are both Roman Catholics."[74]

While not all Rock's laudatory letters came from people who wrote about their Christian faith, many did make specific reference to their religion. One woman wrote in while planning for her marriage. She wanted medical advice about what contraceptive to use, as her husband intended to continue his education for four or five years. "We are Roman Catholics," she wrote, "but we both know that an education is of primary importance for job security and financial success." She further wanted to know whether, when they had completed having their hoped-for four or five children, she could return to taking the Pill without an impact on her menopause and long-term health.[75]

According to responsible parenthood theology, both men and women shared the Christian responsibility to practice contraception; but it was women more than men who wrote to Rock thanking him for the role that the Pill played in their lives. These letters of gratitude did not necessarily address responsible parenthood directly, but they implicitly spoke to its tenets. For example, one thankful woman wrote, "As the mother of two boys, thirteen months apart, I wish to express my gratitude to you and your staff for making the oral contraceptive pill. I am not Catholic, but my husband is, and so naturally we used the rhythm method. After the birth of our second child, who was five weeks premature, my husband consulted the priest who married us. He told my husband that by all means we should use the pill and that we should use it until we wanted another child." For this couple, contraception meant relief. She continued, "The joy and peace that is in our home now is wonderful. Thank you again and may God Bless you and your work."[76] This mother's appreciation begins to point us in the direction of contraception as transformative—a message that was strikingly absent from early Protestant arguments for birth control, but that would become increasingly prominent in future conversations.

After appearing on NBC's *Birth Control: How?*, hosted by David Brinkley, on January 12, 1964, Rock received many more letters from viewers. Mrs. Alden H. Blake wrote that she and her husband used Envoid, the brand name for the first birth control pill, for the first year and a half of their marriage, as he completed his training at Andover Newton Theological School. She noted that Envoid had allowed them to postpone starting their family while achieving "a more than satisfactory adjustment to the normal initiary problems of a good sex life." Blake added that they were looking forward "with the happiest anticipation to our first baby sometime next year, God willing."[77] She concluded:

> My admiration must also be expressed for you as you have stood so firmly in the face of adversity. I think that you have shown great courage in doing so, and I too feel that God does not, and will not condemn you for your wonderful work, but rather walks in step with you as you search to help all mankind. As the wife of a Protestant minister, I should also like to say that you, as a staunch Roman Catholic, are to be commended for all that you have done and are doing in the spirit of ecumenicity. It is people like you who will someday reknit the raveled shreds of this world into the whole cloth of true Christendom.[78]

Mrs. Blake's letter encapsulates much of Protestant thought at the time: She pointed to the need to plan her family, the importance of a good sex life, and the value of ecumenical conversation. To her, Rock's work was godly both because it aided humanity and because, by supporting contraception as a Catholic, Rock was bridging the Protestant/Catholic divide. A woman who signed herself Sarah L. Barnett (Mrs. G. O.) reiterated the ecumenical point when she wrote, "I feel you are doing a great deal to help unsophisticated Protestants and Jews to be open to, and work with, Catholics in this area. I feel that your example is actively encouraging the common people to actively support work in this field. Thank you for your leadership." In another letter, a Mrs. R. Benjamin wrote that she had three children and hoped to adopt a child in need, adding, "Without your pills, I would have 8, and no hope of taking in and educating an extra one."[79] She echoed the godly point, writing, "The envoid pill you have discovered and perfected cannot do anything but good. Goodness is God-ness and so you are right in your position. If you must answer to God and you are wrong, may I suffer for you."[80]

Contraception here was not merely acceptable; instead, it was presented as divinely given, a necessary and wholly Christian obligation. By explicitly divorcing birth control from the language of women's rights, these women made contraception a religious right. While the assertion that birth control was antithetical to a divine concept of the creation of human life was certainly present, casting contraception as a Christian concept was a remarkable—perhaps even radical—reformulation, and one to which the laity, as much as clergy and theologians, laid claim. In addition, the voices of some of these women foreshadow the transformative feminist impact that the birth control pill, and other forms of contraception, would ultimately have.

Women were not Rock's only correspondents. In one letter, a retired teacher and parole officer noted that, in his line of work, he had "got to know the evils of poverty and over-population first hand." The man further said that Rock was "doing a great and a good work and history has shown that the Catholic Church has often been wrong in the past and I think it is presently wrong on birth control."[81]

Protestant clergy wrote to Rock seeking advice for their flocks on the practice of "voluntary parenthood."[82] For instance, after Rock's *Birth Control: How?* appearance, Florida Presbyterian minister Russell Burns wrote to say that after ten years of ministry, he had found that he could "love God, ignore Him, despise Him, and even Crucify Him with my words and deeds, but He remains loving, patient, and merciful. I believe He wants us to be creative, eager, and informed to cultivate and to develop all that He has created."[83] To that end, Reverend Burns told Rock, "I believe if your work or anyone else's were contrary to His will, He, in His own way, would see that it was curtailed. I sincerely believe that you have done no wrong. May our Lord Jesus continue to bless and to use you until He comes."[84] Within two weeks, Rock had written back to thank the minister for his comforting note, and to observe, "I think you and I have about the same idea of the kind of God-man Jesus is. Frankly, I feel very friendly disposed towards him, and within me, I have a sense that he is a friend of mine also. I am sure he is likewise of yours."[85]

In these letters, two men, one Catholic and one Protestant, not only found no conflict between Christianity and birth control, but rather found synergy between them—they both believed that scientific inquiry and development was godly work. Indeed, Rock seems to have drawn emotional comfort in the face of criticism from the support of fellow Christians like Burns, and from his own sense of his relationship with Jesus.

A particularly rich archive of Catholic feelings about contraception and the lack thereof comes from a collection of surveys taken by Pat and Patty Crowley, who were one of the three married couples who attended the final meeting of the Papal Commission on Birth Control. While there were seventy-two members of the commission present at the fifth and final meeting in April 1966, Patty Crowley was one of only five women, three of whom were married. Patty was a fifty-one-year-old mother of five, and she and Pat had been invited because of their leadership in the (Catholic) Christian Family Movement, where they served as the "couple president." CFM was founded in Chicago and South Bend in the early 1940s, and it spread nationally and internationally throughout the 1950s and 1960s. Made up of committed married Catholic couples, CFM chapters met in private homes at least once a month to discuss how members' Catholicism could infuse and inform their marriages, their families, and their lives more broadly in the world. CFM took seriously the idea that, for Catholics, marriage was a vocation in the same way that holy orders were a vocation, and its proponents worked to nurture and support that vocational aspect of marriage and family life.

The depth of the Crowleys' involvement in CFM demonstrates their profound commitments to and connections within Catholicism. At the time of the Papal Commission on Birth Control, CFM had more than 150,000 member couples worldwide. Through CFM, the Crowleys visited people in many countries, speaking with theologians, clergy, and laity alike. In addition to raising their own children, they had served as foster parents through Catholic Family Charities, a role that had given them insight into some of the complications facing families in their community.

Still, the Crowleys decided that if they were going to represent American lay Catholics, and possibly lay Catholics more broadly, they should do so based on something more formal than their own opinions and those of their friends and couples with whom they had spoken. They sent out a collection of surveys to other CFM couples throughout the United States and internationally. The questionnaires were very simple. They asked for the ages of the husband and wife, the number of years that they had been married, and the number of children that they had. The survey then asked whether the church should change its teaching on birth control, offering the option to check off "yes" or "no." The final question was free-form, offering space to respond to the query "What should the church say on the subject?" Some people answered the question about the number of children with a simple number; others noted the number of living children versus dead children, or noted not only the number of living children, but the number of miscarriages suffered. Some responded simply to the question in the space provided; and others used the survey as an opportunity to write a letter to the Crowleys.

Pat and Patty Crowley received responses from across the country, including from California, but mainly from the Midwest and the American South. These responses came sometimes from major cities but also from small towns and small cities. People responded from Los Angeles but also from Fresno, from Birmingham, Alabama, but also from Mobile. While they were sent to couples, it is clear that the surveys were at times answered by the couple together, but more often answered by just one person—most often, but not always, the wife. In some of the responses that seemed to be authored by a couple together, there would be a seamless presentation of a shared view; but at other times, the spouses would record their answers to reflect differences of opinion. When the response seemed to come from one person, sometimes it would be hard to tell whether it noted the shared opinions of a couple. Other times, respondents would include their own thoughts and feelings and their perceptions of their spouses' perspectives. A few responses clearly came from one person and revealed discord and distress in the marriage, as evidenced in how correspondents presented their own stories and their understanding or fears of their spouses' points of view.

Just as the Crowleys' involvement in CFM demonstrates their own commitment to living their Catholicism in their daily lives, the fact that the CFM was the main source of survey respondents suggests that, by and large, the surveys were answered by couples who were profoundly committed to the Catholic Church. Despite that commitment, the questionnaires overwhelmingly depict frustration with the Church's dedication to the rhythm method, and express the respondents' desire for acceptance of the birth control pill.

First, not everyone was supportive of the new technology. Some of the Crowleys' respondents were disapproving, often echoing some version of one writer's point that one "can't change a basic moral principle." [86] Another survey respondent noted being married six years with two children and wrote, "If it is in God's law, as I have been taught: that it is in the bible: how can it be changed! I see a value of the pill for regulations of menstrual cycle so rhythm, perhaps, would be more accurate. I'm against birth control and I was against it as a Protestant." [87] For these voices, contraception was simply not possible because it was against the law of the Catholic Church, which these believers saw as both eternal and immutable. As one response put it, "We accept the Church's teaching authority in the area of artificial birth control but are unable to understand the theology of the doctrine." [88]

Others found beauty and a connection to their faith in the self-discipline required to practice rhythm, writing, "Man should be made to realize that God gave him the will and the faculties to control all of his desires. In the first commandment we are commanded not to have any other gods before us." For this couple, the use of contraception would allow "sex to be important in our lives for sex's sake alone rather than a part of the divine role of matrimony, [so that] we will have elevated sex to the role of a false god." [89] This Gary, Indiana, husband and wife were not alone in seeing real value in the discipline required for rhythm. As one response noted, "It made two people more mature and more in a partnership with God." [90] For these voices, the periodic abstinence of the rhythm was a meaningful practice, both in the discipline that it required and in the joy of sexual reunion.

It is worth noting that many of the people who thought that rhythm should be left in place had been able to use it successfully, at least from the standpoint of child limitation. One response noted, "The church has had a definite point on this subject since its origination by Christ. All men have existed and lived under this ruling until now without changing. Leave it as it is." This couple was close to the end of their reproductive life; the wife was thirty-eight years old, and their nineteen-year marriage had yielded two children.[91] Whatever the constraints of the rhythm method—and many of the people who wrote in support of the status quo did not mention those constraints—they had either been able to limit their families or had desired large families from the start. The successful limitation of children was not, however, a universal characteristic of those who supported rhythm. "There were times, especially when we were younger and poorer, that it seemed like a terrible thing to ask of two young people who were completely in love (self-giving) to not be able to give themselves physically," wrote in one couple who, with the wife at age forty-two, had ten children. "So we gave many times when it didn't seem the prudent thing," they continued, "and God always took care of us. It seems that many young people are forgetting that it takes three, the man, wife, and God, to procreate. Why don't we have more faith?"[92]

Another wife, also with ten children, observed, "If God had made my periods such that we could have limited the size of our family by practicing rhythm and still have somewhat normal (as to the number) relations, we would have been selfish enough to have limited our family to a couple of children." She was glad, however, that "God did not see fit to do this and we are very glad because nothing we have in this life has given us as much pleasure or happiness as the love of our children for us and for each other."[93] This wife presented herself and her husband as having ten children because God saw fit to give them ten children, and they believed that God would then take care of them. As one of the surveys noted, "God has certainly taken care of us in various ways. We feel He does this for everyone who will do what they can do and then depend on God for the rest."[94] These voices were, however, in the minority.

Only a handful of the Catholic survey responses came from people who were using oral contraception—in the section of the CFM questionnaire where respondents were asked to comment on what position they would like to see the church take, they often commented on who in their life had authorized them to do so, possibly a priest or a Catholic doctor. But the majority of the letters came from people who did not use oral contraception.[95] Rather, they wrote about their experiences and struggles with the rhythm method, and its impact on their marriages. For these couples, the birth control pill provided a tool through which Catholics could nurture their marriages. They saw this practice as being in keeping with the Church's emphasis on marriage. Their message echoed the depiction of Christian marriage that Protestants had expounded on from the pulpit, as seen in chapter 1, and made up a key component of Protestant responsible parenthood theology. One couple with six children wrote an impassioned defense of the role of sex in marriage:

> The intimacies of marriage provide for a married person the primary experience with love, and thus with Christ. This is true whether we play together, work together, educate our children together, pray together and especially have marital relations together. One would suspect that many within the church would find any suggestion that Christ shares in the love of marital relations to be at worst obscene and sacrilegious. . . . Does not Christ himself compare his union with the church with that of the bride and bridegroom? How can this be understood in any sense other than as a bond of true spiritual love of the kind known as complementary love with the physical love of marriage?[96]

In this couple's understanding, sex itself drew a couple closer not only to each other but also to Christ. Though this husband and wife had six children born in the nine and a half years of their marriage, they did not think that sex was only for procreation. They believed that "for a married couple, a child is a natural product of that love, much as God's love for Himself is said to have produced a Divine Person." But that did not mean that a child had to be possible with each act of intercourse, for they went on to write, "The proper purpose of the marriage is every bit as much the development of the whole person, caused in part it seems by the contact with the opposite sex, and fulfillment of the most complete love known to man as man, the love of one spouse for the other."[97] That love, the couple stated, served as "our contribution to Christ's greatest commandment, and it accomplishes that command as between husband and wife whether or not there is a child as a product."[98] In other words, the love of husband and wife was of central importance to the sacramental relationship of marriage, even when there was no intention to conceive. This couple observed that while for them their children had been, "over the long range, though not every day," a "joy," they were aware that such was not the case for all of their friends.[99] Marital intimacy needed to be possible, even when having more children would be a cause of strain.

Other couples offered similar thoughts, framing their desire for contraception to control their own fertility in directly religious terms. "In prayer and study, a couple should alone decide upon that method which is consistent with the growth of their love and fulfilling of their responsibilities as parents," wrote a Los Angeles husband and wife who had been married just under twelve years and had five children. "The focus should be upon the entire marriage and family in making this decision," they observed, "not upon the individual act of intercourse."[100] For this couple, the "birth control method should serve the marriage relationship, its growth, its harmony, its expression, and its health. If it does not, it should be discarded and another method considered and tried."[101]

Another couple, from Hartford,[102] emphasized the importance of marriage and family, writing that they were "about the most stable things in our entire universe," and that "everything must be done to strengthen these."[103] Lest the Crowleys take their comments as anticontraception, the respondents, who had been married ten years and had four children, continued, "Birth control need not weaken these if there were certain conditions under which a couple with good conscience and guidance might occasionally make use of it."[104] Those conditions, they went on to say, were not "materialistic," but rather "reasons of health, mental health or emotional stability of a family."[105] This couple clearly saw birth control as a tool that could, if used in certain ways, strengthen the family. The distinction between materialism and the family's mental health and emotional stability is interesting because, as many Protestant clergy argued and, indeed, as other letters and surveys in the Crowley papers demonstrate, financial strain could negatively impact the emotional stability of the family. Letters like this raise the question of whether the writers came from a comfortable class position, such that they were not aware of the potential financial strains of a large family, or whether they meant something a bit different—the desire to live a decadent life, for instance.

In the surveys, some respondents supported expanding the range of contraception acceptable for Catholics, perhaps beyond even the Pill, but these opinions did not mean that they had a weak connection to the institutional Roman Catholic Church. For instance, one Los Angeles couple, the husband age thirty-four and the wife age thirty-two, who had been married eleven and a half years and had five children, wrote to the Crowleys that the Catholic Church should encourage "married couples to select that method (be it pills, rhythm, contraceptives, etc.) that will, for them, *strengthen their mutual love, increase their generosity, and be compatible* with their personal expression and circumstances." At the same time, the Church should encourage those same married couples to "increase their frequentation of the Sacraments as they pioneer this broader understanding of mutual love and responsible parenthood."[106] The implication of their argument was that, in fact, a closer sacramental relationship to the Church would be of use as spouses developed their sense of how to be together, both as lovers and as parents.

While couples showed a clear interest in the potential that the Pill might offer to strengthen marriage, they also made it very clear that the absence of reliable contraception could weaken the marriage and family. One Los Angeles couple commented, "Abstinence from intercourse for fear of conception puts an unnatural strain on marriage and tends to destroy it."[107] Meanwhile, a couple from Beach Grove, Indiana, noted, "When the real reason for indulging is not a spontaneous support but the nagging belief that it might be the last chance for three weeks, the act that is supposed to be building a firm foundation for a lasting love is somehow missing its mark."[108] A San Francisco husband and wife observed, "It is unworkable in many cases, including ours (whose cycle runs from 30 to 90 days), and only causes anxiety, a fear of intercourse due to possible pregnancy, dissension, and a disruption of family life that destroys its ends and affects all members, including the children."[109] These letter writers contended that the Catholic Church should embrace birth control, at least the contraceptive pill, as a tool that would support rather than detract from marriage and family—a message that echoed the sentiments of Protestant responsible parenthood.

While many letter writers explained that abstinence was hard on both the husband and the wife, others noted that the work of the rhythm method, and its anxieties, fell disproportionately on the wife. One woman wrote that using rhythm made her "panicky" and "nervous."[110] A young couple, the husband twenty-eight and the wife twenty-five, who had been married for five years with three children, asked why the wife should be the "policeman of the marriage bed," suggesting instead that "the church should emphasize the husband's responsibility and allow him to use artificial means of contraception." This statement that seemed to imply support for condoms in addition to, or perhaps instead of, the Pill.[111]

The strain of having to act as the gatekeeper to her body at the "unsafe" times was not only an unequal division of labor, but one that could cause women to be in a difficult position vis-à-vis their husbands. As one woman wrote, "I have kept on using rhythm with relations only once or twice right after my period and one week before the period was due with my husband saying he agreed and yet becoming angry at times and threatening to leave. I still became pregnant three more times."[112] As another mother who had given birth to six children in fifteen years, three of whom were born with cleft palates, noted, "We love the children dearly [but the sheer *panic* that a woman of 40 goes through (or any age) after having a number of children and being five, six days or a week or two late having a period can hardly be described."[113] She noted, "[There is] a monthly session of being frantic during which time it is most difficult to be even civil to the children or husband you have. An understanding husband is a great asset at these times, but not everyone is as fortunate as I am in this regard."[114]

Even the most understanding husband, however, could not help with one unfortunate fact: The rhythm method required abstaining from sex during ovulation—the very moment when women are often most interested in sex. As one woman wrote, "The time of the month when I ovulate is the time I most desire intercourse. It is so frustrating to my husband to find me responsive when we can't complete the act of love."[115] She went on to note that she and her husband drifted apart during the times when they could not have sex, and that they "make love when we don't really feel like it because the next day we must abstain or my period is due. I don't like to have intercourse during my period but sometimes now we do."[116] Another survey response observed, "Rather frustrating to refrain from intercourse during period when wife is most sexually excitable. Love should be spontaneous not indulged in because calendar says it's time. Could cause husband to become impotent because he must refrain when he wants partner most."[117] Still another couple observed, "The time of abstinence is really the time in the women's cycle when she feels and looks the best. Naturally, the husband senses this . . . and is attracted."[118]

These survey responses moved from theology or thoughts about what nurtured families or minimized stress to the very real and intimate realities of desire. These couples wanted to be allowed contraception so that they could act on their desires, which they rightly understood to be set in direct opposition to the rhythms of the rhythm method. One respondent went so far as to point out that the prelates, who lived as celibate men, might simply not understand this reality of married life: "I get a feeling that some of the clergy, since they have no experience in this area, think that we are all filled with overflowing passion that can be released at any time we will. This just isn't so."[119] Not only did these surveys reflect the inherent tension between the rhythm method and a satisfying sex life, but they also underscored the challenge of being expected to discuss those problems with a celibate clergy, made up of men who had often entered celibate life at an early enough age to preclude any licit sexual experience.

If the couples who wrote to the Crowleys did so privately, other Catholic women wrote in more public venues, including women's magazines such as *Good Housekeeping* and *Redbook*, where they discussed both their intellectual, theological, and sacramental commitment to the Catholic Church, and their frustration with the rhythm method.[120] The most prominent of these Catholic women speaking out was Rosemary Radford Ruether, who would go on to become one of the founding mothers of feminist theology. In a piece in the *Saturday Evening Post* publicly stating what many would privately tell the Crowleys, Ruether wrote that many couples found that the rhythm method hampered couples' ability to use sex as lovemaking. Additionally, the moments when a couple might be drawn to each other had to coincide with "safe periods," a reality that weakened the marital sexual relationship, causing it to become "forced." The consequences for a marriage could be severe: "After a few years of struggling with such a system [sleeping in separate beds or rooms in order to avoid temptation], a husband and wife begin to feel their whole marriage somehow twisted."[121]

Ruether reminded her readers that "infertile" periods are not actually times when a woman cannot conceive, but rather when the odds of conception are lower. That meant that even those who practiced rhythm the most assiduously were statistically likely to fail at some point, such that use of rhythm kept many couples in a constant state of stress. "Whenever the period is late or the signs by which the woman tries to predict her cycle are off schedule, there is a time of panic," she wrote. She further revealed, "I know of husbands who have exploded with helpless rage and wives who have become hysterical under these circumstances."[122] Perhaps more importantly, Ruether highlighted the gender inequity of the practice of rhythm. "The woman is cast in the role of, literally, the policeman of the marital bed," and "in using rhythm the couple must avoid the middle of the month, when most women feel the greatest sexual inclination, and confine their relationships to the times when sex is less desirable."[123] In the end, Ruether wrote, the problem with rhythm was not that it required couples to "control their passions," but rather that it destroyed "positive good in the marital relationship." Sex, she asserted, is not simply a means subordinate to the end of procreation. Its purpose is to create "this higher union and completion that has its own union and purpose. And it normally takes far more frequent lovemaking to create this union than procreativity could ever require."[124]

For Ruether, like the couples writing to the Crowleys, birth control was an important tool precisely because it allowed sexual intimacy to strengthen the marital bond, and therefore the family, whereas the rhythm method created anxiety and decreased intimacy that ate away at the marriage, and through it the family. Birth control was once again good and positive in the context of a marriage, but its uses outside marriage were not discussed at all.

Judaism

The national conversation about responsible parenthood was, in the end, primarily a Christian question. Jewish leaders—both Jewish clergy and people who were doctors or reproductive rights leaders who happened to be Jewish—carefully explained the reasons why contraception was not as fraught a religious question for Jews as it was for others. In their discussion of contraception, however, we can see that this topic was also a vehicle for some other concerns that were pressing for Jewish leaders in the 1960s. The late 1960s showed fervent defenses of birth control from two notable figures: Jewish physician Alan Guttmacher, the leader of Planned Parenthood, writing in 1967; and rabbi and doctor of philosophy David M. Feldman, a former US Air Force chaplain, a member of the Law Committee of the Rabbinical Assembly (the professional association of the Conservative movement of Judaism), and a United Synagogue representative to New York state legislative hearings on abortion, writing in 1968.

Both men were writing to reassure their fellow Jews, and doctors providing health care to Jewish women, that birth control was acceptable according to their faith's teaching—and acceptable across all Jewish movements. This basic goal, however, was not the only purpose of their writing. As Jewish leaders, or leading Jews, Guttmacher and Feldman were also navigating the possibilities for Jewish involvement in public discourse in general that had been created by the new Judeo-Christian framing. At the same time, the men were resisting the reality that such a framing tended to trade Jewish distinctiveness for Jewish involvement. As a result, these texts emphasize Jewish difference from Christianity while also trying to assert Judaism as a modern religion whose core values are supportive of marital sex, women's sexual pleasure and health, and medical technology.

In his 1967 article on birth control in *Judaism*, a publication of the American Jewish Congress, Guttmacher noted that the subject was relevant because "what journalists call the 'population explosion' has rendered the question of birth control even more urgent and pertinent."[125] He also focused on

Orthodox Judaism because, "by and large, Conservative and Reform Judaism are in agreement with the liberal attitudes of Protestant Christianity toward the ethical issues associated with the control of contraception."[126] Guttmacher explored the four primary modes of "conception control—celibacy, abortion, contraception, and sterilization"—in order to demonstrate to readers that, even for Orthodox Judaism, there were no prohibitions against contraception, and that contraception was the preferred approach in certain circumstances.[127]

Guttmacher emphasized the marital sex-positive nature of rabbinic sources. He pointed out that these sources stipulate how frequently a man must have sex with his wife, based on the amount of travel required by his profession; noting that these requirements set minimum, not maximum, limits on intercourse. He extrapolated that if pregnancy is not, for some reason, desirable—and Jewish law tends to frame undesirable pregnancy in terms of risk to maternal life—the Jewish answer cannot simply be do not have sex, as it might be in Christianity. Additionally, and perhaps as a result of the importance placed on marital sex, birth control is presented as an established fact in Talmudic sources, on which much of Jewish law is based. Guttmacher emphasized that in Jewish thought, debate has centered on what forms of contraception are acceptable, and under what circumstances they may be used; but not on whether contraception is, at a baseline, permissible. Moving beyond the rabbinic sources, Guttmacher drew examples of birth control in Orthodox life from his own experience as a doctor who, while practicing in Baltimore, had treated the wives of Orthodox rabbis. His observed that even in these very observant communities, where large families were the norm and gendered expectations around modesty seemed out of step with the zeitgeist, rabbis would allow women to use birth control if the pregnancy risked her health.

Guttmacher was writing to a Jewish community that had been hearing the debates about birth control in a secular media largely designed for a Christian country, many of whom were likely not deeply familiar with Jewish law. In the end, he demonstrated for an audience across a range of levels of Jewish observance, even the most religious of his Jewish patients found birth control to be acceptable in particular instances. That said, Guttmacher was also writing as a doctor, one with a knowledge of Jewish law, but not necessarily as an acknowledged authority on Jewish law.

The most authoritative response to birth control from the perspective of Jewish law was Rabbi David Feldman's *Birth Control in Jewish Law: Marital Relations, Contraception, and Abortion as Set Forth in the Classical Texts of Jewish Law*, an encyclopedic treatment of the topic that remains canonical in many ways even today.[128] Feldman drew from traditional sources including "the Tal-mud, Codes and Commentaries, mystic and moral literature, and hundreds of rabbinic Responsa from the earliest times to the present day." He made illustrative comparisons to Christianity in order to interpret the "legal-moral teachings of Judaism on such themes as sexual responsibility in marriage, sexual pleasure as an end in itself, [and] the problems of 'onanism,' and also discussed Jewish law on irregular sex acts, the historical and legal background of the oral contraceptive principle, and the question of abortion."[129] Although Feldman was a rabbi in the Conservative movement, he wrote the book in an attempt to discuss the entirety of Judaism, rather than a specific movement. He directly quoted rabbinic and biblical texts and then noted the range of in-terpretation, both historically and in Judaism during the late 1960s. In doing so, he positioned his text to speak not for a particular Jewish movement or school of interpretation but for k'lal Yisroel, or "all of Judaism."[130] Feldman contended that Jews supported both sex in marriage and the use of contra-ception when necessary. While Christians might disagree about whether birth control was acceptable at all, Jewish disagreement, he maintained, focused on what modes of contraception were acceptable, and exactly what conditions rendered it "necessary."

Rather than being a book exclusively for rabbis or an educated Jewish au-dience, Feldman's study found its way into the hands of the medical establish-ment. When it was reviewed in the *Journal of the American Medical Association*, the reviewer recommended the work highly for rabbis and "physicians educated in Jewish Studies and to those who have some background in Biblical and Talmudic Law," thinking that they might want to read it cover to cover. "For the general medical audience," the reviewer wrote, "this book is best used as a reference work to obtain information covering the Jewish attitude toward specific problems such as marriage, conjugal rights of the wife, spermicides, the pill, coitus interruptus, feticide."[131] *Birth Control in Jewish Law* quickly be-came the authority on the Jewish position on birth control, and on sexuality more broadly.

Feldman articulated two goals. First, he sought to establish some fun-damental differences between Jewish and Christian thought on sex, and therefore on contraception; he was thereby implicitly writing against the idea of Judeo-Christian values. In Feldman's rendition, the Christian Bible argues that it is better marry than to burn; and Catholic teaching holds celibacy as the highest form of human sexuality. Even Protestantism, which frames marriage as the ideal form of human existence, remains skeptical of sex—even within marriage. Because Judaism, Feldman writes, views "marital sex as integral to the relational side of marriage—to *shalom bayit* [peace in the home], that is—as well as to the procreational, a threat to the wife's health in connection with pregnancy must be balanced against" this value.[132]

Second, Feldman demonstrated that Judaism had long acknowledged and accepted the validity of contraception. Ancient sources make reference to an object called a *mokh* and to a "cup of roots" presumed to be herbal remedies for pregnancy. The debates, both around those ancient methods of contraception and around contemporary forms as they were developed, were not based in the question of whether contraception was acceptable but rather in which forms were acceptable and under what circumstances. For instance, how severe did a threat to maternal health need to be? If serious health concerns exist, and the only available birth control is problematic according to Jewish law, when may one decide to use that birth control anyway? Thus, though there was sometimes debate in Jewish communities over birth control, it did not take the same tenor as it did in Christian communities.

Underscoring these differences from Christianity served two purposes for Feldman as a mid-twentieth-century rabbi in the Conservative movement. The formulation of a Judeo-Christian America that had focused on the heterosexual family opened up space for Jews in American public life. Yet the Judeo-Christian framework also subsumed Jewish particularity into the Protestant Christian dominance. By asserting that Jews agreed with Protestants on the morality of contraception, but for different reasons, Feldman could proclaim Jewish difference without disrupting the alliance. By asserting that Judaism had placed a higher premium on sexual pleasure within marriage than had Christianity throughout its history, and by demonstrating that Jews had longer considered birth control acceptable, and even at times necessary and moral, he made an implicit claim for Judaism as ultimately, at its core, compatible with modern American society.

Guttmacher and Feldman were writing in a moment in the late 1960s when most non-Orthodox Jews had come to embrace birth control, and when even Orthodox Jews were often particularly interested in forms of birth control like the Pill, which could be used without posing the halakhic problems raised by condoms. Within a decade, some of these Jewish conversations about contraception would fall apart, as fears about Jewish continuity would seize the communal imagination. But at this moment in the late 1960s, however, Jewish support for contraception was remarkably uncomplicated; and with that support came a path to assert aspects of a public American identity.

Conclusion

In 1968, best-selling novelist and women's rights activist Pearl Buck famously compared the Pill to nuclear fallout, saying, "Everyone knows what The Pill is. It is a small object—yet its potential effect upon our society may be even more devastating than the nuclear bomb."[133] Buck was talking about the impact of the Pill on the moral sensibilities of the nation. She saw in oral contraception the possibility to reshape the social structure of the country. In the years after the release of the Pill, any number of birth control advocates found themselves offering theologies of the drug that would counter the idea that the Pill would reshape society—theologies that, in the end, domesticated the Pill. These theologies created a narrative where the Pill—a form of contraception that women could take and men could not interfere with, and that offered the possibility of consequence-free sex—was not a tool for the radical reshaping of the family. Instead, it was a tool to support and burnish a midcentury ideal of a heteropatriarchal nuclear family with a breadwinning father, domestic mother, and however many children they could raise in an emotionally and financially resource-intensive way.

This understanding of birth control appealed to a wide swath of religious people. For mainline Protestants, birth control created a new realm of moral agency. With control over fertility, couples could plan their families so as to be both better stewards of the earth and more "responsible" members of society. Martin Luther King Jr. saw in the potential of the Pill a tool for racial uplift—for improving the lives of African Americans by increasing the opportunities for economic and educational mobility. Jewish American leadership used Jewish comfort with contraception as a way of staking their claims as a religion that was both modern and American. Even within Catholicism, famously and staunchly opposed to contraception, the Pill offered the possibility of an acceptable contraceptive mode when used in support of marriage and family.

CHAPTER 3

Family Planning for the Human Family

Having solidified the doctrine of responsible parenthood domestically, the United States sought to export the Protestant-inflected American nuclear family to the rest of the world. An eleven-minute animated 1968 educational short film offered one of the clearest examples of how they attempted to do so. The film opens with a disclaimer on a black screen: "The characterizations and situations used in this film may not apply directly to your community, but the basic problems presented are of concern to people everywhere." This is followed by an appearance by Donald Duck as the presenter. Next appears an image of a nuclear family—heterosexual parents with a son and a daughter, in silhouette. Then the title image of Family Planning takes the screen, and an announcement that the film was produced by Walt Disney for the Population Council.

In an illustrated lecture, the narrator asserts that despite their differences, all people—drawn and described as "men"—are essentially the same. The cartoon shows a selection of men in regional dress echoing those in Disney's "It's a Small World" ride, before combining them all into one mustachioed, heavily accented, racially ambiguous "common man." While it seems likely that Disney had in mind a non-white common man, the cartoon does not necessarily rule out an interpretation of whiteness. The film's narrative voice-over, a male voice imbued with scientific authority, points out that men are essentially animals, but that they have something that other animals do not—the ability to reason, and therefore to plan and improve their lot. Man, the narrator states, moves ever upward—as the common man, with an open umbrella, cuts through the rain and ascends into the clouds. The image was literal, but this was an argument about the forward march of progress. Man may become, the film suggests, the master of all he surveys—except, of course, for woman. At this point, the film introduces a woman who only ever speaks to the audience and the narrator by whispering in her husband's ear. Thus, in spite of the suggestion that the common man is not considered to be the master of the common woman, she still stands submissively next to him, often tucked under his arm, and he acts as her voice. The presence of woman in her role as wife, mother, and prop to her husband's family life serves to underscore that this film was directed to the husband as paterfamilias.

The narrator teaches this common couple about the problem of overpopulation. The film presents the goal of a birthrate and a death rate that match, represented by balancing scales, and then explains that very quickly, in the space of a generation, this balance had been disrupted by advances in health, sanitation, and food. Despite the fact that these changes seem positive, the film depicts families suffering and starving; maternal health declined and mothers became "cross"; land was divided between too many living sons. *Family Planning* directly connects increased population to suffering. No comment is made about the fates or futures of daughters, who presumably assumed the role of mother in another family.

By contrast, the families that were able to limit the number of children in the household—the film shows an ideal family with three—not only avoided distress but also thrived, acting as consumers who can take advantage of new technologies that make life simpler and more enjoyable. "Modern science," the narrator informs the man, "has given us a key" to make those smaller families possible. "Any couple who wisely choses family planning will definitely improve the future prospects for their whole family and especially the children," the voice-over concludes, adding, "And, on a larger scale, if enough couples choose family planning, the balance will be restored, but this time, in a better way. Thus, every couple has the opportunity to help build a better life, not just for themselves, but for people everywhere. And all of us have a responsibility toward the family of man." This was a film written to introduce responsible parenthood to a new global audience.

While most actual family planning programs targeted women, this film, designed to legitimate those programs, was aimed at men. And it was designed to equate manhood "not with how many children he [a man] can produce, but how well he takes care of them," with his ability to provide rather than with his virility. If women in the developing world were understood to want birth control, this film was designed to get buy-in from their husbands, and to encourage "parents to consider children as liabilities rather than assets and to view childbearing as Americans had begun to do: as a consumer choice with desirable alternatives."[1] Family Planning, then, directly attempted to educate the developing world about the advantages, both emotional and materialistic, of the kind of American family explored in chapter 2—an ostensibly secular family structure that was in fact deeply indebted to a kind of modern Protestant family ethos. The implication of such an educational film was deeply paternalistic—it valued modern Western heteropatriarchal nuclear families over all other family structures—and also deeply rooted in the belief that this more "advanced" and "modern" family was available to anyone who chose to embrace it.

The Population Council, which had created the film with Disney, was a nongovernmental organization founded in 1952 by John D. Rockefeller III, scion of the large philanthropic (and liberal Baptist) Rockefeller family. He had help from Fredrick Osborn, a noted proponent of family planning as a rebranded form of eugenics that worked through persuasion rather than coercion. The Population Council sought to increase access to family planning technology around the world, and to increase demand and desire for it, largely through educational campaigns. These campaigns largely hinged on globally promoting the kind of family that was idealized by theologies of responsible parenthood. If these family structures worked at home, the Population Council hoped, they would work abroad.

The Population Council partnered with Disney specifically because it was an internationally recognizable brand associated with "wholesome family life." Indeed, Family Planning not only used Disney's distinctive style of multinational people—the "It's a Small World" look, as it were—but also featured the near-constant presence of Donald Duck cutting into the story dressed as a doctor, pulling out a gigantic key to illustrate the "key" of family planning, sketching scales to illustrate balance, and always reminding the audience of the role of family-friendly Disney in promoting family planning. The short, which was translated from English into nineteen languages, was not a "how-to" film about contraception but rather a film designed to explain the problem of overpopulation and stimulate an interest in family planning.[2]

While the film was ostensibly secular, the values underpinning it were inherently tied to a Protestant worldview that, this chapter will show, underpinned much of the seemingly nonreligious conversation about population in the United States in the 1960s and early 1970s. Clergy and scientists believed overpopulation to be a "basic problem" that would lead to starvation, war, and inevitable self-destruction. They also believed birth control to be a new, important part of the promise that science had to offer for solving these basic problems in the middle of the twentieth century. This chapter examines how and why religious leaders advocated this extension of their domestic theology of the American nuclear family globally, through the expansion of family planning programs in the developing world for the benefit of the human family. It explores the concepts of population explosion and population control, their connections to eugenics, and the responses of both Protestant and Catholic leadership to what was broadly understood as a global emergency.

Just as the (Protestant-inflected) American nuclear family was understood to be one of the strongest defenses that the United States could mount against the communist threat in the Cold War era, this effort at worldwide population control was understood by many policymakers and Protestant leaders as a way to properly regulate the human family, and thereby as an important tactic in the battle against communism. Regulating the family could slow or halt the spread of the "godless menace," and also prevent the conflicts that raised the ever-present threat of nuclear war. Ultimately, that conflation of scientific recommendation, government policy, and Protestant theology through the voices of prominent clergy, policy leaders, and politicians, and the responses of Catholic and Jewish communities, demonstrated what was in many ways a growing national consensus.

The Intertwined Histories of Population Control and Eugenics

Population explosion is, at its most basic level, the fear that the world's population will grow beyond the planet's ability to support life. Western science has a long history of concern about growing population, dating to the theories of Thomas Robert Malthus in the late eighteenth century. Malthus worried that the birthrate would outstrip agricultural production, resulting in starvation, poverty, and war, thus leading to depopulation. By the twentieth century, particularly in the aftermath of World War II, the concern about the growing population was framed not only in terms of birthrate but also in terms of decreased child mortality and increased life expectancy. If more children born into a family lived to sexual maturity—because of the invention of and increased access to vaccines and antibiotics, improved sanitation, good obstetrical care, and improved nutrition—that meant that each generation would grow notably in size from the previous one. What's more, increased life expectancy meant that each new life would last longer and consume more resources than in previous generations.

My use of the term "population control" follows the work of historian Linda Gordon, who sees the expression "referring, generically, to the attempt in modern history to lower birthrates on national or regional scales for the purpose of improving standards of living of large groups . . . more specifically, to the population control programs and policies advanced by the United States government, international organizations such as the United Nations, and large foundations, notably the Rockefeller Foundation, as well as, on a national basis, by countries such as India and China."[3] From the aftermath of World War II through the 1970s and beyond, conventional wisdom saw population control as one of the most pressing social issues of the day. People approached the threat of overpopulation with a sense of apocalyptic and existential angst; we continue to see this anxiety today in fears about global warming and climate change.

The terms given to the dramatic rise in population in the middle of the twentieth century, "population bomb" and "population explosion," sound sensational today, prompting many to ask whether overpopulation really was such an urgent problem. Certainly, the decades around the Second World War saw a dramatic increase in life expectancy, a subsequent rise in population, and, as more children lived to reproductive age, even steeper projected population increases. In the mid-twentieth century, the population explosion was largely taken as a given in academic, scientific, and political settings—if not always in activist or, as we shall see, religious settings. Both contemporary and historiographical critiques have focused on the problems of seeing birth control campaigns as the solution to the population problem, rather than, for example, resource redistribution. More recently, some scholars have flipped that script; they see capitalism and resource distribution, rather than rising numbers of people, as the core problem. For people considering the social situation in the 1950s, '60s, and '70s, however, there was widespread agreement in governmental, philanthropic, and academic circles that the growing population was the pressing concern.

That said, many people deeply concerned about the issue did not have the skill sets to interrogate the fundamental science involved. Many politicians, preachers, and policymakers were working from information that they received from experts, largely in the newly developed science of demography.

Most debates did not focus on whether population control was necessary: These thought leaders simply trusted what they understood the science to say about the diagnosis of the program, and about how to implement ethical population measures given the unequal distribution of resources on both the both national and global scales. The institutional Catholic Church was one of the only prominent voices suggesting that the population itself was not a problem. Other thought leaders dismissed this view as the message of an authoritarian and antiquated institution standing in opposition to modern scientific and democratic progress. Informed by sources including their clergy, their politicians, and the cover of *Time* magazine, the broader public shared the belief that the population posed a threat akin in severity to nuclear war. In fact, as we shall see, the nuclear fears that animated the Cold War also sharpened anxiety about the growing population.

Many of the solutions that midcentury thought leaders put forward to address the population problem grew directly out of existing conversations about eugenics, which, as we have discussed, was considered scientific best practice in the late nineteenth and early twentieth centuries. At that time, almost all educated people believed in some form of eugenics, ranging from encouraging the spacing of children and robust prenatal care, to improving the

Poster for Zero Population Growth Inc., used 1968–80. Courtesy of the Library of Congress, Prints and Photographs Division, item no. 2016649241.

health of the population. Some eugenic programs encouraged "fit" elements of the population, which often meant those who were white, middle-class, and morally and physically "healthy," to have *more* children (termed "positive eugenics"), and they urged others perceived as "less desirable," often for reasons of race, class, developmental/mental disability, or perceived moral failings, to have fewer children (termed "negative eugenics").[4] The eugenic campaigns that had characterized the 1920s had often featured state control of reproduction, or attempts to instate state control of reproduction, by populations deemed "less fit." These judgments of "unfitness" were notably not accompanied by a robust commitment to changing the economic structures that created those conditions—such as economic considerations driving women into prostitution, or structural racism undercutting the ability of African American families to live out the American ideal of a nuclear family.

In the 1920s and '30s, many liberal, scientifically minded people had supported eugenics, including, to a limited degree, feminist birth control crusader Margaret Sanger and African American sociologist and NAACP president W. E. B. Du Bois. But by the 1940s, the use of eugenics by the Third Reich had changed public perception of the field. In the generations after World War II, one of the primary questions facing those concerned with population control was how to approach the legacy of eugenics in light of its use in Nazi ideology. The trend, even among those who supported eugenics, moved away from the idea that one would limit racial or social groups. Rather, as Fredrick Osborn, president of the American Eugenics Society, who was also influential on both the Population Council and Planned Parenthood, wrote in 1946, "The ten years between 1930 to 1940 marked a major change in eugenic thinking. . . . The differences between individuals far outweighed any differences which might be discovered between the averages of the larger racial or social groups."[5]

This is to say that by the time the birth control pill hit the market, the idea that one could improve the human race by encouraging certain racial and social groups to reproduce and discouraging others from doing so had turned into something that looked more like a forerunner of today's genetic counseling. The fact that Osborn, who was a major advocate for legalizing and expanding birth control access, did not think that some populations were more valuable than others should not be taken to imply that he thought all individuals were genetically worthy of reproducing. He firmly hoped to build social incentives for those "correct" couples to have larger families. In addition, his focus on social reform undercut the feminist aims of early birth control movements. Osborn was one of the primary figures who pressured Margaret Sanger to change the name of the Birth Control Federation of America to the Planned Parenthood Federation of America in 1941. This change brought the organization notable support from business and medical communities precisely because it shifted the organization's focus "from female sexual and reproductive autonomy to social control over childbearing."[6]

On the social level, Fredrick Osborn remained very interested in shaping reproductive patterns and had largely developed the field of demography to that end, training many population experts who created the data that fueled fears around the implications of the rising population. Many demographers, Osborn and his colleagues included, avoided the overt racism and coercion of Nazi eugenics. Rather, they believed that with proper education, individual couples could be persuaded—even incentivized—to make appropriate reproductive choices. Osborn and his team were also deeply invested in valuing certain social and family structures as modern.[7] Even though the incentives sometimes had the force of compulsion, these demographers thought of themselves as liberal precisely because they were invested in modernity, and because they believed in incentivized, rather than compulsory, family limitation. In the words of Alexandra Stern, these population experts were "a core group of eugenicists interested in salvaging and retooling eugenics with the export of Western-led modernization to the Third World." To do so, they embarked on the neo-Malthusian pursuit of "family planning and birth control abroad" via the International Planned Parenthood Federation, founded in 1948, and the Population Council, founded in 1952.[8]

These demographers analyzed the population and brought their new-eugenic logics to solve the problems they found, that is, of burgeoning population and its attendant poverty and war. Politicians, preachers, and policymakers absorbed that information as the best scientific wisdom of their day, and shared the demographers' belief that in the modern world science could solve any kind of problem. But these leaders, particularly the clergy, generally did not have the skills to examine the studies in their full context.

What, then, do we make of their failures? Global historian Matthew Connelly's critical account of population control movements in this period, *Fatal Misconception*, argues that these movements often did as much or more harm than the good they intended to do. Connelly's work is dedicated to "looking past the slogans" to see how the concepts of population control "evolved into norms, practices, and institutions."[9] The Western and cosmopolitan elites, he argues, thought they knew better than the world's poor what they needed, and that hubris was the fatal flaw. Connelly believes that national governments could not successfully protect their populations from the motivations of international nongovernmental organizations.[10] Connelly's critique of these programs is important, and, indeed, many NGOs have since addressed the historical concerns that he raises. That said, his wholesale condemnation of family planning programs is also overly pessimistic. It runs the risk of conflating the attitudes of these midcentury demographers with the potential of contraception to let people, particularly women, have access to birth control that gives them agency in their own lives; it has the potential to undermine the good work that such programs may do now and in the future.

In any case, in this project, however, I am thinking about the motivations of American clergy and faithful—many of whom did not have access to what lay behind the slogans, and who truly believed that population control would improve and save lives at home and around the globe. They did indeed often fall victim to what Connelly calls the "fatal misconception" that they knew best. But they also really believed that everyone should be given access to and choice around contraception, and that creating true options was likely possible. As work like Connelly's shows, they may have been naive, at least at times, about how coercion functioned. I do not explore their motivations to give them a pass, either on their sense that they knew best or on their naivete. Understanding their worldviews, however, gives us increased insight into liberal religious attitudes toward globalization, women's health, and how to implement stewardship of the earth in the contemporary moment. This insight, in turn, helps us to understand the archaeology of our own assumptions.

To that end: It is very much the case, at least rhetorically, that demographers and the thought leaders who listened to them, including politicians, clergy, and policymakers, firmly rejected both coercive eugenic tactics and racially based inferiority. They held a firm belief that with the proper education and resources, populations that they encountered at home and abroad would appreciate the inherent logic of their views on contraception and essentially fall in line. This viewpoint values some forms of knowledge, priorities, lifestyles, family structures, and cultures coded as rational, modern, and Western over other forms coded as emotional, premodern, and non-Western. Thus, whether or not this discourse had the overt racism of the Third Reich or Jim Crow, it remained deeply embedded within the moral logics of white supremacy, structural racism, and patriarchy.

That said, without minimizing the deeply inherent problems with these viewpoints, a good historical analysis requires us to recall that the demographers and their audiences thought of themselves as racial liberals. Unlike many of the previous generation, against whom they defined themselves, they did not think that the people whom they were studying were inherently inferior because they were Black, brown, urban, or from what was at the time called an "underdeveloped" country. They therefore believed that given the appropriate resources, these individuals and communities could become modern, a process that they believed would benefit those communities and, with them, the nation and the planet. These social scientists certainly were of the paternalist perspective that they, rather than their subjects, knew what an improved life would look like. And while they were certainly simultaneously romanticizing and pathologizing the people whom they were studying, they were also "earnestly" trying to improve their lives. Still, in their conversations, by dint of their very belief that the people they were studying could (and should) be modernized, these actors were at the liberal end of the conversation, at least among the thought leaders, academics, and government bureaucrats. We must, then, take seriously both the worldviews that these social scientists had, including their desire to make things better, and the kinds of knowledge and possible futures that their worldview excluded and eliminated.[11]

Exporting Responsible Parenthood: A Cold War Christian Duty

While the previous chapter focused on the domestic implications of responsible parenthood, here we will turn to this ideology's implications for how Americans—generally Protestants, though sometimes Catholics—thought of their role as global citizens. Not only was responsible parenthood a theology that could and should shape the American family, but on the global scale, it could reshape the human family and, through that reshaping, possibly even end famine and war. At the 1954 annual meeting of the Planned Parenthood Federation of America—six years before the FDA approved oral contraception in the United States—two very prominent voices, one religious and the other medical, demonstrated the intertwined domestic and global potential of birth control. The Reverend Harry Emerson Fosdick, one of the most prominent liberal Protestant voices of the age, framed overpopulation as one of the world's "basic problems," which could be relieved by knowledge of and access to contraception. Fosdick, one of that year's recipients of the Federation's Albert and Mary Lasker Foundation Awards, asserted that "the liberty to use contraceptive control [to build] thoughtfully planned, wisely planned homes" was essential to proper family life.[12]

Harvard Medical School's John Rock, the Catholic doctor who was instrumental in both developing and, once it was approved, marketing the Pill, said at the same meeting that if such a pill could be developed, "we could be virtually assured of obtaining the greatest aid ever discovered to the happiness and security of individual families . . . help[ing] to avert man's self-destruction through starvation and war."[13] For these theological and medical leaders, and for their audience at Planned Parenthood, the Pill was a powerful scientific tool, one that had immense potential to reshape the landscape of marriage, the American family, and the planet, each of which faced its own sets of challenges and opportunities.

If, for Protestants, responsible parenthood should ideally shape the American nuclear family, as described in chapter 2, it also dictated how American Protestants and indeed the United States government should structure their foreign aid in care of the human family. The United States should aid "underdeveloped" countries in starting family planning programs, both in order to stave off a growing population, and to aid those countries in forming modern, capitalist nuclear family units. By exporting the nuclear family, the United States could save the human family.

Congregational minister Richard M. Fagley, who had synthesized the theology of responsible parenthood, also served as the representative of the Commission of the Churches on International Affairs at the United Nations, sponsored by the World Council of Churches (WCC) and the International Missionary Council. He held this position when he wrote his 1960 book *The Population Explosion and Christian Responsibility*, described by its publishers as the "first full-length analysis from a Protestant perspective of the world's most neglected social problem."[14] As Fagley explained, one of his responsibilities was "to provide church leaders in the ecumenical movement with background data and analysis on various international problems which might help them to arrive at informed policy decisions," in this case, around religious responses to the burgeoning population.[15] In his articulation, "population and parenthood are two aspects of the same phenomenon." Parenthood was "the personal and family aspect . . . virtually equivalent to procreation," and responsible parenthood meant "restricted or limited procreation in view of the total responsibilities of parenthood . . . the care and nurture of children, the safeguarding of their material welfare, the training for responsible adulthood, the companionship of family life."[16]

Population, by contrast, was the social aspect, the birthrates and death rates of national and global populations, understood in terms of the resources needed to sustain their rates of growth. Fagley did worry that prioritizing statistics about these populations would erase the "flesh and blood people behind the statistics."[17] He was concerned that the conversation would fail to acknowledge their humanity, their hopes and dreams for different and better lives, and the pain that they would feel if forced to face the poverty, war, and famine of a world that had surpassed its resources. In these concerns we can perhaps see an indication that Fagley was aware of the people of foreign nations as individuals, and perhaps even aware that their hopes and dreams might differ from the hopes and dreams that he or other American Christians might have had. Whether his theology ensured space for those hopes and dreams is a slightly different matter.

In developing the global dimensions of responsible parenthood theology, Fagley's first task was to make the case for why population control was necessary.[18] He acknowledged that there had been other moments of population anxiety over the past century. However, drawing on reports by the United Nations, the World Health Organization, UNICEF (United Nations International Children's Emergency Fund), and others, he argued that the population was growing more rapidly in the time since the Second World War, and mostly in "the continents of Asia, Africa, and Asia." It was in these "poorer countries of the world," Fagley argued, that "four-fifths of the current unprecedented increase in the world's population" was occurring. These nations were already "caught in three revolutionary ferments—the struggle for independence and nationalism, the revolt against outmoded social patterns, and the revolution of rising expectations."[19]

These problems were going to be compounded by a fourth: "the demographic revolution."[20] At the same time, then, that citizens of those countries had "rising expectations" about the consumer-oriented aspects of modern life—the cars, refrigerators, and other consumer items that Western Cold War ideology saw as an unmitigated good—their exploding population made those desires harder to achieve. Protestant clergy worried that this combination would fuel the social unrest that existed in these countries. So did many other white thought leaders at midcentury, in part because the pain and suffering caused by war and famine would, in the words of one minister, be "music to the communists' ears."[21]

Fagley's international theology of responsible parenthood is thus deeply informed by the concerns of the Cold War. Writing as a member of the mainstream Christian establishment in the United States, and as a representative of the World Council of Churches, Fagley acknowledged the very real appeal that communism had for countries whose needs radically outpaced their resources, and who lived with an increasing awareness of the disparity between their own standard of living and that of the industrialized West. Religious leaders like Fagley were often less likely to connect this dissatisfaction, resource poverty, and structural instability to the ongoing reality or immediate aftermath of extraction colonialism. Instead, the specter of communism was a pressing fear for Americans writ large. It underscored fears about the implications of growing populations: Population growth might result in starving populations who might turn to communism as a source of relief. The specter of communism also undercut Westerners' ability to see that colonialism and capitalism had created many of the resource problems that they tied exclusively to population.

The National Council of Churches (NCC) shared many of Fagley's international population concerns, and the organization felt compelled to get its American readership on board with the idea that the United States had an obligation "as Christians and citizens in a world society . . . to help our fellow men overseas."[22] The council's logic was something of a "you break it, you buy it" mentality. This attitude was not tied to the United States' colonial practices but rather to the nation's role in advancing global health. The United States, council members explained, had helped to create the population explosion. The country had paid for public health programs that had "helped to create new population pressures"; and it had supported vaccination campaigns and antibiotic distribution that had increased life expectancy, which meant that more children grew up, and therefore more people reproduced.[23]

Thus, the NCC argued, it was American Christians' duty to help. Representatives to the council emphasized that requests for help were coming from the countries themselves: In their minds, this guarded against Western coercion of less affluent countries. It did little, however, to ensure that those countries' elites were not coercing their own populations. "Therefore," the National Council of Churches concluded, "at the request of people in other countries, we believe our government and voluntary agencies have a duty to assist with various measures to alleviate population pressures and to extend family planning."[24] In the same paragraph, the council connected this duty to Christianity: "Christian responsibility indicates that, when requested by other governments, governmental and intergovernmental aid for family planning should be given favorable consideration as part of a wise and dedicated effort to advance in the underprivileged regions of the earth the essential material conditions conducive to human dignity, freedom, justice, and peace."[25]

Again, responsible parenthood was only responsible if it was a freely chosen moral act, and therefore it had to be requested and could not be coerced. In this formulation and self-understanding, developed nations were to give family planning assistance to "economically less developed countries" only when asked. They were not to do so in an attempt to impose population restrictions, but rather to bring the less developed nations into modern conditions allowing for "human dignity, freedom, justice, and peace."[26] That said, the new field of demography was primarily based in the United States. It brought students from countries like India and China to learn the principles of demography and population control at American universities, more or less ensuring that at least some sections of those countries' educated elites would make requests for contraceptive technology.[27] Sharing birth control technology and providing resources to set up birth control clinics, then, were understood to be similar to sharing vaccines and antibiotics—and, indeed, to be necessitated by having already shared the latter.

American Aid as Care for the Human Family

Though in many ways the 1960s represented an era of ecumenical collaboration in the face of the perceived threat of "godless communism," the question of contraception in international aid marked a clear division between Protestant and Catholic thought. While Protestant political activity in favor of responsible parenthood carried weight, that theology's proponents constantly needed to engage Catholic opposition to birth control initiatives. For instance, in 1961, "a possible worldwide dissemination of birth control information" was proposed as an agenda item for the sixteenth United Nations General Assembly.[28] In response to both the UN General Assembly and to the National Council of Churches' February 28, 1961, endorsement of responsible parenthood, the mainline Protestant *Christian Century*, in several unsigned articles that seem to speak with the magazine's editorial voice, articulated strong support for birth control: "In many nations, the population explosion is the most serious of all social problems . . . so immense that they cannot be solved without the aid of the world organization."[29] The magazine made a point of discussing Vatican opposition to the UN proposal. The Vatican's secretary of state had taken steps to oppose discussing birth control, and when Argentina had declared itself "categorically opposed" to the UN's adoption of birth control policies, the "Holy See praised" the country's statement as a "noble document."[30] The *Christian Century* articulated a strong sense that "the Vatican will exert pressure wherever possible to prevent the discussion of birth control by U.N. delegates."[31] The periodical informed its readers that the Vatican's pressure "must be resisted."[32]

To note what this resistance might look like, the magazine highlighted the example of the Protestant Episcopal Church in the USA, which, at its 1961 General Convention that past September in Detroit, had explicitly separated the issue of contraception from abortion and infanticide, both of which the Church condemned. The *Christian Century* declared, "We believe that methods of control which are medically endorsed and morally acceptable may help the people of these lands [less economically developed nations] so to plan family life that children may be born without a likelihood of starvation, and we approve the rendering by our government of assistance to this end wherever it is sought."[33] For the magazine's editorial voice, the piece about "wherever it is sought" was central. Breaking with their coverage of the Episcopal statement, the editors stated, "Birth control information should not be thrust upon people who do not want it," but at the same time, it was the "'duty of the better-developed countries such as our own' to help other peoples burdened by population increases."[34] In the eyes of the Christian Century, the United Nations was an organization that was well equipped to decide when the information was desired, and to facilitate that aid.

Embedded in this reportage, however, was a bit of a contradiction. While the editors of the Christian Century did not think that birth control should be forced on a population, when Argentina objected to birth control measures, they saw that objection as simply a result of the country's Catholicism and pressure from the Vatican. While it is true that Argentina's Catholicism may have shaped its position, and while it is a fair question whether countries should be able to block conversations about contraception or simply abstain, the magazine did not ask on what other grounds Argentina might have been protesting. Nor did the Christian Century see the Vatican's teachings as a just reason for the majority-Catholic country to raise objections to contraception.

Protestant responses to shortages of resources abroad tended to demonstrate that the developed world saw rising population in the developing world as the primary problem, and not the increasingly resource-intensive lifestyle of the West—a lifestyle that the responsible parenthood theology, with its implicit upward mobility, functionally endorsed. Additionally, prominent Protestant voices like Fagley's asked how to curb the growing populace, particularly in South America, Africa, and Asia, rather than trying to figure out how to project the likely population growth and then increase food production accordingly. Fagley's point of view addressed both of these questions, if unsatisfactorily from the standpoint of his opponents. He worried that while "the potentialities for new nutritional resources are not discounted, despite the difficulties, the main issue is the problem of time. It is not easy to feed a hungry baby on the future expectations of a larger larder."[35] Evangelical minister Paul King Jewett agreed, noting that "the cry of the undernourished and underprivileged will abate little of its claim to be heard by the promise of some future utopia created by science."[36] As a result, he came to the conclusion that, "at least in the densely populated countries, no strategy can win which fails to include a real program to control and reduce fertility."[37] In these formulations, the humanitarian need was stark and family planning the most foolproof solution—other ideas, like increasing food production, were depicted as both too risky and too slow.

Theologians like Jewett and Fagley would at times imply that domestically responsible parenthood meant providing for children in resource-heavy ways. But here they argued that they were not pushing contraception abroad to allow for consumption at home but rather pushing to allow those countries access to American levels of consumption. Fagley acknowledged that "certainly a lessened preoccupation with creature comforts in the richest countries could produce a higher quality of life."[38] Rather, he believed that the "revolution of 'rising expectations'" was "thoroughly indigenous" in the "Eastern countries," and that these expectations were held "just as fervently" there as they were in the "West."[39] Fagley worried that if no country was willing to decrease its materialism, and it seemed unfair to ask the underdeveloped countries not to aspire to standards enjoyed by the developed world, then the underdeveloped countries needed to decrease their population. This decrease in population, he believed, would make those countries better able to achieve the standard of living to which they aspired, without overly taxing the planet's increasingly thinly stretched resources. In this way, the family structure of the developing world would come to take the consumption-oriented form of the modern nuclear family. It would allow men to be breadwinners and women to be homemakers who raised children in the labor- and resource-intensive mode that was so central to American notions of responsible parenthood and American anticommunist rhetoric.

In this liberal Protestant formulation, the burden to limit the population fell equally on the poor countries and the wealthy countries; however, the West had already embraced the form of family life most likely to aid the human family. As the National Council of Churches put it to American readers, a major reason for family planning was "the social situation, when rapid population growth places dangerous pressures on the means of livelihood and endangers the social order."[40] Underscoring that its American audience should both practice family planning and support initiatives to share contraceptive technology with less affluent countries, the Christian Century printed an article titled "Family Planning Is a Christian Duty," reporting on a World Council of Churches call to systematically address the relationship between family planning, population explosion, and starvation.[41]

The Christian Century's support for the doctrine of responsible parenthood was sustained. The publication offered editorials praising Fagley's work and statements from the National Council of Churches endorsing responsible parenthood. It also printed Jewett's argument that "if we believe that the decrease of infant mortality and the higher valuation of a woman's life are pleasing to God, then we cannot also believe it is pleasing to God that natural fecundity should run its unimpeded course, with its wretched train of poverty, suffering, and degradation."[42] It was, he claimed, "'one thing to replenish the earth,' but quite another to burden the earth with an irresponsible prodigality."[43]

While individual Protestants had to make their decisions in a global context, Fagley and other proponents of responsible parenthood were careful not to dictate individual family choices in a stringent fashion. He noted that no council or commission had the right to dictate to individual churches, as such a stance was counter to the "ethos of the Reformation and to the nature of the present fellowship of Churches." Rather, the ecumenical statements only had merit in commending themselves to church leaders. The Protestant consensus around responsible parenthood rested on the fact that no religious leader or institution framed it as a "substitute for the responsibility of husband and wife to make their own prayerful and conscious decisions in this area." After all, the potential parents were the people who needed to determine the nature of their "vocation"; this was a conclusion over which "no court of the churches has comparable jurisdiction."[44] A Protestant theological consensus, in other words, could not be used to compel individual Christians.

The firm belief that individuals could not be coerced in their family planning decisions for their own nuclear families extended theologically to state control of the human family. The ecumenical Protestant consensus carefully condemned state coercion around family planning. Fagley and other supporters of contraception were well aware that previous generations had at times been deeply invested in state-sponsored eugenics, usually through sterilization programs. They were likely aware of state-sponsored eugenics in their own moment, particularly directed against African American communities. Fannie Lou Hamer, the prominent civil rights activist who had herself been forcibly sterilized in 1961, coined the term "Mississippi appendectomy" during this period. The Protestant theologians who were articulating the centrality of prayerful choice to responsible parenthood were doing so against this broader political context in which forced sterilization was part of the medical terrain.

Advocates of responsible parenthood on a global scale were also aware that liberal Protestant isolationism had contributed to the United States' delayed entry into the Second World War, which meant that liberal Protestants had delayed the attempt to halt the genocide of the Third Reich. It was therefore essential to take a stand as Christians against eugenics. "It is to husband and wife," Fagley argued, "that God has given the responsibilities of parenthood, and any effort by the state to arrogate unto itself the authority of husband and wife is an invasion of fundamental and God-given rights."[45] This focus on the rights of the couple managed, at least in the minds of those crafting the theology, to simultaneously guard against compulsory eugenic programs and the specter of communist-esque state control, while upholding the agency central to Protestant moral action. Responsible parenthood's advocates contended that "the term 'population control' need[ed] to be delimited and defined if it [was] to serve as the subject for a useful analysis from the perspective of Christian doctrine." And if what "population control" meant was that "the state has a prerogative to determine the size of its population and to exert control through corresponding policies, . . . there was little to be said about it from a Christian point of view, except to condemn it."[46] It was, however, perfectly appropriate and necessary, according to these thought leaders, for the state to monitor the growing population, to educate about its dangers, and to make modes of birth control readily available.

Despite these concerns about coerced forms of birth control, Fagley's theology of responsible parenthood still retained a subtle eugenic cast. To be sure, explicit racialized language was strikingly absent from the theological arguments that mainline Protestant clergy presented to their flocks about the need to control reproduction. By framing birth control in terms that advocated for the "moral good" of society as a whole, however, Fagley and others implicitly privileged a certain type of family. This family—middle-class, typically white, and residents of North America and Europe—was the focus of this Protestant ethic of responsible family planning. At the margins of this discourse was another type of family, one located in Latin America, Africa, or Asia, all places that birth control advocates named as most vulnerable to global shortages. These references implied a racialized dynamic that authors like Fagley seem to have carefully avoided stating directly, perhaps out of sensitivity to the postwar links between birth control and eugenics. But the coded message belied the supposed neutrality and race-blind rhetoric: Population control was supposed to be for everyone, but the problem was located in the non-white developing world, while the answer was found in the prudent choices of white American families. Thus, the religiously inflected language of birth control, population control, and morality all reiterated an idealized family that was implicitly both white and middle-class.

Catholic Responses to Population Growth

Fagley's articulation that no religion should or even could govern the birth control choices of individual couples was framed in terms of not being able to dictate restrictions on procreation, but it was also an implicit criticism of Catholic institutional responses to these issues. Fagley, like other Protestant critics of the Catholic Church, specifically objected to the idea that a religious institution would dictate moral choices, either to a congregation or to a believing Christian. As a result, the argument that the ecumenical Protestant consensus could not compel congregations to take particular stances around contraception, any more than clergy could dictate to a couple how to enact their vocation as parents, was in part a critique of the Catholic Church's stances on birth control and religious authority.

In the immediate postwar years, the Catholic Church had a clear message on contraception: It was not permitted. This applied domestically and internationally, such that the Church was "primarily concerned with protecting the image of the United States in the word as well as with promoting Catholic doctrine regarding sexuality and human life in the United States."[47] While the Church was in sympathy with some of the pronatalist and antifeminist forms of eugenics that focused on "building a strong and healthy population," it was strongly opposed to negative eugenics "that sought to restrict reproduction among the poor, the disabled, immigrants, and minority races through sterilization and birth control."[48] In fact, the Catholic Church maintained its opposition to family planning outreach, despite the fact that some commentators argued that the developing world was very interested in gaining knowledge about contraception. As early as 1940, India's National Congress Party's National Planning Committee had wanted the government to "spread knowledge of cheap and safe methods of birth control" and establish clinics.[49]

In the United States, the Catholic Church's opposition to birth control took the form of its official stances on US aid policies. On November 25, 1959, "the Roman Catholic Bishops of the United States announced their opposition . . . to the use of public funds to promote the use of artificial birth control at home or abroad."[50] The 1,500-word statement, which had been approved by more than 200 bishops at a conference at Catholic University in Washington, DC, "denounced what they called 'a systematic and concerted' campaign of 'propaganda' for the use of foreign aid funds for the encouragement of birth control in the under-developed countries."[51] The basis of the bishops' statement, which was published by the National Catholic Welfare Association, was the belief that, in the words of Pope Pius XI, "the conjugal act is destined primarily for the begetting of children." To inhibit this process by using contraception other than the rhythm method was to "sin against nature and commit a deed which is shameful and intrinsically vicious."[52] Crucially, doctrine was not understood as pertaining only to Catholics in contemporary times. In the words of Pius XI, this condemnation of contraception "will hold tomorrow and always, for it is not a mere precept of human right but the expression of a natural and divine law."[53] Rather, the bishops' statement was based in teachings that the Catholic Church depicted as universal and eternal.

Temporally, however, the message was very much rooted in its moment. The 200 US bishops issued their statement in response to a study by a Stanford University "study group" to the Senate Foreign Relations Committee and a recommendation to President Dwight D. Eisenhower by a special commission on foreign aid. Respectively, the study group and the commission advised the "large-scale foreign" testing of contraceptive devices and the sharing of "means curbing rapid population growth" should be given to nations requesting it. Eisenhower had clearly stated that as long as he was in the White House, the United States would not use foreign aid funds to promote birth control in "underdeveloped countries." So it seemed that a statement from the Protestant World Council of Churches calling for "the widespread introduction of both natural and artificial [birth] control" in response to worldwide "population explosion" had been even more upsetting to the bishops than these reports.[54] The bishops were particularly troubled that "some representatives of Christian bodies" were encouraging the inclusion of birth control in foreign aid, and they were also distressed that some "national and international figures" had claimed that contraception was increasingly acceptable within Catholic marriage. They wanted to make it explicitly clear that the former was unacceptable and the latter simply untrue.

The bishops opposed the very premise of overpopulation, which they framed as needlessly alarmist. The problem was not the overabundance of people, they countered, but rather the undercultivation of the land. "When the Indians roamed the plains, the entire country had a population of about 500,000," the clergymen asserted, "but would have been regarded as 'overpopulated' according to the norms of the exponents of planned parenthood."[55] The bishops pointed out that, at the time of their writing, "those same plains are being retired into a 'land bank' because they are over-productive in a land of 175,000,000 persons."[56] The goal should be to help the underdeveloped countries scale up their food production so as to be in the situation the United States was in, where the land was more than productive enough to feed the population. Tapping into the Cold War fears of the day, the bishops also argued that the Soviet Union was not encouraging the use of birth control but was helping countries to increase their productivity. The Catholic Church, the bishops reiterated, would oppose any and all use of foreign aid to promote artificial birth control.

Both Protestant clergy and scientists immediately swung into action to demonstrate that the Catholic Church was out of step with scientific consensus—and even with other Catholics. Social scientists refuted the Catholic Church through demographic data. In February 1960, Kingsley David, professor of sociology and social interactions at UC Berkeley and US representative to the Population Commission of the United Nations, and Judith Blake, author of *Family Structure in Jamaica*, published a piece in *Commentary*. Founded by the American Jewish Committee in 1945, this opinion magazine would by the 1970s emerge as a prominent neoconservative platform. The article, called "Birth Control and Public Policy," served to refute the bishops' statement, which had, in Davis and Blake's words, "attack[ed] the idea that an American or international agency should use United States funds to help underdeveloped countries lower their birthrates."[57] The authors argued—incorrectly, as I hope I have demonstrated in chapter 1—that previously the birth control movement had been primarily a "ladies' volunteer affair, publicly regarded as either inconsequential or embarrassing." But as it turned out, a 1943 *Fortune* poll demonstrated that 85 percent of American women believed that birth control should be legal for use by married couples; and a University of Michigan and Scripps Foundation poll suggested that 94 percent of all reproductive-aged white couples in the United States were either trying to regulate conception, intending to do so, or not doing so because they were struggling with infertility.[58]

This study also noted that 85 percent of Protestant wives and 45 percent of Catholic wives approved of the use of contraception within marriage, and four-fifths of Catholic couples had used some form of birth control, with 50 percent of that number using something explicitly forbidden by the church.[59] Forty percent of women who regularly went to Mass had at some point used "artificial" contraception, while 83 percent of women who rarely or never attended Mass but still identified as Catholic used contraception. While birth control was a widely held piece of American life, according Davis and Blake, it was not often spoken of. The authors continued, "Protestants and Jews at home have grown increasingly restive under laws and regulations that prevent them from acting in accordance with their own religious precepts as regards family planning, and they resent having those precepts denounced as immoral."[60] To Davis and Blake, the statement of the US bishops represented an attempt on the part of the Catholic Church to impose its views through "political pressure and legislative coercion" and through an "infringement of democratic values," if and when they could not convince people directly. This debate, which had publicly played out domestically with the diaphragm battles in New York City (chapter 1) and through the Supreme Court case of *Griswold v. Connecticut* (chapter 2), entered foreign policy conversations through the realm of birth control.

Protestant leaders framed the Catholic position as anachronistic and immoral. They did not refute the Church's points so much as reject them out of hand. John C. Bennett, dean of the prominent Union Theological Seminary in New York City, called the bishops' statement "tragic," claiming that it had "no sound moral or religious belief," and that it represented views that "had been rejected by most other religious groups."[61] In objecting to the US bishops' statement on birth control, the Right Reverend James A. Pike asked whether the "policy laid down by the Catholic hierarchy was binding on Roman Catholic candidates for public office."[62] This question was particularly relevant because of the presidential candidacy of Massachusetts Senator John F. Kennedy. Kennedy was only the second Catholic to hold a major party nomination, and he would become the nation's first Catholic president.[63]

Kennedy's Catholicism made many Americans nervous for reasons well beyond its implications for his family planning policies. Famously, during his presidential campaign in 1960, the senator spoke to members of the Greater Houston Ministerial Association to assure them that he would be able to make important policy decisions independently of his personal faith or political pressure from Rome. Kennedy argued that his Catholicism had obscured more important issues facing the country, like the global spread of communism, and then promised his audience, "I believe in an America where the separation of church and state is absolute, where no Catholic prelate would tell the president (should he be Catholic) how to act, and no Protestant minister would tell his parishioners for whom to vote."[64]

Given this building concern and the opposition by the US bishops, it is perhaps unsurprising that Kennedy was asked about his position on whether the United States should include funding for birth control in its foreign aid. He responded, "Our government should not 'advocate' that other countries limit their population . . . a kind of mean patriotism, which I think they would find most objectionable," though he indicated that if a country asked for contraception, that would be different.[65] Indeed, Kennedy was the first US president to offer governmental support for "birth control as a means of coping with world population problems."[66] While Kennedy was the era's most prominent example of an American Catholic breaking politically with the Catholic Church over birth control, he was not the only Catholic to believe that the issue of population complicated the Church's stance on contraception.

Catholics and Population Control: Lay Responses

When Pat and Patty Crowley collected surveys from 3,000 Catholic couples in the Christian Family Movement as part of their work for the Papal Commission on Birth Control, they both asked participants specific questions about their own reproductive lives and experiences and left a place where respondents could answer free-form questions. The answers to those queries demonstrated that Catholic couples understood the issue of birth control not only in terms of their own lives but also with reference to the growing global population. Not everyone thought that the population crisis was a reason for the Church to change its position on birth control. As one survey respondent noted, "We feel that man should not try to change God's way of making new life."[67] This did not mean, however, that these individuals were unconcerned about the potential shortages caused by a growing population, or about the responsibility of developed nations or the Catholic Church in the face of those needs. Rather, they wrote, "We should find other means of helping people, such as teaching them how to grow more food using this time, money and effort to help these people to help themselves acquire the material things necessary for life. We feel that birth control would not be pleasing to God."[68]

For many of Pat and Patty's respondents, however, the rising population was a reason for the Church to change its stance on at least some forms of contraception. A survey respondent from Boston observed, "It seems to us that the emphasis on 'giving life' can, and indeed morally should, be subordinated to the other needs of society: population density, ability of the land and the economy to sustain minimal standards of life."[69] For this couple, giving life was only one of the moral responsibilities that the Catholic Church needed to weigh, and in the end, it was not the most important need. A Rockford, Illinois, couple agreed that the church should take into account these other social needs, particularly "a population explosion, which results in famine, poverty, etc." They went on to morally fault the Church's position on contraception, noting, "This situation is in itself a moral issue and the Church's outdated position on birth control contributes to the development of families which are too large to be adequately fed, clothed, educated (including religious education)."[70]

For these couples, there was no distinction overtly made between the situation in the United States and abroad. Indeed, many of the couples who wrote to the Crowleys wrote about the economic hardship of large families in the United States without making overt links to the population explosion, as chapter 2 demonstrates. Rather, it was a call to understand both the "world food and health and over population problems," and to accept that the "the logic for the change is the new scientific discoveries which allow man to modify the natural bodily processes. Man should be allowed [by the Catholic Church] to use his mental powers and free will to take best advantage of all mankind."[71] Science, these couples seemed to assert, had created problems like overpopulation by decreasing infant mortality; and science could be used to solve the problems through contraception.

For other Catholic couples, the worries about population were firmly set in places other than the United States. As one San Francisco husband and wife observed, "Underdeveloped nations have different problems from that of couples in the US. Specialists in sociology, ecologists, and demographers should aid the church in population limitation where vital."[72] This framework suggested that the Church should perhaps do outreach around contraception in other parts of the world. Still others pushed for different needs for different communities, writing, "The Church can and should emphasize, teach, preach, and re-iterate each society's needs, urging increased conception in under-populated, productive, fertile areas, and decreased conceptions in overpopulated, marginally productive areas."[73] This attitude echoed earlier positive and negative eugenic movements. These respondents avoided framing their comments in racial terms, and were perhaps thinking only of averaging out birthrates—the countries that were depicted as suffering the effects of overpopulation were by and large Black and brown; and the ones with low birthrates, barring Japan, were largely white.

Other survey respondents were clearer in expressing their belief that contraception was wrong in the United States, but that it might be morally permissible elsewhere. As a San Diego couple commented, "There are situations where the church should give special dispensation to areas of the world where overpopulation exists. In no other situation should it be allowed."[74] A Mobile, Alabama, couple was even more adamant. When asked if the Church should change its stance on birth control, they responded, "No! Can't change a basic moral principle!" But the respondents also allowed, "Maybe in India and the Far East a concession could be made where so many are starving to death but in our society God takes care of his children."[75]

In these cases, it seems possible that the double standard for the West versus the rest of the world was based in the suffering, real or imagined, in those other places. As one letter from a couple who had written extensively about their own experiences and those of American couples whom they counseled put it, "Thus, far, our comments have been of a personal nature, but widening our horizon to the world, we cannot close our eyes to the population explosions. We can't pretend it doesn't exist. It does—with all the poverty, disease, dissention, etc. 'Catholic' South America is not going to solve its problems just by trusting in God. There aren't that many saints among us."[76] Their argument was essentially that desperate times called for desperate measures, and in some places, the times were more desperate than in others, and therefore rules could be relaxed and changed when necessary. There was certainly a touch of superiority, for example, in the comment that "in our society God takes care of his children," begging the questions of whether those other societies are not the children of God, or why they are less favored. But generally, these comments demonstrate an understanding that the rhythm method is hard, and sacrifices can be great—because "there aren't that many saints among us."

A few responses, however, demonstrated a real sense of racial or social hierarchy. Contraception could be allowed in the "underdeveloped" world not because these countries' need was greater, but because, as one couple put it, in places like India and China children were "starving to death," and "it would be almost impossible to teach uneducated persons or parents facts of the rhythm system."[77] One survey respondent from Santa Clara put it even more sharply: "Although rhythm is successful as contraception, it requires that those using it be enlightened, self-sacrificing and highly motivated." In the view of this respondent, "The areas of the world where family limitation is the most needed are areas where the population is not enlightened or motivated. Most people needing this also are most likely not practiced in self-denial and therefore not capable of the most heroic self-sacrifice required at times."[78]

This response gives a window into how at least some of the American public saw the developing world. If the leaders were often very careful not to use overtly racist language in framing the perceived needs of the developing world, the broader population was not always as careful. And if, in turn, some of the language of those leaders contained dog whistles about the inferiority of the recipients of the aid, comments like this one demonstrate that some people heard those messages. While these responses came from Catholics, there is no particular reason to think that the Catholic views would have been different from the broader national views, particularly as the Church often used the language of eugenics to underscore the problems with birth control campaigns. The combination of the structural racism embedded in the very notion of healthy family life underpinning formal family planning campaigns and the bigotry demonstrated in the more informal attitudes of Americans created great skepticism about what birth control might mean in the lives of non-white Americans.

Population Control Debates in Black Communities

During this period, debates about whether population was a problem and, if so, whether access to birth control was a desirable solution proceeded in different terms among communities of color, particularly in African American communities. It was also in the conversations within Black communities that the distinction between family planning at home and population control abroad—as Fagley would put it, between "parenthood" and "population"—collapsed. The desire to enforce certain family structures (parenthood) on impoverished and marginalized communities had the goal of limiting the number of children born into those communities (population), both at home and abroad. While some Black leaders advocated for contraception, often because of the high Black maternal mortality rate and because they hoped that smaller families would allow Black families to improve their economic prospects, other voices considered birth control to be genocidal. They assumed that the goal was not to help improve the lot of Black communities but either to eliminate them entirely or to shrink their numbers, so that there would ultimately be fewer Black people at the voting box or to bring about a revolution. Black nationalist groups, at least initially, strongly opposed contraception. For instance, Nation of Islam (NOI) leader Elijah Muhammad framed the birth control pill as "a scheme promulgated by whites to eliminate future black families."[79] He also saw the legalization of abortion through *Roe v. Wade* as "a further plot by the devil to shore up the birth-control pill" in its task of Black genocide.[80]

Muhammad, however, was not the only voice within the Nation of Islam, even though he was its leader. No less a figure than Malcolm X met with Planned Parenthood officials in 1962.[81] Field consultant Wylda Cowles wrote a memo describing the meeting between herself, Marian Hernandez, then-director of the Harlem Planned Parenthood Clinic, and Malcolm X, which she sent to Planned Parenthood president Alan Guttmacher. She noted that Malcolm X did not think birth control was necessarily in conflict with NOI

teachings; but he suggested that the term "birth control" offered what was essentially a branding problem. He recommended a switch to "family planning"
on the grounds that "people, particularly Negroes, would be more willing to
plan than to be controlled."[82]

In this conversation, Hernandez and Cowles downplayed the use of birth
control to address the population explosion, because "the mention of overpopulation reasons evoked questions on why major efforts to control population
are directed toward colored nations."[83] This hesitation recognized that Malcolm X, like many American Black nationalists, was highly attuned to the fact
that international population control movements targeted non-white countries, and Hernandez and Cowles were quick to try to anticipate Malcolm X's
reaction to such efforts. They noted, however, that "Malcolm X looked more
favorably on the Maternal–Child Health approach and economic reasons for
Negros using our services."[84] In other words, Malcolm X was very concerned
about the racial implications of attempts to curb international population
explosion, but he did not see birth control as universally unacceptable. Indeed,
he was interested in it as a tool that could improve life for Black women and
children, and therefore for Black communities more broadly.

If the Nation of Islam's leadership had a diversity of views on contraception, the Black Panthers' position changed over time. A 1970 issue of the
Black Panther addressed dangerous side effects of birth control, particularly
the birth control pill, arguing, "We will not gain the necessary information
until scientists stop worrying so much about their paychecks and start being
concerned about the people whose lives their work and finds are affecting
and doctors stop allowing themselves to be used as agents to perpetuate this
underhanded form of genocide against the oppressed people of amerikkka."[85]
But more importantly, the magazine critiqued the concern about population
growth, contending, "The entire idea of the 'population explosion' is only
another attempt at deceiving the masses. . . . The idea is to make the people
think that the problems we are facing are due to overpopulation and the
gross misuse of the natural resources, so that we will turn away from our fight
against capitalism and imperialism and try to deal with ecology."[86] For the
Black Panthers, the problem was not so much too many people as rampant
capitalism, extraction colonialism, and unequal distribution of resources.
The Black Panther here made the precise critique that Martin Luther King Jr.
would avoid making in his Sanger award acceptance speech.

While the Black Panther Party maintained its critique of capitalism, within
a year it had started to walk back its rejection of birth control, largely because
women members pointed out that the time and money necessary to care for

large families could otherwise be contributed to the movement.[87] Additionally, throughout the 1970s, women became more prominent in the Black Panthers. Elaine Brown assumed leadership when Huey Newton left the United States for Cuba, creating more space for women's authority, as did the loss of men who were killed and imprisoned as the FBI focused more attention on the Black Panthers.[88] Reflecting on the mid-1970s, Brown writes in her autobiography, A *Taste of Power*, that it was during this period that she came to realize that "even men who were themselves oppressed wanted power over women."[89] That realization led Brown to decide that she would "support every assertion of human rights by women—from the right to abortion to the right of equality with men as laborers and leaders." "I would declare that the agenda of the Black Panther Party and our revolution to free black people from oppression specifically included black women," she recalls.[90] Brown does not specifically write about birth control, but her declaration about abortion suggests a support for contraceptive access as long as it is used to support the dignity and equality of Black women, rather than to diminish it.

Black nationalists had a variety of views on the question of birth control or family planning, ranging from seeing it as genocidal; to seeing it as a tool that could be used for good purposes like maternal health and economic growth, or ill purposes like population restriction in Black and brown countries; or to seeing it as a source of dignity for Black women. The Reverend Martin Luther King Jr., however, placed the mainstream civil rights movement squarely within the movement for international population control. When King was awarded the Margaret Sanger Award in Human Rights from the Planned Parenthood Federation of America, he sent remarks that supported the project of population control. These remarks began with the observation that the news had been full of reports of flying saucers. King did not give credence to such UFO sightings, but he took them as an inspiration for imagination. He wondered what visitors from outer space would think of a planet that spent "billions" on war, "millions" to cure disease, but "paltry sums for population planning, even though its spontaneous growth is an urgent threat to life on our planet."[91]

King's view of birth control was inherently global—planetary, one could say—combining the ideas of "parenthood" and "population," and he recognized implicitly that Black Americans were part of a larger African diaspora. That said, unlike the more militant Black nationalists, King believed that just as birth control could help improve the lives of African Americans, it could also benefit those abroad. Thus it was for him a moral imperative to both treat the growing population as a global problem and share the potential solution of birth control globally.

King imagined that, in reporting on us to their home planet, these aliens would see us as insane, for "there is no human circumstance more tragic than the persisting existence of a harmful condition for which a remedy is readily available."[92] He then made a strong statement in favor of population control. "*Family Planning, to relate population to world resources, is possible, practical and necessary,*" he wrote, in italics. "*Unlike plagues of the dark ages or contemporary diseases we do not yet understand,*" King continued, "*the modern plague of over-population is soluble by means we have discovered and with resources we possess.*" He concluded, "What is lacking is not sufficient knowledge of the solution but universal consciousness of the gravity of the problem and education of the billions who are its victims."[93] For King, contraception was not, in and of itself, a problem. It was a tool that the human race could use to protect itself from growing beyond the planet's resources. While in other contexts King delivered blistering critiques of capitalism and its effects on Black and brown communities within the United States and internationally, in this moment, he did not point to the way that capitalistic consumption shaped the balance of resources and population. Rather, he pointed to population as a problem for which a contraception society had the tools to solve—should education be able to spread an awareness of the need.

King supported contraception, including as a solution to the population problem. He also sought to de-escalate white fears that Black nationalist groups were opposed to birth control because they wanted to increase their numbers in order to seize political control. He denied that Black Americans sought power through population. Rather, he argued, because African Americans "were once bred by slave owners to be sold as merchandise," they would not "welcome any solution which involves population breeding as a weapon."[94] Rather than rejecting birth control because they sought domination through numbers, King argued that African Americans were "instinctively sympathetic to all who offer methods that will improve their lives and offer them fair opportunity to develop and advance as all other people in our society."[95] Again, if anything, King wanted to underscore that African American communities were pre-disposed, rather than opposed, to contraception as a matter of human dignity.

Overall, survey data seems to bear out King's argument, while suggesting that Black communities did have a distinct preference for Black-run birth control clinics. A 1972 article in the *American Journal of Public Health* tried to tease these responses out, reporting that 63 percent of Black Americans thought that there were acceptable modes of birth control, while 13 percent thought that birth control was designed to eliminate the Black population.[96] Though the vast majority thought that at least some forms of birth control were acceptable, African Americans were also skeptical of racial bias in gynecological medicine: 69 percent of respondents believed that birth control clinics operated by Blacks would be more acceptable to Blacks than those operated by whites.[97] Their skepticism was quite reasonable given the ongoing history of forced sterilization and the Black maternal mortality rate.

In Black communities, there were clearly some people who saw birth control as undermining both masculinity and community. Frances E. Ruffin, writing in a 1972 issue of *Essence* magazine dedicated to exploring the question of birth control, framed most of the objections to it in the Black community as coming from young Black men. They had been encouraged to "acquire strong ethnic pride—consciousness of Black manhood was stressed in an attempt to break away from what was considered a 'matriarchal society.'"[98] Birth control, Ruffin argued, challenged that sense of manhood. Additionally, governmental investment in social services made birth control available to many Black women for the first time on the heels of urban uprisings, and this reality made many community members suspicious that contraception was an attempt to undercut Black Power by undercutting the size of the community. Despite this, according to Ruffin, "many of the nation's Black people consider birth control a basic right of all women as an alternative to prevent unwanted pregnancies, as a means of strengthening the family-life and achieving a quality life-style."[99] Ruffin marshaled the voices of experts in favor of contraception in her piece before concluding, "It is true that the cry of genocide, raised by many of my brothers and sisters can't be ignored. But in my life . . . I have made the choice to have my children when I can economically and emotionally give them the best chances for survival in this world."[100]

Dr. Douglas Stewart, the Black doctor who headed Planned Parenthood's Community Affairs Department, argued that "freedom of choice" underpinned all of the options made available by the organization, including the rhythm method. He explained that, although until 1966 Planned Parenthood had received very little government funding, that funding expanded after a survey identified family planning as a top priority for low-income families.[101] In 1969 and 1970, the federal government increased the money available for family planning, reserving "enormous sums for a program which may be viewed with some hostility by some of the community."[102] Stewart tried to mitigate this hostility with "a 'Black to Black' family kind of dialogue" in which participants "examine and discuss the negative or hostile reactions." Based on those workshops, Stewart observed, "Most of the negative dialogue comes from young, militant males and because of Moynihan's assertion that ours was a matriarchal society, a public quarrel between our men and women was to be avoided. Black women tended not to say anything in public, and there was a belief that they were not interested in utilizing family planning services."[103] He further observed that the interest in Planned Parenthood clinics had proved otherwise, and even noted the irony that pushback against birth control clinics had served to make women more aware that they were available: Claims that contraception was Black genocide had actually increased the numbers of Black women seeking contraceptive services.[104]

Stewart's purpose was to use the women's magazine platform to explain that birth control was good for the Black community—rather than being genocidal. "I put it in the same context as I would economic power and political power," he explained, "because in each case, the element of choice exists."[105] Stewart put that choice in both personal and familial terms: "And if I, as a Black Father, and I am that—I have four, am unable to take care of six, and have no means to avoid six, I am jeopardizing the well-being of that four because of the realities that exist out there."[106] In framing his observations in the context of the family, he steered away from the conversation about nonmarital sexuality. But perhaps more importantly, Stewart's response described birth control as a way to offer options for Black fathers. Many Black communal objections to contraception had come from Black men who saw contraception as essentially emasculating. Stewart's comments directly reframed that interpretation, offering contraception instead as a way to be a man, to ensure that one could adequately care for one's family. For Stewart, birth control, instead of being a product of racism, gave Black families a way of dealing with racism. As he asserted, "Society should make available all of the resources that I need, and my family needs. It hasn't done so up to this point, it does not appear to be doing so within the foreseeable future, so that, in the long run, birth control is a strengthening factor for the Black community."[107]

If Stewart saw birth control as a method of navigating structural racism, other medical providers suggested that when the government provided birth control without any other form of aid, then birth control did seem to take on shades of genocide. Ella MacDonald, whom *Essence* described as the "spirited, afro-coifed" administrative director of fifteen clinics run by the Family Planning Unit of the Human Resources Administration of the Community Development Agency of New York City, explained that her clinics, located in the poorest Black and Puerto Rican neighborhoods, were based on the idea of community control. These clinics were often the only health services available, and "if it's a situation where women cannot get any other health services for [their families] but a birth control device, then the entire question of genocide is a live one."[108] In what looked like a forerunner of the reproductive justice movement, MacDonald believed in birth control, but she also wanted to make sure that the family planning provided by her clinics expanded to include all of the services women needed to have healthy families, including nutrition and other health needs. MacDonald, who spoke of seeing women come to her clinic "butchered" from illegal abortions, made it clear that her vision of Black community health had to include birth control, but that birth control had to be part of a holistic system of care.[109]

While *Essence* provided Ruffin a platform to argue in support of contraception, the fact that she needed to do so pointed to just how controversial the topic of birth control could be within the Black community. Indeed, in 1971, the same magazine had published an in-depth interview with a Mrs. Aileen Hernandez of San Francisco, who had been appointed to the Equal Employment Opportunity Commission by Lyndon Johnson in 1965 but had resigned in 1966. She said in this interview, "It [the whole debate about population growth] seems to be another way of saying 'we do not want you to expand your influence in society by increasing your numbers'—the kind of thing that smacks of genocide."[110] In her comments, which were republished in the *Chicago Daily Defender*, she also pointed out that when the Kennedy clan had twelve children, no one suggested that they were being "obscene."[111] Hernandez was wrong to suggest that no one was criticizing Catholic families for being large—much of the organized Protestant movement for contraceptive access framed Catholics as being irresponsible—but she was absolutely correct to note the double standard with which the American media treated the Kennedy clan as opposed to large families of the urban poor.

In the late 1970s, Black communities debated the role that birth control should play in their lives. Many feared that birth control initiatives were, in fact, covert or even overt attempts to limit the Black population at home. Contraception, in this formulation, was another tool of white supremacy designed to keep African American communities small and disempowered. For others, contraception was a tool that Black women, Black couples, and the Black community more broadly could use to assert agency and improve their lot, individually and collectively, in the face of structural oppression. Few African American voices shared King's concerns about the global population. They focused instead on what contraception initiatives meant for Black communities in the context of American race relations. While some of those voices wanted Black women and communities to have the same access to contraception as their white counterparts, others saw birth control as an imposition limiting the size of Black families for more nefarious reasons. These voices saw themselves as responding to the threat of global eradication—or at least disempowerment through diminished numbers—rather than a threat of global overpopulation.

Population Panics and Jewish Continuity Crises

On January 24, 1974, the *New York Times* reported that Sol Roth, newly elected president of the New York Board of Rabbis, compared birth control to the Holocaust.[112] Specifically, the Orthodox rabbi, according to the *Times*, said that "Jewish families should have at least three children and asserted that the frequently projected goal of zero population growth 'should find no application in the Jewish community.'"[113] The paper reported that Roth saw the declining size of Jewish families as a threat "to the spiritual and cultural future of the American Jewish community." Directly referencing the six million Jews killed in the Holocaust, he said, "The Jewish population in the United States is the same now as it was 30 years ago. There should have been, if we had merely kept pace, 12 million Jews in America today, but there are only six million." The article closed with his rhetorical question: "Is it not obvious that in terms of Jewish survival, the European Holocaust [Nazi murders of Jews], of the war years and the Holocaust-size loss in America during the last three decades produced the same results?"[114]

While Roth did not directly reference contraception, it was, of course, the tool that made movements like Zero Population Growth (ZPG) possible. Roth did not precisely dispute the idea that the world population was growing and that something must be done about it. "[I am] not saying whether or not I oppose zero population growth for the rest of the human family," the *Times* quoted him as saying.[115] He explained his position to *Time* magazine: "Since Jews constitute only three-tenths of 1% of the world's population of 4 billion, the Jewish community will not solve the world's problems by applying Z.P.G. to itself."[116] Unlike Catholic leadership, Roth was not weighing in on the validity of population concerns. Rather, he was searching for reasons not to hold Jews to the global need to limit their families.

Roth was not alone in linking the declining Jewish birthrate, and therefore Jewish use of contraception, to the Holocaust.[117] In 1973, at a conference sponsored by the Federation for Jewish Philanthropies of New York, Rabbi Walker S. Worzburger, vice president of the Rabbinical Council of America, observed, "Having lost one-third of the population to the Holocaust and lacking sufficient population to settle the land of Israel—the Jewish community does not reproduce itself adequately."[118] The Holocaust lent gravity to Jewish discomfort with ZPG and, as we shall see, also served a strategic purpose.

ZPG was a response to concerns about the "population bomb," or the idea that the world's population would rapidly outstrip its resources. The movement encouraged zero population growth, that is, keeping the number of people born each year more or less equivalent to the number that died. This movement took many forms, ranging from the idea that couples should have two children, doing no more than reproduce themselves, to the idea that many should not have children at all.

ZPG was a movement popularized by the publication of *The Population Bomb*, a title that not so subtly connected the rising population to the primary fear of the atomic age. The movement was popular with college-educated young Americans, in part because environmentalism and population limitation were understood to be intimately connected. This point was repeatedly made at campus "teach-ins," where "college students of the time heard repetitious proclamations on the necessity of stopping the US population growth in order to reach environmental goals."[119] All college students were exposed to ZPG, but young Jews attended college at nearly double the national rate, and enough of them found it compelling to worry Jewish leadership.[120]

While we shall consider the full scope of the Jewish response to ZPG and other perceived threats to the survival of the Jewish people in the next chapter, it is worth noting here that Jews were part of the broad-based consensus that a rising population was likely a threat to global stability, both environmentally and politically. That said, this was a community that had been the subject of a eugenics-based genocide only a generation earlier. In addition, the same Protestant groups with whom Jewish groups were in tight alliance in the 1960s were groups whose isolationism had contributed to the United States' delayed entry into World War II. It seems reasonable to assume that the experience of eugenic genocide might make members of the Jewish community anxious about applying population restrictions to themselves. Given the popularity of ZPG among young Jews, this reaction was not universal. However, as the examples of Roth and others demonstrate, at least for some who had been adults in the 1940s, there were resonances between Nazi eugenics and the potential implications for the Jewish community of a full-throated embrace of population control. Many Protestant religious leaders felt guilt for their role in delaying the American entry into the Second World War. This guilt made mobilizing the massive losses that the Jewish community suffered during the Holocaust an unassailable reason—at least not assailable by their Protestant allies—for why Jewish families might believe in the need for population control but refuse to apply it to themselves.

White Jews and African Americans had very different histories and experiences of eugenics, and they had notably different social locations in the United States of the 1960s. Yet both communities had been subject to eugenic projects over the course of the twentieth century, projects that were arguably ongoing in some African American communities. These experiences made members of both communities skeptical about the broader motivations of those looking to promote birth control, however interested individuals might be in gaining access to reproductive technology.

The Political Implications of Religion and Population

On March 16, 1970, President Richard Nixon established the Commission on Population Growth and the American Future, in order to conduct and sponsor research on population growth in the United States with an eye toward its effect on "the economy, government resources, and environmental pollution."[121] Chaired by John D. Rockefeller III, cofounder of the Population Council, and made up of representatives of the House and the Senate, as well as nineteen additional people appointed by the president, the commission presented a report after two years and disbanded two months later.[122] The group was made up primarily of academics, along with some nonprofit leaders, students, and two women listed as "housewife, volunteer."[123]

The commission did not include any clergy, but its members did solicit a report entitled *Ethics, Population and the American Tradition* prepared by Daniel Callahan, a philosopher and the founding director of the Institute of Society, Ethics and the Life Sciences at the Hastings Center. The nonpartisan, nonprofit multidisciplinary think tank was founded in 1969 and was influential in creating contemporary bioethics. In the memorandum accompanying the report for the Commission on Population Growth and the American Future, Callahan detailed for Rockefeller its primary implications. He explained that people did not think of the question of population on the level of systems and global statistics, but rather considered what it meant for their own families and their "private, personal lives."[124] Any policy that the commission developed was therefore going to "have a major impact on some deeply-held and fervently-felt values" about "sexuality, procreation, government and their own conception of the good and decent life, for themselves and everyone else."[125]

The result of that reality was, in essence, that the commission was not going to win. No policy was going to satisfy everyone. Callahan therefore recommended that a policy giving "central place to a recognition of the diversity of values present in America," showing "sensitivity to different needs and strains in our national life, would probably gain a majority acceptance." He argued that, whether or not people could speak articulately about their values—specifically, the American values of "freedom" and "justice"—those values nevertheless matter deeply to them, and therein lay the potential success of a population program. Callahan contended that if a population program could be framed in a way that enhanced those key values of what we might call an American civil religion, that framing would silence many of the potential criticisms that such a program would otherwise call forth.[126] He was only partially correct.

On March 15, 1972, Monsignor James T. McHugh, the director of the Division for Family Life of the United States Catholic Conference, wrote that the Population Commission's "pre-occupation with finding an effective way to get rid of the 'unwanted child'" had led its members "into an ideological 'valley of death.'" Focusing on abortion rather than birth control, and emphasizing what he referred to as "eugenic abortion," McHugh asserted, "Despite occasional platitudes about human dignity, moral values, and religious convictions, the Commission is highly utilitarian in the policies that it recommends."[127] Seeing the report as "naïve in its assumptions and punitive in its recommendations," McHugh advised Washington to treat the report with "benign neglect."[128]

By contrast, the following month, Bishop John Wesley Lord of the United Methodist Church, Washington Area, wrote to Richard Nixon on behalf of himself and a collection of "national church leaders" to commend the president and to request a meeting to discuss the report of the Commission on Population Growth and the American Future. He reminded the president that a "number of leading figures of the religious community" had recently issued a statement "welcoming" the report "as a valuable stimulus to the public discussion necessary for the development of population policies adequate to the challenge confronting humanity."[129]

More important than the contents of the letter were the signatories—who were, perhaps as an indicator of the declining status of the clergy in American public life, denied their requested audience. Joining this Methodist bishop were the presidents of the National Council of Churches and the National Federation of Temple Sisterhoods; the moderator of the United Presbyterian Church, USA; an American president of the World Council of Churches; the bishop coadjutor of the Episcopal Diocese of New York; the executive vice-president of the Synagogue Council of America; the president of the American Baptist Convention; the executive secretary of the Board of

Social Ministry, Lutheran Church in America; the executive secretary of the
Christian Life Commission, Southern Baptist Convention; the president of
the American Union of Hebrew Congregations; the director of the Office of
Church and Society, Presbyterian Church in the USA; the suffragan bishop of
Washington for the Episcopal Church; the general secretary of the Board of
Christian Concerns, United Methodist Church; the executive director of the
National Federation of Temple Sisterhoods; the secretary of the general board,
Church of the Brethren; the president of the United Church of Christ; the gen-
eral minister and president of the Disciples of Christ; the executive director
of the Division of Christian Social Concern, American Baptist Convention;
the executive secretary of the American Baptist Home Mission Society; the
president of the Board of Bishops, African Methodist Episcopal (AME) Zion
Church; and a representative of the Commission on Social Action, Union of
American Hebrew Congregations.[130] I have reproduced this list in total to
demonstrate how pervasive religious support for population control was in
this moment. This list includes a broad range of Protestant denominations
and a number of Jewish organizations, from the North and the South, representing a range of liturgical practices, from traditional to innovative, and
having a broad variety of governance structures.

Despite their concerns about population control, Jews, whose coreligion-
ists had just decades earlier suffered a eugenically based genocide, signed on
to the letter: the Reform movement and the National Federation of Temple
Sisterhoods, an organization that crossed Jewish movements. While the
majority of the Protestant denominations listed were largely white religious
communities, though none of them were exclusively so, the AME Zion movement is a Black church movement. I say this not to dismiss the critiques of
birth control that were certainly already present, particularly in some Black
communal conversations, but rather to note that there was a broad consensus
about the urgency of population control. It also seems worth noting that, just
as in the 1940s, this interfaith coalition, which includes Jews, refers to the
community as a whole as "churches."

The threat of global population explosion created a stunning religious
consensus, absent the official Catholic Church, on the question of contraception. Contraception as a moral, even a salvific, good allowed Protestants
from across the religious, racial, and political spectrum to unite in the idea
that the United States should promote family planning at home and abroad.
Though individual Black people worried that population control could be
turned on their own communities, denominational and movement leaders
like Martin Luther King Jr. saw enough need for contraception in the growing

population that they could endorse family planning as a necessity in the fight for social justice.

While the Catholic Church condemned such measures and Jewish leaders were ambivalent about applying the logic of family planning for population control to their own households, individual Catholics and Jews found the logic of population control to be compelling, a fact that caused concern for their leadership. That said, Jewish leaders, however concerned they were about the Jewish laity's embrace of ZPG, were convinced enough of the global threat of overpopulation that they could sign on to a statement encouraging the government to take it seriously as a moral issue. These concerns were deeply entangled with morally rooted understandings of the family, and with deep fear of communism, both as a way of life and in the context of the Cold War. All of these reasons for supporting contraception were, however, couched in social control, and were very much separated from the rights of women and the changing sexual patterns of the country. These factors were among those that sowed the seeds of a backlash against this religious near unity on contraception as family planning, and on family planning as a social good.

As women were able to better control their reproductive lives through accessible birth control, both domestically and abroad, it became clear that while readily accessible contraception could be used to create carefully planned families, it could also be used to liberate women from the cultural constraints of patriarchy. For all the problems embedded in exporting contraception abroad, as soon as women in developing countries got access to it, they used it to improve their standard of living and that of their children, particularly their daughters. Domestically, birth control also expanded the options available to women. While women could and did use contraception to space out their children, and to limit the number of children in their families, they also used it to delay childbearing in order to get more education and build careers. These goals were in tension—or at least, they were perceived by many to be in tension—with the inherent goals of responsible parenthood.

CHAPTER 4

Contraceptive Backlash

In the early 1970s, Margaret Sanger was elevated to become no less than an "icon of feminist art" when she was given a place at Judy Chicago's famous *The Dinner Party*. Chicago, a Jewish feminist artist, and her team of collaborators had taken five years to create the iconic mixed-media art installation: a giant triangular table set with thirty-nine place settings, each of which represented an important woman in history or myth—often through an artistic representation of her vulva—and each lying on place mats and table runners embroidered with images relevant to the woman's work and impact. On the side of the triangle representing the American Revolution to the 1970s sits Margaret Sanger's bright bloodred plate. It is described as representing "the female reproductive organs and the blood that is involved in the reproductive process, as well as the battle for reproductive freedom."[1] The red also denotes death—in childbirth or from illegal abortions—and the struggle of activists who were and are arrested and jailed fighting for women's rights. Sanger's plate lifts up at the edges, representing her "efforts to lift up her sex."[2] Her section of the table runner depicts a butterfly, symbolizing the freedom that she gained but also the freedom that women more broadly gained from her work.

Margaret Sanger's presence in *The Dinner Party* represents a shift in the public face of birth control with the rise of the women's liberation movement. Contraception had gotten its early start as a feminist issue, and certainly it had been carried forward by many feminist groups. During the middle of the century, however, advocates, particularly liberal religious ones, had worked hard to tie birth control to the Protestant-inflected theology of responsible parenthood. The rise of second-wave feminism, as represented by artists like Chicago, brought the feminist dimensions of birth control dramatically back into the public eye—often at the cost of its hard-won respectability.

This chapter asks how contraception went from being understood by many as a public good, to becoming the subject of right-wing attacks, and how the cause was largely abandoned by the religious left in the face of those attacks. It considers the increasing association of contraception with second-wave feminism, and the implications of that association for both liberal and conservative religious actors. Up to this point, this book has traced religious support for, and sometimes opposition to, contraception, demonstrating that a broad-based but politically middle-of-the-road support for contraception existed in in American religious and political life. That consensus fell apart in the 1970s and 1980s, setting the stage for attacks on access to birth control. The decrease in public support for contraception can largely be traced to three factors: the increasingly visible feminist implications of contraception, the decline of the religious left, and the parallel rise of the religious right. Together, these factors eroded the consensus that birth control was a social good, and created further reason and opportunity for backlash.

Feminist Uses of Contraception

In the midcentury, any number of social actors brought their own motivations to birth control, and feminist reasons for supporting or using contraception were often not the most salient reasons for religious leaders to support birth control access. But by the 1970s, birth control was inextricably linked to the women's liberation movement. While there had been feminist organizing and community around birth control throughout the twentieth century, the period from late 1960s through the early 1980s marked the century's most intensive periods of feminist organizing in general since the suffrage movement of the early 1900s. Most histories depict two main prongs of feminist organizing: an older and perhaps more conservative approach, represented by the National Organization for Women and drawing from a base of political, union labor, and professional women; and the younger, more grassroots and radical women's liberation movement. But it is better to think of this historical moment as characterized by a "complex array of feminist movements" representing all races, classes, and sexual orientations of women.[3]

While these numerous feminist movements had different agendas born of their profoundly different social locations, many shared a common organizing technique: consciousness raising, or CR. The technique involved women gathering in small groups to share about their lives; and through this process, many of them learned that the discontent that they felt under white supremacist heteropatriarchy was not "just them," but rather experienced by other women—that the problems were systemic.[4] It was through these realizations that women's discontentedness was normalized; their grievances could be approached as structural, rather than individualized, problems. It was through the combined forces of all these movements, along with other social forces, that women were able to access to a broader range of educational opportunities and to normalize their presence in the professions. It was in these spaces, too, that they were able to identify and give voice to problems that have not yet been solved—or whose solutions began to be dismantled in the first quarter of the twenty-first century—such as unequal sharing of domestic and emotional labor, the gender wage gap, lack of respect and opportunity for advancement in the workplace, or limited access to parental leave and reproductive health care.

In addition to gender-based concerns, working-class women and women of color had both economic and race-based discrimination to navigate, and they were sometimes caught between solidarity with their communities and wishing to name the sexism they experienced in their communities. Those tensions would play out differently in different contexts: For instance, the women of the Black Panther Party were able to leverage their power and organizing to increase mutual aid; and the women of the Young Lords used a sex strike to get women into the organization's leadership.[5] That said, the media tended to focus only on the aspects of the moment represented by white middle- and upper-class women, many of whom neither wished to exclude women of color nor were willing to make room for their concerns when they did not align with their own. And that media focus tended also to dwell on aspects of feminism that stoked public fears: women's desire for lives and careers outside the home; a new emphasis on female sexual pleasure; the valuing of relationships, including sexual relationships, between women; and reproductive rights, in particular, because of the media attention to white women, the right to an abortion.

In her foundational history of contraception, *The Moral Property of Women: A History of Birth Control Politics in America*, feminist historian Linda Gordon put it this way: "The major reason for the heightened passion about reproductive issues is that they seemed to express the core aims of the women's liberation movement and thus became the major focus of backlash against feminism."[6] Gordon asserts that this backlash occurred in part because, from the late 1960s to the 1970s, "feminism's ideas shifted considerably from an emphasis on personal freedom to a concern with the values that underlie our whole social order and an understanding that reproductive rights could not only provide individual rights but also promote social goals such as equality."[7] Working-class feminists and feminists of color would legitimately argue that the mainstream feminist movement did not go far enough in focusing on social goals—paying more attention, for instance, to the right to not have a child than to the right to have a child, and to the need for social support to raise that child in a safe and healthy environment. But it was this broader vision of equality, along with the ramifications of women having personal freedom, that likely ruffled religious feathers.[8]

The feminist potential of the Pill was in many ways completely obvious: In gaining the ability to control their own reproductive lives, women gained control over other aspects of their destiny as well; they could use contraception to obtain education or build careers, goals that might or might not exist in concert with the creation of upwardly mobile nuclear families.[9] In practical terms, the Pill did not usher in a sexual revolution, nor did it immediately, positively change the average woman's experience of heterosexual sex. However, more readily available contraception did better allow women to control pregnancy, and therefore improved their access to education, careers, and economic autonomy. This reality existed in tension with the use of contraception only for family planning of the sort espoused by the ideals of responsible parenthood.

While these tensions already created anxiety about contraception in mainstream, establishment circles, some of the optimistic popular depictions of what the Pill potentially meant for women's sexuality further stoked that unease. Perhaps the most famous example of this optimism about came in Loretta Lynn's 1975 hit song "The Pill." As a country singer whose repertoire often depicted her childhood as a poor coal miner's daughter, Lynn seemed a far cry from "women's libbers," but her song still pointed to the Pill as a way out of a marital double standard. The song tells of a wife whose husband promised, while courting, that he would show her the world. Instead, marriage found her confined to his bed and their children's nursery, flat broke from the doctor's bills from so many pregnancies and children, all while he ran around having fun. Not only was her husband keeping her pregnant, he caroused while she had babies! The Pill freed her from this cycle of childbearing. She planned to trade in her maternity dresses for clothing with less yardage—hot pants and miniskirts. With the Pill, Mama was going to have her fun—though, as the song implies, Daddy still did not need to worry, because she had the protection of the Pill. What the song fails to make clear is why Daddy did not need to worry. Was it because they could now have fun, as a couple, without the fear of pregnancy, or was it because, as Mama headed off to find her pleasure, the Pill would ensure that she did not bring another man's baby home?

Aspects of Lynn's song reflected reality: Certainly, the pill, and the diaphragm before it, had ended cycles of endless pregnancy and had both removed anxiety from, and added spontaneity to, marital sex. The Pill did not, however, usher in the kind of sexual freedom in the song. But reality often matters less, or at least not more, than perception. Contraception really gave women greater reproductive autonomy, and therefore the possibility of greater economic autonomy. It also gave the appearance of allowing women much more sexual freedom—an appearance many mistook for reality at the time. The prospect of neither autonomy nor sexual freedom appealed to a religious conversation that had framed birth control in terms of a tool for the safeguarding of marriage and the family. While the story of the backlash against contraception is perhaps the best-known piece of the story of religion and birth control, a close examination of the apparent religious about-face on the issue demonstrates that even the most liberal of religious voices had, if nothing else, created a rhetorical messaging on birth control that made it difficult to loudly support its continued accessibility.

Sex and the Single Girl

The 1972 Supreme Court case of *Eisenstadt v. Baird* made it illegal to deny birth control based on marital status. William Baird was charged with violating a Massachusetts law forbidding the distribution of contraceptives to unmarried people. In a planned violation of the law, Baird gave a nineteen-year-old woman a condom and contraceptive foam during a lecture on birth control and population control at Boston University on April 6, 1967. The case worked its way through the court system over the next several years. On March 22, 1972, the Supreme Court decided: "If the right of privacy means anything, it is the right of the individual, married or single, to be free from unwarranted governmental intrusion into matters so fundamentally affecting a person as the decision whether to bear or beget a child."[10] It therefore stood to reason that "whatever the rights of the individual to access contraceptives may be, the rights must be the same for the unmarried and the married alike."[11]

In short, *Eisenstadt v. Baird* made it illegal to deny contraception to people on the basis of marital status. Practically, that meant that a woman who asked her doctor for the birth control pill would be legally entitled to be prescribed the drug, regardless of whether she was married, no matter what the doctor thought about premarital sex. Similarly, if someone who owned a corner store disapproved of nonmarital sex, he could decline to carry condoms, but he could not decide whether to sell someone condoms based on the presence or absence of a wedding ring. In addition to removing legal distinctions between the married and unmarried in the purchasing of contraception, the case functionally recognized in law the right of single people to sexual activity.

While *Eisenstadt v. Baird* was a legal victory for many of the activists who had been looking to expand birth control access, it posed a problem for religious groups that had supported contraception. The very many religious groups that had supported contraception did so by and large to support the institutions of marriage. Marital sexuality was lauded as important to helping couples build intimacy in a sacred and holy relationship, and birth control was described as a helpful tool in allowing for sex for that purpose. But as I have discussed in chapters 1 and 2, sexuality was only described as valuable in the context of marriage. Birth control laws vary by state, and so there were plenty of places in the United States that did allow contraception regardless of marital status. But prior to *Eisenstadt*, the language used to legalize birth control on the national level had connected contraception to marriage with the Supreme Court case of *Griswold v. Connecticut*. *Griswold* ended the State of Connecticut's ban on birth control for married couples by establishing the "heterosexual act of intercourse in marital bedrooms as protected by a zone of privacy into which courts must not peer and with which they must not interfere."[12] As long as the legal language around contraception echoed the religious language, and the law at least in some places provided the assurance that birth control was intended primarily for marriage, clergy could publicly support the increased access and availability of contraception because it would create stronger marriages, rather than implicitly giving license to nonmarital sex.

With *Eisenstadt*, however, the law of the land no longer followed the marital logic of the religious leaders. It was now illegal to deny unmarried people access to contraception. Functionally, that meant that any expansion of birth control access meant access was more possible for nonmarried people, including young people. Most liberal Protestant denominations and Jewish groups did not actively condemn this development, and some campus chaplains actively supported it. Yet the fact that contraception was no longer restricted to marriage made it harder for clergy and other religious leaders to actively campaign for birth control as a moral good.

Protestant sexuality education under, for instance, William and Elizabeth Genné, had advocated that adolescents learn about contraception, but as a tool for their eventual marriages (see chapter 2). Clergy were similarly trained, often by the Gennés, to talk about contraception in premarital or marital counseling. None of the mainline Protestant denominations or the liberal Jewish movements had robust theologies addressing nonmarital sexuality. At best, they simply hoped that it was premarital, rather than nonmarital or extramarital; and when speaking privately, even the most supportive clergy turned largely to psychology for support of birth control access, rather than to theology.

The Decline of Liberal Religion

Part of the reason that the religious left largely fell silent on the issue of contraception in this period—other than its members' rhetorical inability to support contraception for everyone—came from its declining power in the public sphere. For the majority of the time covered by this book—the 1940s, 1950s, and 1960s—all clergy, including liberal Protestant, Catholic, and Jewish clergy, had a kind of moral force. Before the end of the century, they would lose that cultural relevance, in part because the religious left also began to lose membership. Some was lost, as we shall see in a moment, to the growing religious right; but other members simply left organized religion. The post–World War II years had been characterized by higher-than-usual religious participation. More Americans of the Greatest Generation belonged to churches and synagogues in the 1950s than in any other decade of the century, and this numerical strength gave religious leaders a kind of political power. But that power waned with the next generation, the baby boomers, who were less likely to join religious institutions than their parents had been. The baby boomers were often what sociologists of religion term "religious seekers," people who either did not join or moved between religious communities, "in search of a holistic, all-encompassing vision of life."[13] One effect of this generational trend was fewer people in the more traditional congregations, a situation that gave these denominations correspondingly less power.

Other historical factors also contributed to this waning power. The religious left had been a very diverse collective, what scholar of religion and media Diane Winston refers to as a "mighty river of progressive Evangelicals, mainline Protestants, Roman Catholics, Unitarians, Jews, and much of the African American church"; and it had come together in striking unity under the profoundly compelling, charismatic, and erudite symbolic leadership of the Reverend Martin Luther King Jr.[14] After his assassination, that movement fractured into a number of other movements ranging from antiwar activism to feminism to Black nationalism.[15] Simultaneously, ego-driven conflicts undermined some of the alliances.

As a result, the religious left started speaking with a much less unified voice: Individual religious groups created their own social justice organizations and their own independent priorities, rather than necessarily collaborating on a shared set of goals. This also made it difficult for Protestants to create ecumenical partnerships with Jewish and Catholic groups, who were faced with an increasing plethora of potential partners. It was not so much that these groups disagreed with one another as that they no longer had the immediate infrastructure to allow them to create strong ecumenical alliances.

Winston also notes another reason why the religious left lost power and traction at the same time that the religious right was coalescing into a unified power with a clear agenda. In general, the Left liked complex arguments. Liberal or progressive religious communities had responded to feminist, racial justice, and economic justice movements by coming to understand that there was rarely one shared position across complicated identities. The thinking of religions about morality, but also about organizing, thus became multivocal rather than univocal.

This valuing of diversity introduced complexity into political or theological messages, and often people do not like complexity—they like simple answers. The religious right provided these answers, with its simplification of the Bible and clear messages of heaven and hell. And as Winston explains, the kind of messages that the Left created did not work well with the media. They did not make for good sound bites on the nightly news, or pull quotes in newspapers. By contrast, the kinds of messages that the coalescing religious right favored made for better media communications—it was easier to report on simple statements, and it was easier to turn them into sound bites.

Liberal religions were also often paralyzed by the inherent complexity of issues. Think, for instance, about debates in communities of color about how to understand contraception. On the one hand, you have figures like Martin Luther King, who argued that contraception was a human right and that Black communities deserved access to that medical technology. On the other hand, segments of the Nation of Islam and the Black Panthers were more dubious about birth control; they took into account the historical relationship between contraception and eugenics, the history of gynecological experimentation on Black women, and also the history of the relationship between the Black churches and the politics of respectability. At the farthest end of the spectrum were those who saw contraception as genocidal.

The fact that communities of color did not speak with a unified voice on contraception—and the reality that many Black religious communities, as the work of Monique Moultrie tells us, were liberal on many social issues but not necessarily on sexuality—made it hard, again, for the Christian left to speak with a unified voice. Contraception access was a complicated issue for Black communities to navigate; and they often did not see it as their most pressing issue, so they did not take strong public stances. Meanwhile, white liberal communities, who were at least somewhat aware of their own complicated racial histories, were cautious about addressing issues that they knew might fragment their relationships with Black religious organizations.

Thus, a combination of a wide range of factors—the religious left's own hesitation and discomfort with the feminist implications of contraception, the organizational fragmentation, the lack of media coverage, and the complexity of messages   contributed to declining numbers for the religious left and to the rising power for the Right, such that the religious right increasingly set the terms of debate and engagement.

Ronald Reagan, the Religious Right, and Declining Reproductive Rights

The fact that the religious right was setting the terms of the debate also meant that contraception became linked with abortion; that linkage also undercut the liberal religious groups who were generally pro-choice, but for whom abortion was also a more challenging topic than contraception. Therefore, it was not so much that liberal religious congregations and denominations stopped supporting contraception in this period—religious education material still talked about contraception, as did premarital counseling in family planning. But they had lost their public platform and public power. Besides, in many ways, liberal congregations assumed that the contraception battle had been won, and so they put their decreasing capital elsewhere. The voices that continued to protect family planning from the Left begin to speak as secular voices, even when many of the participating activists were, in fact, privately religious. In doing so, however, they lost the quality of moral authority that came from the pulpits.

Moral authority was important, because more conservative religious actors were arguing that that *Eisenstadt v. Baird* was actually going to erode moral authority very significantly. As has been established, the Supreme Court case extended the right to contraception to people regardless of marital status.

Although this happened with the support of some clergy, it undermined what had been a key piece of religious conversations about contraception over the preceding decades: that contraception was an important tool for marriage and family life that would not necessarily lead to sexual promiscuity. The idea that contraception was for marriage also offered social assurances that it would be for adults. Once birth control was legally protected for single people, it raised questions and concerns about whether teens could access contraception.

During this period, as contraception for unmarried women was becoming the norm, birth control was becoming a secular question available for public discourse outside the meetings of clergy or advocates. One of the most prominent voices offering insight into how the public saw birth control was that of Herblock, the nom de plume of Herbert Block, the Chicago-born son of a Catholic mother and a Jewish father. Herblock was a Pulitzer Prize–winning political cartoonist who spent fifty years drawing for the *Washington Post*. He was particularly known for his critiques of those in power, even more so for his critiques of the federal government.

In 1983, Herblock drew a cartoon for the *Washington Post* that pictured what was likely a caricature of Richard S. Schweiker, the secretary of the Department of Health and Human Services, as a Vincent Price–esque, sinister-looking man, writing a letter that read, "I guess maybe you didn't know about your dear little daughter being interested in contraceptives. Just thought you . . ." A placard on his desk read "Department of Health and Human Disservices." Herblock's cartoon was criticizing a policy put forward by the Reagan administration called the "Squeal Rule," or sometimes the "Tattle Tale policy": It obligated any reproductive health clinics providing federally funded Title X services to report in writing to parents anytime a non-emancipated minor received contraception in the form of birth control pills, a diaphragm, or an IUD (intrauterine device).[16] Schweiker announced his decision to "make the rule final" on January 10, 1983, and then resigned the following day. His successor, Margaret Heckler, had opposed the rule as a member of Congress, but she did not repeal the rule when she took over the Department of Health and Human Services.[17]

Title X, which had been authorized in 1970 as part of the Population Research and Voluntary Family Planning Act and was renewed annually, provided federal funding in the form of grants to public and private family planning clinics.[18] Until the Squeal Rule, all Title X services were required to be both confidential and provided regardless of age. With the act's 1978 renewal, Congress explicitly included adolescents in its language out of a concern for teen

Department of Health and Human Disservices. A Herblock Cartoon,
© The Herb Block Foundation. Courtesy of the Library of Congress,
Prints and Photographs Division, LC-DIG-hlb-10511.

pregnancy.[19] In 1981, Congress added the lines "to the extent practical, entities which receive grants or contacts under this subsection shall encourage family participation."[20] Likewise, a Congressional Conference Committee report emphasized that, "while family involvement is not mandated, it is important that families participate in the activities authorized by this title as much as possible."[21] The report went on to recommend that those receiving services be encouraged to include their families in counseling and decision-making, but made it clear that they were not required to do so. Despite that, Schweiker, the secretary of the Department of Health and Human Services, used the insertion of this family language to justify policies around parental notification.[22]

The Squeal Rule was opposed by more than 900 groups, ranging from the Girls Clubs of America, to the American College of Obstetricians and Gynecologists, to the Salvation Army, to the American Civil Liberties Union and the Center for Constitutional Rights.[23] Oregon took steps to replace federal funding with state funding to protect its clinics from the policy.[24] While the Squeal Rule was never enforced, and the courts ultimately struck it down, the conversation that it occasioned provides useful insights into the issues surrounding birth control access in the early 1980s.[25]

Teen access to contraception played a prominent role in Reagan's remarks at the Annual Convention of the National Association of Evangelicals (NAE) on March 8, 1983—as a problem. He opened by telling a joke about a preacher and a politician arriving in heaven, only to discover that heaven was much more excited about the politician. Preachers were a dime a dozen, according to Saint Peter. The politician was the first they had ever had in heaven![26] Reagan, however, did not "want to contribute to a stereotype," saying, "So, I tell you there are a great many God-fearing, dedicated, noble men and women in public life, present company included."[27]

He told the assembled Evangelical audience that his administration was "motivated by a political philosophy that sees the greatness of America in you, her people, and in your families, churches, neighborhoods, communities—the institutions that foster and nourish values like concern for others and respect for the rule of law under God."[28] The Reagan administration was, however, in opposition to the many "who have turned to a modern day secularism, disregarding the tried and time-tested values upon which our very civilization is based."[29] He asserted that while these people may have louder voices than "ours," they remained in the minority, with a value system that was "radically different from that of most Americans."[30] While these secular voices "proclaim that they're freeing us from the voices of the past," Reagan argued that they were, in fact, "superintending us by government rule and regulation."[31]

In this section of the speech, Reagan fused secularism and big government, positing that the same people who want those things have values that are in tension not only with traditional American values but with the moral sensibilities of their fellow Americans. His language also evoked the threat of communism, a recurring preoccupation of his presidential campaigns and his presidency. He did not go so far as to label his fellow Americans communists; but his description of a secularism that empowered the state and discarded "traditional values," which should be read, particularly in the context of this speech to the Annual Convention of the NAE, as religious values, is a clear dog whistle to communism.

Who, then, were these dangerous big-government secularists who were taking the country in a direction reminiscent of communism? They were, according to Reagan, proponents of reproductive health clinics: "An organization of citizens, sincerely motivated and deeply concerned about the increase in illegitimate births and abortions involving girls well below the age of consent, some time ago established a nationwide network of clinics to offer help to these girls and, hopefully, alleviate this situation."[32] Reagan agreed that illegitimate births and abortions were a problem, and he noted that he "did not fault their [clinic proponents'] intent." He explained, however, that these clinics were providing "birth control advice and birth control drugs and devices to underage girls without the knowledge of their parents."[33] It is worth emphasizing that the birth control available at clinics, both birth control pills and devices like the diaphragm, acted on the female body. The Reagan administration, then, sought to control young women's access to the contraception that they could use to prevent pregnancy without the help or consent of their partners, or simply without their dependence on them. There was not similar scrutiny of condoms—the contraception that any young man might buy at the drugstore.

Reagan did not talk about why the clinics had made this choice. A study had reported that 25 percent of their clientele would stop seeking prescription contraception if their parents were notified—but only 2 percent of them said that they would stop having sex.[34] As a New York Times opinion piece pointed out, it would be ironic if the firmly antiabortion Reagan administration created an uptick in teenage girls accessing abortion because they had been restricted in their access to contraception.[35]

Instead, the president talked about how the media was treating his proposal; news outlets argued that the administration was in the wrong, and they referred to his policy as a "squeal rule." But, he said, "no one seems to mention morality as playing a part in the subject of sex." This absence of morality was, for Reagan, an absence of religion. "Is the Judeo-Christian [tradition] wrong?" he asked his Evangelical audience. "Are we to believe," he continued, "that something so sacred can be looked upon as a purely physical thing with no potential for emotional and psychological harm? And isn't it the parents' right to give counsel and advice to keep their children from making mistakes that may affect their entire lives?"[36]

Reagan was not, in these remarks, attacking birth control per se but rather its use by sexually active teenage girls. He almost explicitly framed his argument in terms of Judeo-Christian theologies of the family that framed sex as a sacred matter for adults and that assumed that parents, rather than anyone else, were the people best positioned to counsel their children on matters of sexuality. This version of reality failed to take into account the 25 percent of young women who would forgo contraception rather than speak to their parents. A Rhode Island state legislator, writing in the liberal Catholic magazine *Commonweal*, parodied the idea that the policy would promote parent-child communication: "Ma, I'm making it with Johnny and I wanna go on the pill." "I'll break your arm, you little snit."[37]

Reflecting the Cold War tensions that were shot through Reagan's remarks, the above legislator, David R. Carlin, commented that "in a period of economic disarray at home and rising Soviet American tension abroad, it may seem a bit odd that a dispute about something as trivial as teen-age sex rules should be front page news."[38] It was in fact not odd at all, he suggested, as, "like almost all sexual controversies," the question of teenage birth control access refracted "certain broader and more fundamental conflicts in American society and culture." The first, and less pressing, division was about teenage sex itself, with the more conservative, pro-parental-notification side thinking of teen sex with "stern disapproval." Meanwhile, Carlin stated, the side favoring confidentiality between teens and their health care providers, "while not exactly jumping with joy at the spectacle of widespread and increasing sex among school-kids, regards it as a tolerable and fairly normal thing—at worst, a kind of venial sin."[39] This observation highlights something essential to understand in figuring out why the religious left did not continue to advocate loudly and publicly for birth control access—its members were largely not excited about the need for it. Given the reality of sexually active teens, those on the religious left generally thought that birth control for unmarried adolescents was necessary, but they were hardly enthusiastic about it.

Carlin's second point, however, was that society lacked clarity about whether sex was "a strictly self-regarding activity or an activity in which society at large has a legitimate interest," essentially, whether sex is best understood as a public or a private act.[40] Even if sex happens in private, if one thought that "social regulation [by family, friends, neighbors, potential spouses, and society generally] of [sexual activity] was warranted," then one thought of sex as basically public, Carlin argued. The idea that sex, though often occurring in private, is fundamentally a public concern is the stance traditionally taken by many societies, including the majority of the population of the United States. "The traditional rule that sex should be confined within marriage meant that one was not free to act sexually in one's capacity as a mere private or natural individual; instead one acted in virtue of a kind of public office—husband or wife—that society had created and inducted one into," Carlin asserted.[41] By contrast, "sexual activity outside of marriage was an act of private will."[42]

People who supported premarital sex (in this reading, it was presumed that no one really supported extramarital sex) did not think that society could or should have a say or an interest in people's sex lives—even the sex lives of children. In this logic, as Carlin put it, "while parents of minor children may have a legitimate right to worry about the health and possible pregnancies of their sexually active kids, any interference beyond that point could be justified only on the traditional theory that sex is a matter of public interest."[43] This understanding of sex made it different from other areas of concern, such as education or smoking, that in Carlin's rendering remained matters of public interest. Though he was a Democrat writing in a liberal Catholic publication, Carlin disapproved of the privatization of sex—at least in part because he thought that it led to focusing on the individual rather than society in ways that could easily extend beyond sex, into moneymaking and other endeavors.

Jewish Communal Anxieties and a Weakening of Jewish Enthusiasm for Contraception

In essence, Carlin's article posited that the culture was undergoing a shift from seeing sex and reproduction as public matters to seeing them as matters of private concern. The latter interpretation, he suggested, was a troubling new trend. This same concern about the impact of the sexual and reproductive interests of the individual on the broader community also worried Jewish leaders, many of whom clearly articulated their concerns, particularly in terms of the feminist implications of contraception. The question of whether a woman should place her well-being, or a couple should place their well-being, ahead of the interests of the group in making decisions about contraception and reproduction animated conversations in the Jewish space.

While Jewish clergy and lay leaders had been strongly supportive of contraception, once it became readily available, American Jewish leaders faced a new problem. In their view, and in the view of a range of scholars of varying types, predominantly but not exclusively Jewish demographers and sociologists, any number of factors were weakening the Jewish community. Worry about these factors came to be known as concern for Jewish continuity, which essentially meant anxiety about the survival of the Jewish people. These social scientists were scholars of American Judaism, but they were also, by and large, American Jews with their own communal loyalties and concerns.

In articulating what they saw as a crisis of Jewish continuity, these thought leaders identified a range of threats to the long-term health of American (and, in many ways, global) Jewry, including assimilation, interfaith marriage, and a decline in the Jewish family. That decline, they argued, was caused by factors such as increased sexual liberation, such that brides were unlikely to be virgins (no similar concern was voiced about bridegrooms); increased acceptance of same-sex relationships; a decline in patriarchal authority; and the choice that many Jewish women made to pursue professional identities outside the home.[44] These thought leaders identified the declining Jewish birthrate as a primary threat to Jewish continuity. Jews were being lost to the community in many ways; but, also, not enough Jewish babies were being born.

Many of these conversations focused on "declining Jewish fertility" or "the low Jewish birthrate" without making much direct reference to the contraception that was obviously instrumental in bringing about a lowered birthrate. But in case there is any doubt about other potential causes, in 1975, leading Jewish sociologist Marshall Sklare and neocon essayist, editor of *Commentary*, and director of research for the American Jewish Committee Milton Himmelfarb referred to Jewish women as "contraceptive virtuosos" and characterized them as a "survival threat."[45] The following year, the Synagogue Council of America, an organization designed to promote cooperation between the various branches of Judaism from Reform to Orthodox, held a symposium called Zero Population Growth and the Jewish Community.[46]

At this meeting, social scientists noted that Jewish women were following the same trends as other American women, but more dramatically. If American women generally were increasingly likely to go to college, Jewish women were more likely to get some form of graduate education. Therefore, they were more likely to join the professions.[47] The years it took to complete the education and establish one's career delayed childbearing.[48] In addition, women were less likely to permanently leave those highly trained professional careers to stay home, raise children, and volunteer at the synagogue or other

Jewish communal organizations. These researchers noted that it was unclear whether these newly educated Jewish women were choosing not to have children, or were more likely to have fewer children, or whether they were simply delaying childbearing.[49]

Even though the possibility that educated women were simply delaying having children meant that the trend would potentially correct itself, increasing the generational spread from twenty years to thirty still meant that the overall population growth would slow. According to these researchers, young Jewish women continued to say that they wanted to have three to four children. Did that mean that, instead of having four children in four years, women would have four babies in eight years? Or that instead of having four children between the ages of twenty and thirty, they would have four between twenty-eight and thirty-eight? Or would starting later and juggling children and career mean that women would have fewer children overall, either because they ran out of time, or because they realized that their desired family sizes were unrealistic if they were also going to have careers?

These scholars argued that both declining Jewish birthrates and the presence of women in the workforce turned out to be "bad for the Jews." Fewer children meant there was less need for Hebrew school classes, for day schools, for all kinds of infrastructure. Similarly, women who worked full time in professions, had less time than stay-at-home mothers of school-aged children did for activities that supported the Jewish community, like membership in the Sisterhood or in the National Council of Jewish Women. Rather than understanding that the lives of Jewish women were changing, and that the infrastructure of the Jewish communal world might need to change in order to meet the needs of the "new" Jewish women—and the needs of the community that those women had previously been serving as volunteers—these social scientists simply hoped that the trends would simply reverse themselves.

They hoped that these trends would reverse because later marriage and access to contraception lead to smaller families, and smaller families meant fewer Jews. The demographers of the Institute for Jewish Policy Planning and Research found reason to hope that some of the trends leading to lower birthrates would simply disappear. For instance, in an article called "Fertility Trends and Their Impact on Jewish Education," Harold S. Himmelfarb hoped that since there were soon to be more college graduates than jobs requiring college degrees, it would no longer make financial sense for women to go to college; and therefore, he stated, as the "declining subsequent financial value of going to college mounts, women may be less likely to postpone starting a family in favor of getting more education," in the case of Jewish women, postgraduate education.[50]

The institute's demographers, also all men, placed these concerns for continuity—both the literal production of children and the labor that maintained institutions—squarely on the shoulders of women. They were not alone. Two months after the symposium that we just discussed, the New York Jewish Women's Center sponsored a talk called "Zero Population Growth and Jewish Survival" at Hebrew Union College in New York. The previous February had seen a conference on Jewish fertility that largely tracked the declining fertility of American Jews, in some cases against other American religions.

In most of these conversations, comments about contraceptive virtuosity aside, birth control was not viewed as a problem in and of itself: The problem was using too much birth control. These articles maintained that the difference between having two children and having three was the difference between Jews continuing and Jews dwindling; women were to be encouraged to be pronatal. Social changes that markedly improved the self-determination of women—their ability to experience professional success, to support themselves and their children, to leave unhappy or abusive marriages, and to control their own bodies—were regarded not as positive change but rather as problems for the Jewish community.

In part because of this kind of scholarship, William Berman, a graduate of the Jewish Theological Seminary, founded a group called PRU, or the Jewish Population Regeneration Union. The acronym was also a pun on the Hebrew phrase *Pru Urvu*, "be fruitful and multiply." The organization incorporated in 1975, and by 1978 it had enough prominence that Shirly Frank wrote about it in *Lilith* magazine. PRU created pamphlets that encouraged American Jews to eschew zero population growth (ZPG) "before it is too late."

While it is tempting to see these debates as largely the product of male leadership in the Jewish community asking women to be the solutions to larger demographic realities like assimilation, women's voices also echoed the need for Jews to avoid ZPG by having many children. When the Women's Division of the American Jewish Congress met on April 25, 1977, Blu Greenberg, the modern Orthodox feminist who twenty years later would become the founding president of the Jewish Orthodox Feminist Alliance, warned the assembled about the dangers of delaying childbirth and, worse, of ZPG. "The Jewish community has the lowest birthrate of any religious or ethnic group in the country, yet many Jewish women put off having children until their middle thirties so they can pursue careers," Greenberg stated. "For the rest of the world ZPG is a wonderful thing. For the Jewish people, in view of the huge losses our people have suffered in our own lifetime, it is a form of suicide, a death wish. Perhaps the Jewish thing to do, in light of our community's population needs, would be to begin our families early, with part-time or delayed career for husband or wife. Starting a family ten years earlier would add a new generation of Jews every thirty years."[51]

Greenberg is widely considered the mother of Orthodox feminism, and so there is an irony in that her desire to hasten the regeneration of the Jewish community after the Holocaust places a burden on Jewish women. Yes, she suggested that husbands might shoulder some of this challenge, but she basically placed the burden of Jewish continuity squarely on the shoulders of Jewish women. On some level, she attributed the contemporary population problems to the selfishness of women, to their desire to put career ahead of maternity, and their failure to sacrifice their professional needs on the altar of community growth. Greenberg was not the only Jewish feminist to strongly support continuity; and it was perhaps the seeming urgency of population regeneration postgenocide that caused some Jewish feminists to support a discourse that so strongly burdened women.

Of course, as demonstrated by the fact that Zero Population Growth served as a trigger for many of these debates, this Jewish conversation took place against a backdrop of what was going on in American life more broadly. For instance, while we have already seen Himmelfarb hoping that the recession would lead to a dearth of jobs that would cause Jewish women to marry instead of going to graduate school, the reality is that many middle-class American women entered the workforce in the 1970s precisely because of the recession. Yes, many women went to work because of the feminist desire to have an intellectually satisfying career, but many came to feminism because of the gender discrimination that they experienced in the workplace—a workplace that they had entered out of financial necessity.

It is also the case that by the 1970s, the first generation of Jews to grow up in the suburbs was reaching adulthood and marrying. They had grown up with Protestant and Catholic friends and were far more assimilated into American life than their parents had been. And while, yes, Jewish communal leaders most certainly worried about the force of assimilation, they expected Jewish women—and, as we saw earlier, Christian women married to Jewish men—to have and raise the Jewish children who would replace the people who were leaving Jewish communal life for life as unaffiliated Jews.

As attractive as assimilation was for this generation of Jews raised in Herberg's tri-faith America, secularism was also deeply appealing. The baby boom was the generation of what Wade Clark Roof and Robert Wuthnow have described as "religious seekers," those who did not tend to join their childhood religious communities at high rates, at least not as their sole and all-encompassing community. This does not mean, for seekers who were Jews, that they ceased to identify as Jews or to care about having Jewishly rooted lives. It does mean that they did not tend to root their Jewish lives in the large suburban synagogues that their parents' generation had so enthusiastically built. They stopped participating in Jewish communal life as institutional life, a trend that echoed what was happening in Protestant and Catholic life. Rather than exploring the myriad social factors that led young Jews to make lives outside of the Jewish community, however, communal leadership turned instead to Jewish wombs to make up for a range of communal losses.[52] This focus on raising the Jewish birthrate did not cause Jewish leaders to condemn contraception outright; but it certainly caused them to discourage its use in the Jewish community, at least implicitly.

Bringing Catholics Back in Line

Like Jews, Catholics discovered that their institutional structures were less accommodating than they might have expected. Most Catholics, laity and clergy alike, believed that the Vatican would take the recommendations of the Papal Commission on Birth Control and approve some forms of contraception, particularly the birth control pill. Instead, on July 29, 1968, Pope Paul VI issued the encyclical *Humanae Vitae*, which reaffirmed the inadmissibility of all artificial contraception, including the birth control pill. Historian Leslie Woodcock Tentler argues that, in fact, the encyclical softened the Church's stance in many ways: It more strongly affirmed the value of marital love, speaking of it in "lyrical" terms; acknowledged the changing status of women; accepted global population concerns; and hoped that "medical science" would help to make the rhythm method more dependable. In addition, *Humanae Vitae* allowed that couples may struggle with the desire to use contraception, and it expressed the hope that couples who had used contraception would not stay away from the sacraments and priestly counsel—at least not if they hoped to overcome their struggle and live in accordance with the teachings of the church.[53] That said, Tentler acknowledged that most Catholic Americans likely did not read the text of *Humanae Vitae* itself, and therefore they were left with what the media said about it. And the media had said that the Catholic Church had denied the faithful the right to use contraception.[54]

Almost immediately, priests objected, as did the lay members of the Papal Commission on Birth Control. This was, in and of itself, unusual.

ITEM 67 · ©1968 PANDORA PRODUCTIONS · BOX 407 · WAYZATA MN 55391

"The Pill Is a No-No." Courtesy of the Library of Congress,
Prints and Photographs Division, LC-USZC4-3846.

Generally speaking, only theologians tend to react to encyclicals. But in this case the laity responded, often with a level of indignation that could only be attributed to a sense of betrayal. The lay members of the commission held a press conference in Washington DC, where John T. Noonan, acting as their spokesman, compared *Humanae Vitae* to other encyclicals that had been subsequently discredited—perhaps most notably, given its role in couples making their own decisions, one denying the right of conscience.[55] A Gallup poll taken the following month found that 54 percent of Catholics disagreed with the encyclical; only 28 percent supported it, and the remaining 18 percent registered no opinion.[56] Tentler notes that the encyclical had remarkably little impact on the contraceptive practices of the laity. Use of contraception continued to increase, until the solid majority of married Catholic women were using a form of birth control forbidden by *Humanae Vitae*.[57] She suggests that by the time of the encyclical, the laity had grown comfortable not only with contraception, but also with "independent decision making." Priests reported that fewer and fewer people brought questions about contraception to them, either in the context of counseling or in the confessional.[58]

The issue of birth control was more complicated for priests, since they were officially part of the Catholic Church's hierarchy, directly subject to its rules, and trained in obedience to authority. Even so, many priests were deeply troubled by the *Humanae Vitae* decision; and over time, many came to simply disregard it. The amount of freedom any priest had to express concern about *Humanae Vitae* depended in large part on his bishop—both the bishop's own feelings about the encyclical and his tolerance for dissent. Still, over 600 priests signed a letter of protest issued by members of the theology faculty of Catholic University in Washington, DC. While a handful of the signers permanently or temporarily lost their positions, none of them were removed, even temporarily, from the priesthood.[59]

Perhaps more telling than the priests' immediate objections was the longer-term unwillingness of the priesthood to enforce the teaching of *Humanae Vitae*. In 1972, shortly after the encyclical was released, Andrew Greeley, Catholic priest, sociologist, columnist, and mystery author, completed a two-year-long study of the "attitudes, beliefs, and teaching on the part of priests" in the American Catholic Church for the National Opinion Research Center.[60] The statistics were, perhaps, surprising. In the time covered by the study, 1970–72, only 40 percent of priests in the United States supported Catholic teaching on birth control. Even among bishops, the support was not complete; although 83 percent of bishops overall supported a ban on contraception, only 42 percent of bishops were willing to deny couples absolution if they confessed to using, and planning to continue using, birth control. Even more importantly, the younger the priests, the less likely they were to support the policy: Only 13 percent of priests under thirty-five and 30 percent of priests between thirty-six and forty-five supported the encyclical.[61] The younger the priests, the more likely they were to grant absolution to birth-control-using couples. Ninety-seven percent of priests under thirty-five would grant abso-lution to users of contraception, and 92 percent of priests between thirty-five and forty-six would do so. Only a third of the priests who said that they would grant absolution said that they would, in that circumstance, still counsel against using artificial contraception.[62]

Greeley pointed out that one of the more surprising results of Humanae Vitae was that, overall, it made the American priesthood more liberal on the issue of birth control. Prior to the encyclical, many priests had counseled their parishioners to wait, secure in the knowledge that permission to use birth control would soon come from the Vatican. When Humanae Vitae instead reiterated the ban on contraception, priests believed they could no longer in good conscience counsel patience; 27 percent of priests in the United States responded by becoming more liberal on the subject of birth control, and only 3 percent became more conservative.[63] An additional 29 percent of priests did not change their position on the permissibility of birth control, but they did become more liberal in the confessional, absolving people who planned to continue to use contraception.

Perhaps the most interesting aspect of the article is that Humanae Vitae, which was supposed to create a unified position on birth control for the Catholic Church, in fact moved approximately 25 percent of American priests to the left on "both birth control theory and birth control procedure in the confessional," as Greeley put it.[64] The loss of the clergy was "an extraordi-narily dramatic change, especially considering that the prohibition against artificial birth control was the central concern of the American Church as far as practical catechetics was concerned," Greeley wrote. He added, "In less than half a decade the majority has swung away from support of this central moral position to a refusal to try to enforce it. It may be one of the most dra-matic shifts in the entire history of human ethics."[65] In the decade between 1965 and 1975, birth control went from being a central topic of Catholic life, one which many Catholics defined themselves against, to an issue on which much of the American Catholic leadership was silent: They could not publicly oppose the teachings of the Church, but they also would not endorse them.

Instead of following the Church teaching, these priests directed their parishioners to the right of conscience as the way to navigate marital sex and contraception.[66] The right of conscience, which was repeatedly referenced by couples as the best way to handle birth control decisions in the surveys collected by Pat and Patty Crowley in the 1960s, was the internal and subjective counterpoint to the morally objective and external law of the Catholic Church. Law and conscience served as the two pillars that governed moral life within the Church. Within the strict adherence to Church doctrine, the right-of-conscience movement did not allow Catholics to escape the law, but at the same time, the fact that priests had stood for the right of conscience did "seriously curtail" the "capacity of the law to define reality."[67] Traditionally, the balance between law and conscience was worked out between priest and penitent in the confessional; and thus ideas about the appropriate balance between law and conscience varied widely.[68] Some priests even moved to have parishioners bypass the confessional altogether, at least as far as birth control was concerned.

According to Catholic journalist and author Patricia Miller, between the issuance of Humanae Vitae and John Paul II's installation as pope, the Catholic Church took something of a "don't ask, don't tell" approach to birth control, one that was, according to theologian Anthony Padovano, a standard approach to a doctrine that most people understood to be unworkable. "The general Vatican approach to something highly controversial," he told Miller, "is to make your statement and then ignore it."[69] By and large, American Catholics came to consider birth control part of the realm of conscience; certainly, many American priests both helped them come to that conclusion and supported them in those decisions, either overtly or by quietly and deliberately looking the other way.

When Pope John Paul II ascended to the papacy in 1978, he sought to crack down on the flexible relationship that the faithful had to Humanae Vitae. His reasons for doing so likely had to do with two factors. First, in the words of Andrew Greeley, from the standpoint of the Catholic Church, Humanae Vitae was an "ill-advised disaster," a tragedy because it undermined the trust that the faithful placed in the ecclesial structure and caused them to look elsewhere, perhaps to their own consciences, for supreme guidance as to how to live their lives.[70] Vatican II had taught Catholics that rather than being eternal and unchanging, the Catholic Church could change. Once it became clear to many Catholics, clergy and laity alike, that some teachings could change, this raised the question of why other teachings could not change, too, and effectively brought all pronouncements into question.

Greeley suggested that, after all of the changes of Vatican II, in Humanae Vitae Pope Paul VI had overreached his authority. He had issued a pronouncement and expected obedience rather than explaining his logic. In addition, Greeley's survey data suggested that the priesthood had concerns about the ecclesial process through which Humanae Vitae had come about. Only 36 percent of priests thought that Humanae Vitae was a "competent and appropriate use of papal teaching," while 18 percent did not object to the ruling per se but thought that it was bad timing. A striking 33 percent of priests saw Humanae Vitae as a misuse of papal authority, "because the Pope had failed to act with appropriate collegiality" through his disregard of the Papal Commission on Birth Control.[71] Once again, age was a factor: While almost three-quarters of bishops found Humanae Vitae to be a competent use of authority, only 14 percent of priests under thirty-five and 23 percent of priests between thirty-six and forty-five agreed.[72] In fact, while in the long run Humanae Vitae would raise moral concerns, most initial concerns were about process. In cracking down on Humanae Vitae, John Paul II may well have been trying to assert his own authority as pope, getting back some of the authority that his predecessor had lost.

Second, Miller points out that Humanae Vitae was, in fact, a powerful statement from the Church about the nature of both gender and the family. Reasserting Humanae Vitae and trying to bring the Church back in line with its teaching on contraception were attempts to enforce Catholicism's conservative teaching on gender. In his 1961 book Family Planning, Stanislas De Lestapis, SJ, one of the few members of the Papal Commission on Birth Control to oppose oral contraception's approval by the Catholic Church, and one of the four authors of the commission's minority report, coined the term "contraceptive mentality." Contraceptive mentality would eventually expand to include couples who used natural family planning "too well," but in this initial usage, Lestapis cautioned that "allowing women the freedom to regulate when they got pregnant would lead to a decline in women's maternal instinct and a hostility toward children, [as well as] increase female promiscuity, and 'confusion between the sexes.'"[73] Miller, herself a Catholic pro-choice activist, argued persuasively that for John Paul II, part of the reason to crack down on birth control was to crack down on the implications of feminism for the Catholic family. Tying women back to the rhythm method would make it more difficult for many sexually active women to pursue educations and careers outside the home.

Two of the most public demonstrations of this desire happened on the international stage. In 1979, shortly into John Paul II's papacy, Hans Küng, liberal theologian and member of the Catholic theology faculty of the German University of Tübingen, published a letter in Italy's largest newspaper criticizing the Vatican's positions on a number of issues, including birth control. Notably, Küng critiqued the church's position because of both population control and, more unusually, women's rights. On population, he wrote, "Can we intervene in a believable way, in Latin America and in the Third World, against poverty, unemployment, diseases—all problems that are linked to the high increase in births—if we do not engage strongly in favor of a reasonable and human planning of births?" In terms of women's rights, he argued that Catholicism could hardly advocate for human rights "in the world" if it denied women human rights within the Catholic Church. Küng also defended the use of contraception on the grounds of the right of conscience.[74]

While the Vatican did not respond directly to the letter, on December 15, 1979, it suspended Küng's "authorization to teach as a Catholic theologian," though it did not cite his letter in doing so.[75] Küng contested his suspension. Ultimately, the theologian and the Vatican reached an agreement whereby he could continue to be employed at the University of Tübingen and could continue to direct the ecumenical center that he had founded, but he would no longer be allowed to teach Catholic theology.[76] Küng was a popular and well-known priest with a large following in both the Catholic Church and among the Protestant denominations. His public disciplining was therefore a very strong statement of the Catholic Church's position.

Contraception also took center stage at the 1980 World Synod of Bishops. Prior to the 1980 synod, the Vatican consulted with individual bishops and episcopal groups in putting together a working paper that was intended to set the parameters for the meeting's conversations on the subject of family life. The document was then circulated throughout the various clerical conferences around the world so that they could determine the "mind of the faith," both priests and laity.

According to Francis X. Murphy, CSsR, writing in the *Atlantic Monthly*, the statement received quite a bit of criticism globally. Congregations in the Global South saw the statement as privileging European nuclear families, rather than taking into account the extended kinship networks common in other parts of the world. Other constituents argued that the document neglected to take into account a changing world, specifically failing to treat "married love, divorce, the sexual revolution, homosexuality, and the population explosion in a realistic fashion."[77] The faithful believed that the "Roman document repeated pious platitudes about the sanctity of marriage and that, while dodging the reality of the population explosion, it insisted on the virtues of 'natural methods' of family planning as a type of conjugal asceticism."[78] They further expressed frustration with "the ease with which these clerical experts, with no experience of the pains of childbirth, the incessant worries and tragedies of rearing teenagers, and the thousand and one difficulties of conjugal cohabitation, spoke so glibly of the Cross as part of a family's Christian witness."[79] In the United States, the doctrine of conscience had slightly cushioned the laity from *Humanae Vitae*. Globally, however, people were frustrated with the Catholic Church.

According to Murphy, the Vatican had originally framed the World Synod of Bishops as a chance for John Paul II to hear from the clergy about the state of marriage and family life throughout the Church. Once the pre-circulated document received so much pushback, however, the Vatican carefully hand-picked the voices allowed to speak at the event. This ensured, for instance, that only doctors and couples who found "natural birth control" to be effective were included, and every attempt was made to restrict conversation closely to the legal interpretation of the Church. The synod began on September 28, 1980, and the pope's opening remarks suggested that there might be space for some freedom of discussion. However, at the actual inauguration of the synod, John Paul II appointed Cardinal Joseph Ratzinger as the relator.[80] The relator is the person responsible for providing a fulsome outline of the synod's theme, for presenting topics for ecclesial consideration, and for summarizing the speeches of synod members before the collective moves from conversation to formulating concrete proposals for the pope.[81]

The relator, then, has quite a bit of power to frame the discussion of the issues, and Ratzinger was a conservative thinker whose endless responses of "no" to the liberal wing of the Church would eventually get him the nickname "Cardinal No." Ratzinger would also acquire the nicknames "the Hammer," "the Enforcer," and "God's Rottweiler" for the fervency with which he defended the laws of the Church against liberal theology.[82] In fact, he was one of the primary opponents of Hans Küng.[83] Placing him in charge of the agenda thus demonstrated clearly where the Vatican stood in terms of marriage and family life, and, indeed, Ratzinger noted for the assembled that "doctrinally speaking . . . the majority of the bishops were satisfied with the Church's teachings on the family."[84] He also noted the "need for a profound restatement of the truths contained in *Humanae Vitae*."[85] At least in Murphy's telling, the structure of the synod did not create space for the question that the Catholic community had raised around the pre-circulated document.

While bishops from Cincinnati, Ohio; Thailand; and Madrid all spoke out for more attention to family life, and for creativity in addressing human embodiment and sexuality, it was Archbishop John R. Quinn of San Francisco, outgoing president of the United States Conference of Catholic Bishops, who "faced the fact that this teaching [Humanae Vitae] was contested by priests and people whose faith, practice of their religion, and good will simply could not be called into question."[86] While Quinn denied that he was attacking *Humanae Vitae*, he pointed out that 75 percent of American Catholic women used birth control, and less than 30 percent of the American priesthood thought that they were sinful for doing so. The Vatican's lack of flexibility on the issue, he claimed, was both alienating Catholics and undermining the credibility of priests. Quinn argued that "Pope Paul's hope that 'people of good will' would see the validity of his teachings had not been fulfilled."[87] He maintained that the Church should move toward a doctrine of responsible parenthood, much as the Papal Commission on Birth Control had argued more than a decade before.[88]

Quinn's speech received support from bishops from New Delhi and Tanzania, to Indonesia and Ecuador, to England and France. They spoke of poverty and of the difficulties of rhythm. Others, however, spoke in opposition, noting that "statistics do not make morality" and arguing that "the synod cannot substitute compassion for morality."[89] Despite Quinn's words, and those who agreed with him, he was ultimately forced to back down. The World Synod of Bishops pledged allegiance to the "prophetic" encyclical *Humanae Vitae* and committed to better explaining it to Catholics. As Murphy wrote in the *Atlantic Monthly*, "Despite pleas from liberal prelates around the world, the Vatican-dominated synod reaffirmed the precedence of law over compassion."[90]

The following year, in November 1981, John Paul II issued the apostolic exhortation *Familiaris Consortio*, in which he noted that there had been attempts to compel Catholic approval of contraception in the name of population control, and because of the use of contraception by Catholic couples themselves. Of the latter, he wrote, "When couples, by means of recourse to contraception, separate these two meanings that God the Creator has inscribed in the being of man and woman and in the dynamism of their sexual communion, they act as 'arbiters' of the divine plan and they 'manipulate' and degrade human sexuality—and with it themselves and their married partner—by altering its value of 'total' self-giving."[91] Contraception, according to the Catholic Church, undercut the divine plan and demeaned both the couple and their expression of their sexuality. Furthermore, the pope wrote that the use of contraception constituted a "falsification of conjugal love."[92] The statement moved beyond criticizing the use of actual contraception to censuring a "contraceptive mentality," condemning even those couples using the rhythm method, eventually called "natural family planning," for placing their desire for personal fulfillment, sexual or otherwise, above welcoming new life.[93]

But Sending Birth Control Matter Would Be Immoral. A Herblock
Cartoon, © The Herb Block Foundation. Courtesy of the Library of
Congress, Prints and Photographs Division, LC-DIG-hlb-12098.

This Vatican doubling down on the impermissibility of contraception was, as the examples of Küng and Quinn demonstrate, coupled with a doubling down on the acceptability of dissent. Because of the extent to which the health care system in the United States was run by Catholics, the Vatican crackdown on nonconformity had immediate relevance for Americans, regardless of their religion. For instance, according to Miller, the year that John Paul II became pope, the largest nonprofit health care system in the United States was run by the Sisters of Mercy, an order of Catholic nuns. Tubal ligation was an increasingly popular form of birth control for married women—by 1982, it would be the most popular form—and so, despite the fact that it was banned by the Church, the Sisters of Mercy in 1978 "decided that good medical ethics required that they provide the procedure when the patient and her doctor determined it was 'essential to the overall good of the patient.'"[94] If a woman was having her child at a Sisters of Mercy hospital, tubal ligation could be performed as a relatively minor surgery after childbirth. The sisters thought that it was an "unjustifiable risk" to ask the woman to have a second, more invasive, surgical procedure at a non-Catholic hospital at a later date.[95]

The Sisters of Mercy decided to test the Vatican's determination to enforce contraceptive bans by allowing tubal ligations in their hospitals. The Vatican responded by threatening "to dismiss their entire leadership and put all their hospitals, schools, and other projects under Vatican control."[96] In order to protect their broader progressive agenda, the Sisters of Mercy backed down and banned tubal ligations; and the following year, the National Council of Catholic Bishops banned tubal ligations at any Catholic hospital, for any reason—including if additional pregnancies would threaten a woman's life.[97]

The Vatican crackdown, then, had effects on American life far beyond the Catholic Church itself. Much of the suppression of contraception happened on the international stage, with defenses of more liberal standards coming from members of the American Catholic leadership, among others. Because of the structure of the institutional Church, however, the international debates and decisions also impacted American Catholic life, and American life more generally, as the hospital example demonstrates. That said, as Greeley's data demonstrated, the majority of American Catholics had changed their birth control practices, with the tacit and sometimes active support of their priests. Yet the official position of the Catholic Church put conservative American Catholics in a position to create alliances with other conservative Christian groups.

The Policy Implications of the Religious Right

The Reagan administration's assault on family planning, nationally and globally, was widely understood as a consequence of his alliance with the religious right. In another 1984 Herblock cartoon captioned "Be Fruitful and Multiply," Ronald Reagan, in riding gear, stood next to a horse on the edge of a cliff. His loyal steed looked on proudly as he declaimed from a piece of paper labeled "World Population Policy." At the base of the cliff stood the recipients of his message, the world's poor and dispossessed—skeletally thin figures sometimes shaded in to imply dark skin, many of them mothers holding children. In the throng of people off to the side stood an oil drum and a shanty with a stovepipe, both evoking the developing world.

The image evoked both Reagan's history as a movie star known for Westerns and Jesus's Sermon on the Mount, implying that America, with its wealth and largesse, was something of a white savior offering help to the poor. But instead of family planning, which might offer hope to this emaciated crowd, the United States offered tone-deaf advice: "Be fruitful and multiply." It promised nothing but more of the same—starving children in the arms of starving parents. This portrait underscored that although Reagan's global population policies did not say much, if anything, about religion, the press understood it to be rooted in his alliance with Evangelicals, and that while the messaging about this policy was overtly packaged around limiting the United States' funding for abortion, it was also broadly understood as an assault on family planning.

The Reagan administration's complicated relationship to family planning played out on the international stage with a policy statement to the United Nations International Conference on Population, which was held that August in Mexico City. This policy statement "strongly oppose[d] abortion and coercive measures of population control such as forced sterilization."[98] The draft that reached Congress suggested that "the key to population control" was a "thriving economy." In the words of the *Washington Post*, the draft simultaneously "support[ed] and discount[ed] family planning programs."[99] In a meeting of the US House of Representatives Subcommittee on Census and Population of the Committee on Post Office and Civil Service, held the month before the UN Conference, the Honorable Katie Hall characterized the draft, which would come to be called the Mexico City Policy, before Congress thus: "The President's position for the U.N. International conference on Population diminishes the role of voluntary family planning. It places reliance on adoption

Be Fruitful and Multiply. A Herblock Cartoon, © The Herb Block Foundation. Courtesy of the Library of Congress, Prints and Photographs Division, LC-DIG-hlb-10850.

by developing nations of free market economic policies to resolve pressures these nations experience from growth in their populations. It follows that the White House advocates curtailment of U.S. family planning assistance to any nongovernmental organization which, as a component of its health and family planning programs, funds abortion-related activities."[100]

Specifically, the policy demanded that any nations receiving financial support for population control ensure that all of that money—some $38 million— be fully accounted for, and that these nations offer "'concrete' assurances" that none of the money had been used to "promote abortion."[101] Second, the plan threatened to cut off federal funds to any private organizations—for instance, the International Planned Parenthood Federation—that funded programs to "actively promote" abortion, even if the money these groups sent came from other fundraising efforts and not from the US government. While a 1974 policy already ensured that US funds could not be used for abortion, opponents of abortion considered the new policy a "sham." They argued that Planned Parenthood and other organizations could simply move money around in accounts such that US funds continued to promote abortion, however indirectly.[102] Yet opponents of the policy argued that the existing protections successfully created a firewall between US funds and abortion, and they worried that the abortion restrictions abroad were a slippery slope that would lead to restrictions on family planning agencies at home.[103]

In addition to the actual policy implications, which Congress suggested would result in millions of dollars' worth of cuts to family planning programs abroad, some members of Congress saw this plan as overreach on the part of the executive branch, stating, "The initiative and leadership in voluntary family planning services overseas, as well as domestically, has always been in the Congress of the United States."[104] The Reagan administration's proposals were not overtly rooted in religious rationales—though they periodically made reference to morals. Instead, the agenda was part of Reagan's staunch, if newfound, opposition to abortion, which was part and parcel of his role as the candidate and figurehead of the newly established religious right.

The Catholic-Evangelical Alliance

This new religious right was shaped by Evangelicals, but it also included conservative and establishment Catholics. The Evangelical-Catholic alliance behind the religious right was working to dramatically curtail women's rights, as Herblock depicted in a 1987 cartoon of Ronald Reagan having a convivial chat with Pope John Paul II. The two men sat in wing chairs and held newspapers

That Kind of Natural Population Control Saves Us Several Dollars. A Herblock
Cartoon, © The Herb Block Foundation. Courtesy of the Library of
Congress, Prints and Photographs Division, LC-DIG-hlb-13202.

with photos of women emblazoned on the front pages. Reagan's headlines read "Family Planning" and "No to Reagan and Bork," and John Paul II's read "Equality in the Church." The Gipper was shown leaning over to the pontiff and saying, "Women! I don't know what's come over them either!" This image underscored the right-leaning religious alliance that had formed in American politics between Reagan, the public face of Evangelical manhood, and the Catholic Church. It also pointed to one of the primary targets of that alliance: women, and a growing public awareness of their desires for equality, both in religion and in control of their own bodies.[105]

The depiction of contraception in this cartoon differed sharply from the image of contraception that clergy had put forward twenty years earlier. This was not an image of birth control as a tool for couples trying to thoughtfully plan the timing and number of children in their family. Though the headline read "Family Planning," there were no men or carefully spaced children in the image. Family planning, here, was no longer associated with a nuclear family such as one sees in *Leave It to Beaver* or *The Donna Reed Show* or the Disney population film: a working paterfamilias and a homemaker wife and mother, harnessing the best advances of science and technology in service of her family. Instead, family planning, whatever it was called, was clearly back to being birth control, a tool through which women could control their own reproduction to their own ends in order to pursue their own economic, social, and sexual liberation. The linkage of family planning with equality in the church suggested that birth control was a tool that women need to free them from the yoke of male control.

Indeed, the feminist implications of contraception helped to finesse the unlikely alliance between Catholics and Evangelicals. The two groups generally shared an opposition to abortion—and to economic pressure and liberatory desire bringing more women into the workforce, changing the middle-class family structure by, among other things, putting more children in childcare—but they did not agree on birth control. Evangelicals had, by and large, supported birth control expansion throughout the middle of the century, and they continued to see it as a helpful tool in marriage. What they did not support was the expansion of birth control to unmarried people. They found this expansion particularly concerning when it meant that teenage girls could access contraception without their parents' knowledge or consent. So the cultural moments that highlighted birth control being framed in terms of feminism, such as Judy Chicago including Margaret Sanger in *The Dinner Party*, were also highlighting a shift in emphasis that had made Evangelicals more likely to ally with Catholics in forming the religious right.

Women! I don't know what's come over them either! A Herblock Cartoon,
© The Herb Block Foundation. Courtesy of the Library of Congress,
Prints and Photographs Division, LC-DIG-hlb-11506.

This alliance was made more possible not only by framing birth control as feminist, but also by collapsing birth control and abortion into each other. Abortion had never been entirely absent from the conversations about birth control in groups like the National Council of Churches, but it was not a primary conversational thread; and when abortion did appear, it sometimes was used as a justification for contraception. Birth control was good, the logic went, in part because it reduced the need for abortion. Some denominations found this fact good because abortion was stigmatized and not always legal and readily accessible; and others found it satisfactory because they thought abortion was a moral wrong.

The fusion, then, of abortion and family planning in conservative religious rhetoric through the public funding of women's health clinics, which did not ask questions about why people wanted birth control; the concern that birth control would be pedaled to "children"; and the feminist uses of contraception made possible the creation of the Catholic-Evangelical alliance. This alliance had actual policy repercussions, such as the Supreme Court case of *Rust v. Sullivan*, which allowed the government to limit free speech of federally funded programs: in this case, restricting the ability of women's health clinics to counsel patients about, or refer patients for, abortions. Previously, the clinics could not use federal funds for such purposes. Starting in 1991, they could not offer the services at all if receiving any federal funds.

While this ruling did not affect the legality of abortion or address birth control at all, its effect was to limit the access to both, in part because with the legalization of abortion, they were increasingly linked together both in rhetoric and in imagination. This linkage had real and dangerous implications for women's health centers. From 1977 to 1988, there were 110 cases of arson, firebombing, or bombing at American family planning clinics.[106] In addition, from 1977 to 1988, the National Abortion Federation additionally reported "222 clinic invasions, 220 acts of clinic vandalism, 216 bomb threats, 65 death threats, 46 assault and batteries, 20 burglaries, and 2 kidnappings."[107]

In 1984, there were twenty-nine discrete attacks on women's health clinics in the United States, 98 percent of which provided abortions. Several of these 1984 attacks were directly connected to religious actors, including a Mother's Day attack on a clinic in Birmingham, Alabama, by Edward Markley, a Benedictine priest who was the coordinator of the diocese's pro-life activities. Markley did not physically injure anyone, but he did do approximately $8,000 worth of damage (in 1984 dollars) to clinic equipment. Later that year, on Christmas Day, the Ladies Center, a reproductive health clinic in Pensacola, Florida, was bombed, as were two doctors' offices. The four bombers would later explain that they had intended the bombings as "a birthday gift to Jesus."[108] While these acts of violence explicitly targeted clinics and doctors' offices because they provided abortions, in doing so, the attackers also made it more difficult for the clients to access contraception.

Opposition to the Religious Right

Along with the hypocrisy of the religious right in general, other critiques were leveled at specific religious organizations. In 1978, two years after the year of conferences about Jewish fertility and Zero Population Growth, Shirley Frank, managing editor of the Feminist Press's Women's Studies Newsletter, published an article in Lilith magazine called the "Population Panic." It was a play on broader societal concerns about the population explosion and the population bomb. Frank, however, was not thinking about overpopulation. She was writing about the Jewish panic about the dropping birthrate.

Frank wrote that, although the Jewish people have survived for 3,000 years, "we seem to regard [our survival] as an inexplicable anomaly, and our mind-set is one of perpetual vigilance against threats to our continued existence." In other parts of the world, she explained, those threats had often been obvious and physical: pogroms, forced conversions, the Holocaust. In the United States, the threats had been subtler: apathy, assimilation, intermarriage, and ignorance. But she sarcastically said, "A new threat has appeared on the horizon and is spreading over us like a malignant black fallout cloud. This new danger is an insidious three initialed foe more to be feared than the KGB, the PLO, or the KKK—namely the ZPG or the Zero Population Growth Movement. Young Jewish people, it seems, ever concerned about all the problems of humanity, have thoughtfully, though misguidedly, taken it upon themselves to volunteer, en masse, to do their share by not adding to the world's 'population explosion.'" She kept going, in a similar tone, to talk about the declining Jewish birthrate—lower than that of other Americans, far lower than in the rest of the world. She pointed out that Jews had not recovered their pre-Holocaust numbers, that Jews were barely replacing themselves, especially accounting for "defectors," and that "immanent extinction" was nigh.[109]

Frank was very clearly convinced that the rhetoric around continuity and the Jewish birthrate was more than a tinge hysterical. But more than that, she saw it as an attack on the women's movement. In her article, she argued that Jews have always been a small remnant; and while they might be a smaller percentage of the global population, there were actually more Jews in the 1970s than at many other points of Jewish history. She looked at several decades of data showing that the Jewish birthrate had long hovered slightly below that of Protestants and Catholics; and although the Holocaust had occurred more than thirty years earlier, it was a relatively new factor in conversations about the Jewish birthrate. Frank also pointed out that it seemed odd, at best, to assume that couples made their own personal reproductive decisions with an eye toward what was best for a people, rather than for themselves and the family that they hoped to create. People in general did not, she argued, make their reproductive decisions based on what would be best for the human race; nor should Jews be asked to do so.

While Frank's comment was intended to critique the claim that people should have more children because to do so was in the interest of the Jewish people, her attitude also contrasted sharply with the idea, held by proponents of both responsible parenthood and ZPG, that people should limit the number of children they had because of the implications of a growing population. Her argument pointed, once again, to the feminist possibilities of birth control: the ability of a woman or a couple to shape their family with an eye toward their own desires, rather than to the broader society.

Frank argued that although the women's movement and its ramifications were largely absent from the Zero Population Growth conversations, the reason that all of these issues seemed salient in the 1970s was, in fact, the rise of the women's movement. She suggested that when feminism was mentioned, it was passed over quickly, treated essentially as a lifestyle trend rather than as a movement that was shifting the terrain of American social life. Real feminist analysis, she argued, would take into account the idea that women, no less than men, should not be asked to sacrifice the "the pursuit of personal careers and other indulgences" over the more "traditional joys of family life and the transmission of Jewish heritage to the next generation." A feminist analysis would argue that women's careers are not indulgences: If a man's career is an important component of his full personhood, so might a woman's be. And even more pressingly, women's incomes were no longer providing only for extra luxuries, if, indeed, they ever had. Women's incomes were quite often necessary for maintaining a middle-class lifestyle. And while Frank did not go on to say this, so was limiting family size.

Frank's feminist analysis pointed out many elements that were left out of the ZPG conversation, and pointed to the need for feminist voices in the conversation. Note that I am deliberately separating the idea of feminist voices from the idea of women's voices, since Blu Greenberg and other women had certainly pushed for Jewish continuity over professional careers; however, I also think that one of the ways to get more feminist voices in the conversation is to have and value women's voices more prominently. Now, clearly, Frank had a platform to write, but it was not an academic or mainstream platform. She was not part of the conferences where the experts spoke about trends in Jewish demography; while Lilith is the most prominent Jewish feminist publication, it is also, by its very nature, something of a niche market. Her voice would not go on to affect or shape Jewish demography or sociology and, because that research undergirds much of Jewish communal decision-making, many of the resulting initiatives. Instead, what would happen is that while Jewish women would continue to use birth control, Jewish doctors would continue to prescribe birth control, and the leadership of the Jewish movements would continue to support birth control and abortion, they would also actively push for large Jewish families.

Popular Critiques of the Catholic Church

While Shirley Frank tried to persuade the generally liberal Jewish community to take seriously the claims of feminism, various pop-cultural texts depicted the Catholic Church as being out of step with modern life. To get an idea of how the general population viewed the Catholic position on contraception, let us consider its portrayal in two cultural works: the one-act play Sister Mary Ignatius Explains It All for You by Christopher Durang, first performed in New York City in 1979; and the prime-time television show Picket Fences, which aired for four seasons from 1992 to 1996. While the two works represent strikingly different forms of media with what one might initially suspect to be fairly different audiences, they both represent similar frustration, and even anger, with the position of the Catholic Church on birth control.

Sister Mary Ignatius was Christopher Durang's first major success, winning him an Obie Award, the highest honor given to an off-Broadway production. The play is largely a monologue by Sister Mary Ignatius, a nun dressed in an old-fashioned habit in the style of the nuns from The Sound of Music, based on the premise that she is answering questions from the audience. During the course of the performance, she interacts with seven-year-old Thomas, whom she asks questions out of the catechism, and also with four adult former students who are dressed to perform a Christmas pageant from their childhood. The students return in order to attempt to hold Sister Mary Ignatius responsible for the pain the Catholic Church has caused in their lives. The play elevates its rage at the strictures of the Catholic Church to absurdist effect, as Sister Mary holds forth on elements of Catholic doctrine such as the difference between the Immaculate Conception, the idea that Mary herself was born without original sin, and the Virgin Birth, the idea that she gave birth "without the prior unpleasantness of physical intimacy." The fact that people confuse these two concepts "makes me lose my patience," Sister Mary tells the audience.[110] She also sidesteps the question "If God is all powerful, why does he allow evil in the world?" in order to tell horrific stories of growing up with twenty-six siblings and indifferent and abusive parents.

It is in the context of talking about her parents that, on page five of the script, Sister Mary Ignatius takes a swipe at birth control. Her mother, she tells the audience, "hated little children, but they couldn't use birth control."[111] She goes on to explain: "Birth control is wrong because, whatever you may think of the wisdom involved, God created sex for the purpose of procreation, not recreation. Everything in the world has a purpose. We eat food to feed our bodies. We do not eat and then make ourselves throw up immediately afterwards, do we? So it should be with sex. Either it is done with its proper purpose, or it is just so much throwing up, morally speaking."[112] Sister Mary's monologue then goes tearing on to other topics. She gives brief answers to questions such as "Do nuns go to the bathroom?" and "Was Jesus Christ effeminate?" Both of these questions are answered yes. Her remarks on birth control are not the point of the play—the point of Durang's portrayal is to lampoon the authoritarianism of Catholicism and the arbitrariness of its rules. That arbitrariness is underscored by the fact that some rules, like the one that condemns unborn babies to limbo or the one that forbids eating meat on Fridays, were changed with Vatican II, while others, like the rule about birth control, were not. The play points to the Catholic Church's rules about birth control, then, as a way to ridicule the Church's policies overall.

Reviews of the play were generally positive. Frank Rich wrote in his 1981 *New York Times* review, "Anyone can write an angry play—all it takes is an active spleen. But only a writer of real talent can write an angry play that remains funny and controlled even in its most savage moments."[113] Of a Providence, Rhode Island, production, Kevin Kelly wrote in the *Boston Globe* that "Christopher Durang's Catholic-snapping satire . . . sparkles like votive lights in a dark church echoing with laughter."[114] He went on to describe the play as "like religion itself . . . an evening dramatically between the message and the myth, the real and the surreal, the rational and the irrational."[115] In 1983, when Durang won the Kenyon Theater Festival's first Kenyon Award, the play "was in its 547th performance off-Broadway, with additional productions in Chicago, St. Louis, Los Angeles, and Seattle."[116] At the time, according to the *Boston Globe*, the $25,000 award "would seem to be the richest single grant designed for playwrights."[117] *Sister Mary Ignatius Explains It All for You* was the breakout play that launched the thirty-two-year-old Christopher Durang's career.

That said, the critics' acclaim was not universally shared by the public, or even by all critics. Protesters from the right-wing Catholic League for Religious and Civil Rights picketed the Charles Playhouse production of *Sister Mary* in Boston, where they were "very vocal and tried to engage people in conversation as they go into the theater."[118] The protests had the support of the city's mayor, Raymond Flynn, who wrote on his official stationery to the president of the league's Massachusetts branch. Flynn had read a copy of the play and found it "blatantly and painfully anti-Catholic." He further stated, "Catholic beliefs, practices, and institutions are ridiculed and portrayed in cruel and bigoted stereotype. It is difficult to imagine this type of religious bigotry being presented on the public stage."[119] The mayor went on to "join the Catholic League for Religious and Civil Rights in repudiating all forms of religious and ethnic prejudice, in this case as represented by *Sister Mary Ignatius Explains It All For You*."[120]

The Catholic League condemned the St. Louis performance as well and protested in St. Louis and Boston.[121] In both places, the Jewish Anti-Defamation League of B'nai B'rith (ADL) joined the Catholic League for Religious and Civil Rights in its criticism, according to a letter that Christopher Durang sent to the *New Republic*, with the ADL arguing that the play was "misrepresentative of the Catholic faith and of those who believe and practice it."[122] Ironically, the objections that conservative Catholics and their allies raised to the play generated publicity that almost certainly increased its ticket sales and extended its run time.[123]

Durang, himself raised Catholic, objected to the idea that his play misrepresented the Catholic faith. He told the *New Republic* that, while he believed the ADL had the right to criticize his play, he found its statement that he had misrepresented Catholicism to be an "arrogant" opinion. "I based my opinions in the play on my 12 years in Catholic school. I was taught the things I wrote about in that play, as were scores of other Catholics and ex-Catholics who have strongly identified with my play," Durang wrote in a letter to the editor.[124] He had used almost identical language the year before in an article in the *Boston Globe* in defense of *Sister Mary Explains It All for You*. There, he had also pointed out that the *National Catholic Reporter*, "a liberal, but by no means radical" newspaper, had noted that the play "offers much to think about for Catholics and non-Catholics alike—not only the theological question about the benevolence of God, but questions about the meaning of teachings and the value of open-mindedness."[125] Durang both staked out his own claim to Catholicism and pointed out that not all Catholics disapproved of his creation.

Durang specifically used his treatment of birth control to argue that his play was critical, not bigoted. "The Catholic bishops, with whom I am often in agreement, recently spoke eloquently for the rights of the poor," he wrote. He added, "If I agree with them, but point out that the Catholic Church, by its pigheaded and illogical stance on birth control, adds to the suffering of the poor by being a block to population control, that is not bigotry; that is called criticism."[126] Durang pointed out later that his use of the word "pigheaded" here was "kind of rude."[127] His rudeness, he argued, strengthened his point "more strongly than if I just left it at illogical." That, he explained, was how his plays worked—he used strong language and biting satire to make his criticisms of Catholicism as forceful as he could.

Durang had lost his faith in God, both because of the suffering of civilians in the Vietnam War, and because his mother's prolonged suffering with and death from cancer was not ameliorated by her own or his sister's prayers.[128] The fact that Durang was gay likely also contributed to his disaffection. Even so, he wrote that he had not written the play in order to offend, but to express his feelings of anger, "disbelief that I had ever believed some of the things, and sorrow, because I missed the sense of security that belief gives you."[129] Despite Durang's loss of faith, his play was profoundly rooted in his Catholicism.[130] As a letter to the *Boston Globe* from Evelyn Wolfson, a Wayland, Massachusetts, woman who had been raised Catholic, pointed out, the play also encouraged those within the Catholic Church to talk about places where the Church teaching seemed internally inconsistent. "If the Church's teachings can't stand up to examination, ask why," she wrote. "If the Church's stance on birth control places a burden on the poor or unfortunate," she continued, "do something about it. Talk about it. Face it. Make it an issue."[131] Durang's sharp critiques, including his critique of the Church's stance on birth control, show how strongly some within the Catholic sphere of influence disapproved of its stance on contraception, and how controversial criticism of the Church could be.

Picket Fences, which ran from 1992 to 1996, was a television drama depicting life in the small fictional town of Rome, Wisconsin, and centered on the intersecting family and work lives of the town's sheriff and doctor. Both a Protestant minister and a Catholic priest appear as recurring characters. *Picket Fences* won fourteen Emmys and one Golden Globe. "Duty Free Rome," episode two of the second season, focuses on the experiences of a Catholic couple who were both carriers for Hurler's syndrome, a fatal genetic disorder that can be diagnosed in utero. The couple had previously lost a child to Hurler's, a child who, in the words of the town doctor, "should never have been born." When she makes this comment to the priest, he responds, "I did not go to them preaching anti-abortion. They came to me, wanting to know the position of the Church." Despite this opening, the bulk of the show does not focus on abortion but rather on the Church's position on contraception. The husband and wife are unable to face the loss of another child; however, because of the wife's commitment to Catholicism, she refuses to use birth control. Unwilling to risk pregnancy, this left the couple unable to have sex.

The show offers insight into both the private conversations that the couple has with the priest, and the conversations carried out in front of other members of the town. The priest, who often shows up as a unit with the Protestant minister, is portrayed as accessible and reasonable throughout most of the show. During this episode, he is presented as sympathetic to the couple's dilemma, even as members of the town, ranging from the doctor to the stern but liberal-leaning judge, express frustration at him for what strikes them as an inhumane and out-of-touch Catholic policy. He, too, indicates that the policy was cruel; but as a priest, he explains, he cannot misrepresent the formal position of the Church, a reality that leaves him unable to alleviate the couple's pain.

This dilemma comes to a head in one of the closing scenes of the episode. Patty, the wife, tells Father Barrett that her husband has left her because of her refusal to use birth control, and his refusal to be trapped in a sexless marriage. She tells the priest, "He said he's not coming back—if we are not going to be husband and wife, then we are not going to be husband and wife. I don't know what to do. I do not want to lose him. Joe is all I have." The priest asks Patty whether she wanted to have "conjugal relations" with her husband, and she reiterates, "Of course I do, but I can't risk having a child with this disease, I cannot."

Faced with her pain, and clearly wanting to offer her assistance, Father Barrett responds, "Patty, please listen to me very carefully. Ninety percent of all Catholics use contraception. The Church is even considering letting nuns use birth control in Bosnia because of the threat of rape. Now, I take that consideration to mean that exceptions can be made. The fact that both you and Joe have a gene for Hurler's? I think our Lord would be very forgiving of you." She responds by asking him point-blank, "Are you telling me to use artificial contraception?" He explains that, as a priest, he could face excommunication for telling her to do so. "As a person," he then tells her, "someone who cares about you very much: Save your marriage, Patty."

Patty, however, does not listen to Father Barrett—he cannot tell her that the Church supports contraception, and she cannot disobey the Catholic Church. Ultimately, her husband leaves her, and she tells the priest that this is good: Their division over contraception demonstrates that they have different relationships to Catholicism. Joe can remarry and have children, since his new wife would be unlikely to be a carrier. Since the Catholic Church does not permit divorce, Patty can never again have a sacramental marriage, and since she will not live outside the Church, she consigns herself to a life alone. In the face of this situation and its immense pain, the Church, and Father Barrett as its representative, are left unable offer any real or realistic solution. Instead of providing a source of comfort to the couple, or support for their marriage, the Church's teachings are portrayed as responsible for the destruction of their marriage and the condemnation of the faithful wife to a lifetime alone. The Church is depicted as at best impotent and at worst ridiculous, cruel, and irresponsible.

The prime-time drama even depicts the Catholic Church's stance as problematic beyond the familial or marital level. As the drama plays out, Father Barrett walks in on his Protestant colleague having a conversation about birth control with Joe. The priest accuses the minister of poaching his clients, and the minister counters, "Gary, Christianity is dying in this country. The Catholics who are leaving the Church, and many of them because of birth control, they are not becoming Protestants. They are forsaking religion altogether in general, and that hurts us all." The Protestant minister is speaking here of the kind of religious unraveling that Diane Winston describes—people leaving liberal Christianity. In the eyes of the reverend, who is sometimes Father Barrett's rival but also his close friend and ally, the Catholic Church's position on birth control is essentially contributing to the secularization of the country. In his eyes, religion at that moment in history needs to clearly enhance people's lives. Religious organizations themselves are too embattled to challenge people or to ask them to take on pain as part of their faith. In the episode, the reverend implies that the Catholic Church is outmoded, and if it wants to survive and be taken seriously, it will have to change and keep pace with the times. At least in the reverend's eyes, losses to Catholicism do not benefit Protestants. Rather, they represent a net loss to the American religious landscape.

How, then, do we understand this depiction of the Catholic Church in the mainstream media? First, and perhaps most importantly, it is worth underscoring that *Picket Fences* did not necessarily represent a Catholic reality. As we have already seen in this chapter, and as scholarship on Catholics and contraception like that of Leslie Woodcock Tentler and Peter Cajka demonstrates—and indeed, as the priest in the series points out—by the early '90s, when the show aired, the majority of Catholics were using contraception. Some were simply not conferring with their priests on the matter, though they often did continue to take the sacraments, and surely their priests—when looking at couples without children or with only one, two, or three children—suspected that many of their parishioners were using contraception. That said, the Church itself was unable to speak in a way that provided meaningful comfort or ethical engagement for many people. The show demonstrated that the American public was receptive to the message that the Catholic Church was a source of pain, rather than of comfort or practical advice—at least on the matter of contraception.

Conclusion

The 1970s and 1980s witnessed the expansion of legal access to contraception. But because that legal access opened the use of birth control to single people, and particularly because it potentially opened it to teenage girls, it became more complicated for religious groups to publicly champion it as a cause. They continued to do so privately: Most religious liberals continued to use contraception in their marriages, and liberal clergy advised the use of contraception in premarital counseling and teen sexuality classes, carefully framing it in terms of marriage. But the feminist implications of birth control were troubling, even for religious liberals, who, being well aware of their declining power in the public sphere, did not publicly continue to advocate for contraception.

Meanwhile, the religious right mobilized against contraception. The conservative John Paul II sought to bring the Catholic Church in line with the policies outlined in *Humanae Vitae,* creating a synergy in the United States between doctrinaire Catholics and an American Evangelical movement that was growing in political and cultural power. These voices, which were both religiously and politically conservative, opposed funding contraception access at home and abroad for numerous reasons: They supported small budgets for social services, and they believed that any money supporting the contraceptive services of reproductive health clinics would implicitly support any abortions these clinics performed. Conservative Catholics did not support the use of contraception at all, and conservative Evangelicals did not support the increasingly liberal access to and use of birth control. These viewpoints came in response to the perception that society was becoming more sexually liberal and to concerns that feminism was eroding the traditional family. While there were cultural responses calling these conservative voices to task for hypocrisy and irrelevance, those voices operated in cultural, rather than legal or political, realms.

Epilogue

In June 2022, I was sitting in a café in Athens, Greece, when I received the news: The Supreme Court had released its decision in *Dobbs v. Jackson Women's Health Organization*. Though a draft of the court's majority opinion had been leaked weeks in advance, and I had written several commentaries in response, the reality still fell like a hammer's blow: The Supreme Court had overturned *Roe v. Wade* and ended the federal right to an abortion. A friend traveling with me had left early that morning, so I sat alone, sobbing.

It was relatively early, and the café had few customers. A woman waiting tables came up to me and asked, "Are you American?" When I answered yes, the woman said she had suspected from my accent, but when I had opened my computer and started to cry, she knew. For the rest of the morning, until the lunch rush began, the server and other women working at the café took turns sitting with me, holding my hand, and asking how such a thing could happen in the United States.

Writing for the majority, Justice Samuel Alito used history to defend the court's decision. Unless a right is mentioned in the US Constitution, he explained, it is only guaranteed if it is "deeply rooted in the Nation's history and tradition."[1] Abortion, he argued, did not meet that standard. But as I and many other historians have written in amicus briefs, scholarly essays, and commentaries, Alito's assertion about abortion's history is untrue. Through most of American history, abortion has been accepted as a fact of life.[2] In addition to being a miscarriage of justice, the court's majority opinion was a misuse of history.

Yet we live with the reality of the *Dobbs* decision and the terrible costs it has exacted. We must similarly live with the reality that despite past religious engagement in support of contraceptive access, the backlash described in chapter 4 has proved more powerful—not only when it comes to abortion rights, but also in subtle ways that the public and scholars of religion have largely missed.[3] Scholars and pundits have tended to focus on data that indicates that support for both contraception and abortion are very high in the United States. According to a 2016 Pew study called "Where the Public Stands on Religious Liberty vs. Nondiscrimination," only 4 percent of the adult population of the United States think contraception is immoral. Among Catholics who attend Mass weekly, 13 percent say that contraceptive use is morally wrong; 45 percent say it is morally acceptable, and 42 percent say it is not a moral issue at all.[4]

Similarly, a study of attitudes toward abortion in the United States between 1995 and 2024 demonstrated that the majority of Americans have consistently thought that abortion should be legal in all or most cases. At its lowest ebb in 2008, just over 50 percent of Americans thought that abortion should be largely legal; otherwise, for most of that time, at least 60 percent of Americans supported legal abortion in all or most cases.[5] Such statistics, alongside the much-touted increase in religious "nones" in the United States, and legal victories such as the Supreme Court's 2015 decision finding in favor of the right to gay marriage, led many scholars and commentators to assume that the country had grown more expansive in its support of sexual and reproductive rights.

But many, if not all, scholars failed to recognize that support for such changes was not always rooted in a logic of liberation. As this book has shown, the expansion of support for birth control was initially tied to the institution of marriage and the strength of the family, not to women's freedoms or to approval of nonmarital sexuality. Similarly, LGBT rights expanded when they were framed in terms of marriage equality; those victories were not based in an acceptance of queer life, let alone a delight in the broad range of ways in which it had blossomed and created new networks of care and kinship. The expansion of reproductive rights, like the expansion of queer rights, worked when those rights were based in more fundamentally conservative logics.

In addition, while the majority of Americans came to support birth control and abortion, a very important minority group did not: 73 percent of white Evangelicals thought abortion should be illegal in all or most cases in 2024.[6] While that number dropped to 65 percent in 2025, the majority of white Evangelicals continue to believe that abortion should not be legal in most cases.[7] A Pew study that looked at cultural issues around the 2024 election did not directly ask questions about birth control—the absence of the question itself suggesting that the people designing the survey saw contraception as a settled issue about which they did not need to ask.[8] That said, studies have also shown that Republicans increasingly favor a "return" to traditional gender roles.[9] Those traditional gender roles can include an interest in creating large families. Such views of the American family are advocated in religious communities; but they are also increasingly promoted on social media, where communities of people calling themselves "TradWives" and "TheoBros" offer a new form of Christian nationalism based on the old idea of complementarianism.

Complementarianism claims that men and women are made to have distinct and complementary roles. While both of these roles are of equal importance, they are not equal in power. TradWives ("traditional wives") promote complementarian culture as an Instagram and TikTok phenomenon: women who primarily define themselves in terms of care for their home and family, and, most importantly, who see their husband as the head of their family, to whom they submit. TradWives tend to eschew prepared foods, and sometimes regulated food. Their feeds tend to discuss their sourdough starters, the benefits of drinking raw milk, and the dream of homesteading. While there is no explicit requirement that TradWives have large families, many do; and they talk about how they leave the number of children in their families up to God. TradWives are as much an industry as a reality, with content creators such as the Ballerina Farm creating followings that valorize this traditional, highly romanticized family structure.

Their husbands, fathers, and brothers are the TheoBros, every bit as omnipresent in social media culture as TradWives and potentially far more powerful politically. *Mother Jones* characterizes TheoBros as "extremely online young Christian men" who "want to end the 19th Amendment, restore public flogging, and make America white again." *Baptist News Global* suggests that TheoBros exist in order to correct women's theology online—which *Baptist News Global* does not see as a good thing.[10] As Kristen Kobes Du Mez, author of *Jesus and John Wayne: How White Evangelicals Corrupted a Faith and Fractured a Nation*, put it, "With this sort of John Wayne masculinity, the ends justify the means: violence, crassness, or in the case of some pastors and theologians, aggressive and even misogynistic rhetoric, can be seen in this light. Civility and gentleness can be seen as interfering with a man's God-given duty to defend the faith against whatever dire threats one identifies."[11] This is a hypermacho form of Christianity that is as much about the subjugation of women back to their "proper" role as wives and mothers as it is about shaping Christian masculinity.

There are legal and political ramifications in this kind of Christianity. *Mother Jones* suggests that in order to understand Vice President J. D. Vance, one must understand the TheoBros' ethos. TheoBros are not necessarily the ones calling for a strict reading of the Constitution—the approach traditionally taken by political conservatives. These are people who see the Constitution as hollow and wish to see it replaced with the Ten Commandments.[12] They do not want simply to reshape their homes or churches in line with this vision of Christianity. They wish to realign the nation along these lines, a move that has serious ramifications for reproductive health. Many TheoBros hope to see the Nineteenth Amendment, which gives women the vote, overturned; they do not believe that women belong in the voting booth, the pulpit, or any number of other places.[13] Like J. D. Vance, they may valorize motherhood; but the flip side of valorizing motherhood is demeaning women who do not choose to become mothers.[14]

TradWives and TheoBros did not create the backlash against birth control; but through their social media presence, they make these more "traditional" forms of masculinity and femininity seem comforting and, especially in in the latter case, "Instagram cute." The segment of American society that holds such extremely complementarian views is in the distinct minority. In fact, for much of the twenty-first century, scholars of religion have shown that organized religion has been on the decline, and both religious "nones" and people who identify as spiritual but not religious are increasing. As people in the United States increasingly chose not to affiliate with religious institutions, popular, and sometimes scholarly, assumptions suggested that an increasingly secular society would also be more politically liberal—particularly, perhaps, in areas of sexuality. However, in focusing on the ramifications of an increasingly religiously unaffiliated society, this account seems to have missed something key. In the first quarter of the twenty-first century, the conservative Christian minority has stopped trying to win the cultural battle by gaining numbers. Instead, it has focused on winning by gaining in power through both legislative and judicial victories. As a result, the fact that conservative Christians' views are dramatically out of step with the electoral majority does not matter. They are still able to bring about profound legal changes around sexual rights and reproductive justice, and they cut funding that supports reproductive health care.

It is in this cultural and religious context that we must read attempts to reverse gains in access to reproductive health care. While birth control may be tacitly acceptable in these circumstances, it is suspect: These communities proudly support large families and remain absolutely against abortion. We must understand that the resurgence of complementarianism as a socially acceptable—or at least social media acceptable—cultural choice is an assault on the bodies and lives of women, whom the TheoBros and their parallels in politics would like to see returned to the roles designated to them by a heteropatriarchal society. We must also understand TheoBros and their political counterparts as a way to further amplify the assaults on the bodies of trans and nonbinary people, who do not fit neatly into the binaries of heteropatriarchy.

The *Dobbs* decision dismantled the federal right to an abortion in 2022; and as I write in 2025, birth control access is also under attack in the United States. According to the National Women's Law Center, "because birth control is widely popular, basic health care that enables people to exercise autonomy and self-determination and is essential to people's health, lives, and futures, those who are attacking birth control are deliberately using tactics that hide their true motives."[15] Birth control opponents attack and control access to contraception through their attacks on abortion.[16] This tactic has had serious ramifications, as exemplified by the 2014 Supreme Court decision *Burwell v. Hobby Lobby*. In the *Hobby Lobby* case, the owners of the craft store chain argued that they had a "sincerely held belief" that intrauterine devices (IUDs) used for birth control caused abortion, which they held to be morally wrong. Although the vast majority of medical authorities, including the American College of Obstetricians and Gynecologists, hold that IUDs prevent rather than disrupt pregnancy and therefore do not cause abortion, this medical consensus did not prove relevant to the case.[17] What mattered was that the Green family, who own Hobby Lobby as a private company, sincerely held this scientifically unsubstantiated belief that conflated birth control and abortion. Because they held that belief, the Supreme Court argued, Hobby Lobby did not have to provide insurance coverage for the IUD to its employees.

The court's 2014 decision in *Hobby Lobby* created a pathway that allowed the first Trump administration to weaken the Affordable Care Act's contraceptive mandate, specifically by allowing employers to claim religious and moral objections to contraception—this time without necessarily conflating it with abortion.[18] The administration also weakened federal programs, such as Title X, that fund elements of reproductive health care, including contraceptive counseling.[19] In the summer of 2020, the Supreme Court upheld the Trump administration's assault on the contraceptive mandate in the case *Little Sisters of the Poor Saints Peter and Paul Home v. Pennsylvania*.[20] As the *Harvard Law Review* (HLR) put it, "The Supreme Court . . . upheld the Trump Administration's sweeping exemptions to the Affordable Care Act's (ACA) contraceptive mandate without discussing third-party harms."[21] This was significant because, "in doing so, the Court reneged on its earlier assurances that contraceptive coverage would not be jeopardized by religious accommodations and, more broadly, signaled that harm to third parties will no longer serve as a check on those accommodations at all."[22] According to the HLR, "It is not clear what limiting principle remains to curb exemptions to any antidiscrimination protection."[23] In other words, for over a century, SCOTUS has held that one person's rights only extend so far that they do not impinge on another person's rights; and with this decision about birth control, that logic clearly no longer applies, at least not for women and other people with the capacity for pregnancy.

Legally, then, contraception is very much under attack, and both the right and the ability to access it is being eroded.

What, then, of *God Bless the Pill* and its story of how religious support helped increase contraceptive access, at least for a time?

Since the culture wars of the 1980s, Americans tend to formulate our historical thinking in binary ways. The Left supports "feminism," and with it, access to contraception and abortion, which women might use to further their education and careers, both out of economic necessity and to advance their own ambitions. The Right, by contrast, supports "family values," defined as a father who is able to support his family in a middle-class manner, and a mother who is primarily engaged in motherhood and homemaking. She may or may not work, but ideally he is the primary breadwinner and she the primary nurturer. These roles are seen as "how it always has been, and how it always should be." The Right, while it is relatively quiet on the subject of birth control within marriage, decries abortion as murder, paints women as selfish for the desire to control their own maternity, and disapproves of sex—and therefore contraception—outside marriage. It most certainly disapproves of teenage girls being able to access contraception without the knowledge of their parents. These lines have shaped the conversation about contraception in ways that now feel completely natural to us.

But understanding American culture and birth control along these lines also obscures history. And as we know from the invented history that Justice Alito placed in the *Dobbs* decision, misunderstood or misrepresented history can be used against us. In addition, if we assume birth control grew solely out of the feminist movement, we miss some of the conservative logics about the family that are baked into much of how our culture justified making contraception available in the first place.

God Bless the Pill points to a time before the modern culture wars codified these ideological lines. It points to a time when contraceptive access was

encouraged in order to decrease abortion, and to do so with aims that did
not dovetail perfectly with the advancement of women's social, political, and
economic equality. The book describes a world in which expanding access to
contraception was seen to support, rather than to undercut, the traditional
family and to uphold a set of white middle-class social ideologies. It also shows
us that those political lines had been drawn in a different way in the past. *God
Bless the Pill* underscores a historical reality that is not immediately apparent
in our current political climate, where conservatives who have made abortion
increasingly unattainable are now coming for contraceptives. Many of the
impulses that led to the expansion of birth control were ones that we would
now see as conservative, even though many of the people who espoused them
at the time understood themselves as liberal, even progressive. Contraceptive
access spread in part because religious leaders, who supported traditional
family structures, endorsed it for reasons that were not feminist. That does
not mean that no feminists were out there fighting for contraceptive access
so that women could achieve bodily autonomy and sexual pleasure, but their
voices were not the voices that made contraception respectable and therefore
mainstream.

My hope is that, in unpacking this complicated history, this book will show
us unsuspected lines of continuity between the past and the present, and help
to explain some of the backlash we are currently experiencing, particularly
backlash against women's bodily autonomy. When we understand that many of
the people who made contraception readily available did not do so for feminist
change, but to enable a particular kind of sexuality and family that they saw
as both the most healthy and most godly, we better understand why, when
feminists were able to make such good use of contraception, the coalition of
religious leaders, politicians, and doctors that had made it respectable began
to fragment. None of this means that the feminist uses of contraception are
wrong or bad—but it does help us to understand that they were not the goal
of most of the voices advocating for access.

We understand that some of the backlash against women's bodily autonomy is a course correction by those who never expected or wanted contraception to lead to women's liberation. The goal for many of the religious, political,
and medical leaders who pushed for contraceptive expansion was not for
women to gain power over their own bodies. It was a form of biopolitics that
regulated the family and society, both American and even global, through
the regulation of women's bodies. Indeed, when feminists in the 1970s and
1980s objected to some particularly invasive forms of birth control, they did
so because they objected to using potentially risky medical technology in

service of social regulation—so that men could have consequence-free sex. There is a steady through line from the attempts to control women's bodies detailed in *God Bless the Pill* to the political efforts to contain women's bodily autonomy that we see today. A clear understanding of how we got here, and the compromises that we made along the way, can help us counter false histories as they are put forth to limit reproductive health care.

We can also better understand how some of the language that we now use to justify rights to contraception and abortion—language about "responsible parents" who need contraception to ensure college educations, or nice women who need abortions because of rape—fall into long scripts. According to those scripts, birth control is deserved by those who make responsible use of it, rather than being the right of any person with a uterus who wants to use their body to experience pleasure. In our contemporary efforts to protect contraceptive rights, we can see how we echo the logics of previous eras, framing some families, bodies, and choices as more responsible and therefore more deserving than others. We need to know and understand the dangerous histories that underpin contemporary conversations about women "deserving" the ability to use birth control or receive an abortion, in order to create a future in which those are understood as basic human rights, not something that good girls and wives might somehow be able to earn.

NOTES

Abbreviations

CHM   Center for the History of Medicine, Francis A. Countway Library of Medicine, Harvard University

PPCP   Patrick and Patricia Crowley Papers, University of Notre Dame Archives

SSC   Sophia Smith Collection, Smith College Archives

Introduction

1. Alan F. Guttmacher, "1970 Commencement Address to Smith College," May 31, 1970, 80. Cla, Smith College Archives, Northampton, MA.

2. David Dempsey, "Dr. Guttmacher Is the Evangelist of Birth Control: Guttmacher Is Gambling That Planning and Freedom Are Not Incompatible," *New York Times*, February 9, 1969, sec. Magazine.

3. Guttmacher, "1970 Commencement Address to Smith College."

4. Davis, *More Perfect Unions*; May, *Homeward Bound*; Coontz, *Marriage*; Coontz, *Way We Never Were*.

5. Hedstrom, *Rise of Liberal Religion*, 143.

6. Hedstrom, *Rise of Liberal Religion*, 143.

7. In thinking about how seemingly secular ideas are deeply shaped by Christianity, particularly as regards sexuality, I am deeply shaped by the work of Janet Jakobsen, both on her own and with Ann Pellegrini. Their work, particularly Jakobsen, "Sex + Freedom = Regulation: Why?," 285–308, and Jakobsen and Pellegrini, *Love the Sin*, unpacks the Christian archaeologies of many American laws and values around sexuality, arguing that the focus on families based in heterosexual marriage and both the regulatory attention and privacy afforded those families are deeply rooted in the Protestant Reformation. My thinking on the relationship between Christianity, Judaism, and the secular in the contemporary United States has also been deeply shaped by both Tisa J. Wenger and Matthew S. Hedstrom. Wenger's *Religious Freedom* powerfully shows how religious freedom talk privileged Protestantism, at the same time that it demonstrates how religious minorities (in terms of my primary interests, Catholics and Jews) were able to create spaces for themselves through

the logics of religious freedom. Wenger has further influenced my thinking about public Protestantism and the role of Jews in creating the American secular through our heated debates while baking the Thanksgiving pies. Additionally, some of the most compelling work on apparently secular values that were in fact deeply connected to the interreligious Judeo-Christian values of midcentury liberal religion is Hedstrom's *Rise of Liberal Religion*. Hedstrom's project is, essentially, to use book culture to demonstrate that, though we associate it with the demise of (non-Evangelical) Protestant power in the United States, liberal religion in fact came to animate a wide array of American values, so thoroughly that their inherent religiosity is no longer clearly evident to the inheritors of "spiritual cosmopolitanism" that was the result of this liberal Judeo-Christianity. Hedstrom also does an excellent job of tracing the archaeology of the concept of Judeo-Christianity, to which my description here owes much. Other important scholarship that provides key analysis on the centrality of the concept of Judeo-Christian America and the religious values undergirding the American secular in the middle of the twentieth century includes Gaston, *Imagining Judeo-Christian America*; Sehat, *Myth of American Religious Freedom*; Schultz, *Tri-Faith America*.

8. Studies of the post–World War II American family were central to the rise of feminist history and were deeply influential in my own career. In fact, it is Elaine Tyler May's *Homeward Bound* that first made me want to study the twentieth century. It is a tribute to both *Homeward Bound*, first published in 1988; to her work on the birth control pill, *America and the Pill*, first published in 2010; and to May's own encouragement of my work at an Organization of American Historians meeting in 2015 that I asked what would happen if we brought religion to the study of birth control. The historical scholarship on the family and sexuality in the middle of the twentieth century that has most shaped my thinking includes May, *Homeward Bound*; May, *America and the Pill*; Bailey, *Sex in the Heartland*; Coontz, *Way We Never Were*; Coontz, *Way We Really Are*; Coontz, *Marriage*; Davis, *More Perfect Unions*.

9. May, *Homeward Bound*, 1.

10. May, *Homeward Bound*, 1.

11. May, *Homeward Bound*, 136.

12. May, *Homeward Bound*, 95–96.

13. For more on Jewish and Protestant embrace of therapeutic culture and the insights of psychology, see Heinze, *Jews and the American Soul*; Myers-Shirk, *Helping the Good Shepherd*; Davis, *More Perfect Unions*.

14. Griffith offers one of the most useful depictions of the relationship between the social sciences and theology. She demonstrates that when Alfred Kinsey did his studies of the sexual practices of Americans, he was interested in whether people's professed religious commitments shaped their sexual habits. When it was published, theologians felt the need to respond to his social scientific study, specifically the discovery that many sexual practices deemed immoral (and abnormal) at the time, for instance, same-sex sexual experiences, masturbation, and nonmarital sex including adultery, were much more statistically normal than expected. Conservative theologians wanted to make it clear that while some practices were statistically more "normal" than previously supposed, that did not make them moral, while more liberal theologians wanted to explore how religious understandings of sexual norms might, at least in some cases, be drawn from or be changed in order to reflect contemporary sexual practices. Griffith, chap. 4 in *Moral Combat*.

15. White, "How Heterosexuality Became Religious," 331–57, looks specifically at the post–World War II period to argue that the links between a Judeo-Christian tradition and

heterosexual marriage date to this time—rather than to the ancient origins of the respective traditions. White points to numerous connections between clergy and the growing psychoanalytic discussion of sexual health in the period. Further, she argues that "the invocation of an ideal of a common heritage took place amid rancorous disagreement about what these three heterogeneous religious groups actually shared as religious viewpoints on marriage and sexual morality" (333). In the end, White compellingly claims that the same process that "redrew the lines of religious pluralism" also "redefined marriage to encompass ideals of health and pleasure" (333). Central here are the links that White draws between psychology and religion in establishing what counts as "health." Griffith and White provide only two examples of the relationship between the theologies of the family and social science research on the family. Perhaps the best example of how communal needs, biases, and perceptions of a religious group (or its leaders) can shape social science comes from Berman et al., "Continuity Crisis," 168–94. Their project is an indictment of how the antifeminist communal concerns of rabbis and Jewish social scientists created a panic over Jewish continuity that demanded that Jewish women place the needs of the community over their own self-actualization. Berman et al. also point to the reality that scholars and clergy created a panic about Jewish continuity that created a demand for solutions that the community could raise money to fund, which in turn allowed the community to fund scholarly studies investigating the success of such solutions. In other words, not only did the perceived needs of the community become the tail that wagged the dog of the research, but they created a funding source that benefited both communal leaders and researchers. Additional scholarship that demonstrates strong links between religious professionals and social science research can be seen in Davis, *More Perfect Unions*; White, *Reforming Sodom*.

16. Particularly useful for understanding the relationship between Jews and Protestants respectively and the field of psychology are Heinze, *Jews and the American Soul*; and Myers-Shirk, *Helping the Good Shepherd*.

17. For an excellent explanation of the long-standing and systemic structures that make the nuclear family ideal less accessible to Black families than to white families, see Stewart, *Black Women, Black Love*. Stewart's synthetic work demonstrates that there were many forces beyond eugenics and birth control that structurally undermined the health of African American families, and that devalued the forms of resilient family structures that Black Americans created in place of the national models, even as many people yearned to be able to achieve the family structures held up as ideal.

18. United States Holocaust Memorial Museum, "The Biological State: Nazi Racial Hygiene, 1933–1939," The United States Holocaust Memorial Museum: Holocaust Encyclopedia, accessed October 31, 2023, https://encyclopedia.ushmm.org/content/en/article /the-biological-state-nazi-racial-hygiene-1933-1939.

19. "Reproductive Justice," In Our Own Voice: National Black Women's Reproductive Justice Agenda, accessed November 1, 2023, https://blackrj.org/our-causes/reproductive -justice/.

20. Griffith, chap. 1 in *Moral Combat*; Klapper, chaps. 2, 4 in *Ballots, Babies, and Banners of Peace*; Washington, chap. 8 in *Medical Apartheid*.

21. Eig, *Birth of the Pill*, 53.

22. Washington, *Medical Apartheid*, 197.

23. Washington, *Medical Apartheid*, 197.

24. Eig, *Birth of the Pill*, 53–54.

25. Washington, *Medical Apartheid*, 197.

26. Davis, *More Perfect Unions*, 33–34.

27. Davis, *More Perfect Unions*, 34.

28. Eig, *Birth of the Pill*, 149.

29. Griffith, chap. 1 in *Moral Combat*; Klapper, chaps. 2, 4 in *Ballots, Babies, and Banners of Peace*; Washington, chap. 8 in *Medical Apartheid*; White, "How Heterosexuality Became Religious."

30. Washington, *Medical Apartheid*, 198.

31. Washington, *Medical Apartheid*, 199.

32. Washington, *Medical Apartheid*, 199.

33. Washington, *Medical Apartheid*, 200.

34. Khan et al., "Story of the Condom," 12–15.

35. In this, I follow the lead of Carol Adams, who used the literary concept of the absent referent in political contexts. See Adams, *Sexual Politics of Meat*. I also draw heavily from Ann Braude's seminal (ahem) essay "Women's History Is American Religious History," which calls attention to the absence of women in the literature about American religious history, despite their very real presence in churches, synagogues, and other aspects of religious life. Braude calls us to pay attention to where women are, even or particularly, when they are absent from discourse. Braude, "Women's History."

Chapter 1

1. Condoms did not require medical supervision, nor did any number of home remedies, for instance, the insertion of a vinegar-dipped sponge into the vagina. These methods ranged in inconvenience, efficacy, and safety. Lysol had an advertising campaign that coyly suggested using the cleaning liquid as a douche to prevent pregnancy, but such uses also carried the risk of inflammation, burning, and death.

2. "Birth Control Defended as 'Christian' by Rector," *New York Herald Tribune*, September 1, 1958, sec. Religious News.

3. Klapper, *Ballots, Babies, and Banners of Peace*, 87–88.

4. For a deep analysis of the sacred nature of the trust that people placed in doctors, and the medical and behavioral standards that maintained that trust, see Imber, *Trusting Doctors*.

5. Since ancient times, science and religion have existed as co-constituting categories for understanding the world. For a (non-exhaustive) list of scholarship exploring this relationship from Talmudic times to the present, see: Neis, *When a Human Gives Birth to a Raven*; Mokhtarian, *Medicine in the Talmud*; Harrison, *Territories of Science and Religion*; Josephson-Storm, *Myth of Disenchantment*; Wells-Oghoghomeh, *Souls of Womenfolk*; Petro, *After the Wrath of God*.

6. There are many excellent works on Margaret Sanger, but for the best depiction of how her work intersected with American religion, see Griffith, chap. 1 in *Moral Combat*.

7. For treatments on Sanger's move to expand birth control access by medicalizing it, see Tone, *Devices and Desires*; McCann, chap. 3 in *Figuring the Population Bomb*; McCann, *Birth Control Politics*; Reed, *Birth Control Movement and American Society*; Kennedy, *Birth Control in America*.

8. Lauren MacIvor Thompson and Heather Munro Prescott, "A Right to Ourselves: Woman's Suffrage and the Birth Control Movement," *Journal of the Gilded Age and Progressive Era*

19, no. 4 (October 2020): 542–58; Thompson, "Abortion, Contraception"; Lauren MacIvor Thompson and Kelly O'Donnell, "Contemporary Comstockery: Legal Restrictions on Medication Abortion," *Journal of General Internal Medicine* 37, no. 10 (June 10, 2022): 2564–67.

9. Tone, *Devices and Desires*, 121–22.

10. Margaret Sanger, The Public Papers of Margaret Sanger: Web Edition, accessed July 4, 2019, https://sanger.hosting.nyu.edu/.

11. Sanger, Public Papers of Margaret Sanger: Web Edition.

12. All diaphragms are pessaries, or soft, flexible objects that fit into the vagina, as described in the text, but not all pessaries function as contraception. In addition to serving to block sperm from entering the uterus, pessaries can also provide support for internal organs including the uterus, bladder, rectum, or vagina.

13. Tone, *Devices and Desires*, 117, 58.

14. Tone, *Devices and Desires*, 122.

15. While chapter 3 engages more directly with Laura Briggs's work, her work is an excellent example of the power that came with framing contraception in medical terms. Briggs, *Reproducing Empire*.

16. Margaret Sanger, The Margaret Sanger Papers Project, accessed June 25, 2024, https://sanger.hosting.nyu.edu/articles/tracing_one_package/.

17. Sanger, Margaret Sanger Papers Project.

18. Sanger, Margaret Sanger Papers Project.

19. While United States v. One Package of Japanese Pessaries created a loophole in the Comstock Act for contraception, it did not do the same for abortifacients, which were also covered by the act. At the time of this writing, the Comstock Act is what is termed "zombie legislation," which means that it remains on the books but is not enforced. The passage of the Supreme Court case *Dobbs v. Jackson Women's Health Organization* in 2022 created fear in many reproductive rights and justice activists that the Comstock Act could be revived and weaponized against mail-order abortion medication such as mifepristone.

20. McCann, *Figuring the Population Bomb*, 56.

21. Gordon, "From Birth Control to Family Planning," pt. 3 in *Moral Property of Women*; McCann, *Birth Control Politics*; McCann, chap. 3 in *Figuring the Population Bomb*; Kennedy, *Birth Control in America*; Tone, *Devices and Desires*.

22. Tone, *Devices and Desires*, 155.

23. Tone, *Devices and Desires*, 136.

24. Tone, *Devices and Desires*, 153.

25. For more on the implications of the Comstock Act and its implications for Margaret Sanger and her quest to legalize birth control, see Griffith, chaps. 1 and 2 in *Moral Combat*.

26. Moeller, "Eugenics and the Approval of Birth Control," 99–100.

27. *Conference of Bishops*; Moeller, "Eugenics and the Approval of Birth Control."

28. Moeller, "Eugenics and the Approval of Birth Control," 100.

29. Anglican Consultative Counsel, *Lambeth Conference*.

30. Anglican Consultative Counsel, *Lambeth Conference*.

31. Anglican Consultative Counsel, *Lambeth Conference*.

32. Fagley, *Population Explosion*, 195.

33. Fagley, *Population Explosion*, 196.

34. Fagley, *Population Explosion*, 196.

35. Fagley, *Population Explosion*, 196.

36. Fagley, *Population Explosion*, 233.

37. Fagley, *Population Explosion*, 233.

38. Fagley, *Population Explosion*, 233.

39. Fagley, *Population Explosion*, 233.

40. The most recent example of this argument that clergy were actively promoting positive and negative eugenics came from Wilde, *Birth Control Battles*. Wilde analyzes the major American periodicals from 1918 to 1965 to argue that "whether a religious group supported legalizing access to contraception depended on whether they were believers in the white supremacist eugenics movement and thus deeply concerned about reducing some (undesirable) people's fertility" (1–2). She notes that the periodicals were interested in expanding birth control into poor neighborhoods but showed little interest in expanding contraceptive use in their own communities. Her dataset is impressive in that she carefully examined many periodicals, but limited in that she only examined periodicals. Wilde seems to have missed both the reality that many of the white middle-class women whose fertility she assumes these denominations hoped to promote were actually already using contraception, and the assumptions that those denominations made about the sizes of the families of their most active members. This evidence was supported by statistics showing a declining birthrate in the middle class and through marriage and child-rearing manuals, which encouraged couples to have a robust sex life, but also assumed relatively small numbers of children. The work of historians such as Leslie Reagan and Lauren MacIvor Thompson challenges many of Wilde's findings. Wilde also argues that these denominations were interested in expanding access to Catholic and Jewish women, without interrogating the attitudes within those communities. Klapper's work is particularly useful in demonstrating Jewish women's interest in and use of birth control.

41. Woloch, *Women and the American Experience*, 606.

42. Klepp, *Revolutionary Conceptions*.

43. Klapper, *Ballots, Babies, and Banners of Peace*, 69.

44. Klapper, *Ballots, Babies, and Banners of Peace*, 69.

45. Klapper, *Ballots, Babies, and Banners of Peace*, 70.

46. Klapper, *Ballots, Babies, and Banners of Peace*, 86–87.

47. Klapper, *Ballots, Babies, and Banners of Peace*, 87.

48. Klapper, *Ballots, Babies, and Banners of Peace*, 88.

49. Stephen J. Wise, "Stephen J. Wise to S. Adolphus Knopf," November 19, 1925, P-134, Box 69, Reel 74–48, Wise Papers, American Jewish Historical Society, New York, NY.

50. For a rich description and analysis of the details of Lauterbach's argument, see Klapper, *Ballots, Babies, and Banners of Peace*, 163–68.

51. D. Kenneth Rose to Dr. Joseph Robbins, February 8, 1943, PPFA I; Florence Rose to Dr. Dwight Bradley, Executive Director, Council for Social Action, February 8, 1943, both in Series III, Box 18, Folder 2, SSC.

52. Planned Parenthood Federation of America, "Agenda and Material for Clergymen's Committee," February 17, 1943, PPFA I, Series III, Box 18, Folder 2, SSC.

53. F. Rose to Dr. Dwight Bradley, February 8, 1943.

54. F. Rose to Dr. Dwight Bradley, February 8, 1943; "Rev. Dr. Robbins Barstow Dies; Overseas Union Churches Aide: Congregational Minister Was 72—Author Formerly Headed

Hartford Seminary," *New York Times*, September 19, 1962; Wolfgang Saxon, "Algernon Black, Leader of Society for Ethical Culture, Is Dead at 92," *New York Times*, May 11, 1993, www .nytimes.com/1993/05/11/obituaries/algernon-black-leader-of-society-for-ethical-culture -is-dead-at-92.html; Sanger, Public Papers of Margaret Sanger: Web Edition.

55. Planned Parenthood Federation of America, "Agenda and Material for Clergymen's Committee," February 17, 1943, PPFA I, Series III, Box 18, Folder 2, SSC.

56. National Clergymen's Committee, Planned Parenthood Federation of America, "Minutes of National Clergymen's Committee," February 17, 1943, PPFA I, Series III, Box 18, Folder 2, SSC.

57. National Clergymen's Committee, Planned Parenthood Federation of America, "Minutes."

58. National Clergymen's Committee, Planned Parenthood Federation of America, "Minutes."

59. National Clergymen's Committee, Planned Parenthood Federation of America, "Minutes."

60. Mary Whitehead, Catholic Charities, to Guy Emery Shipler of the National Clergymen's Advisory Council, PPFA, December 11, 1946, PPFA I, Series III, Box 17, Folder 1, SSC.

61. In thinking about how to approach Black interest in eugenics and population control, I draw from the thinking of Nuriddin, for instance, in "Engineering Uplift."

62. E. Franklin Frazier, "More Birth Control for More Negro Babies," *Negro Digest* 3, no. 9 (July 1945).

63. Frazier, *Negro Family*; Frazier, *Negro Church*.

64. Frazier, "More Birth Control."

65. Frazier, "More Birth Control."

66. Frazier, "More Birth Control."

67. Frazier, "More Birth Control."

68. Frazier, "More Birth Control."

69. Frazier, "More Birth Control."

70. Frazier, "More Birth Control."

71. For those of us in religious studies, the canonical book for understanding the concept of racial uplift and its gendered politics remains Higginbotham, *Righteous Discontent*.

72. M. King, "Advice for Living."

73. M. King, "Advice for Living."

74. M. King, "Advice for Living."

75. M. King, "Advice for Living."

76. M. King, "Advice for Living."

77. M. King, "Advice for Living."

78. M. King, "Advice for Living."

79. Centers for Disease Control and Prevention, "Differences in Maternal Mortality."

80. M. King, "Advice for Living."

81. M. King, "Advice for Living."

82. Edith Evans Asbury, "Birth Control Issue Again Stirs Debate: Hospital Commissioner's Action Rouses Bitter Controversy," *New York Times*, August 24, 1958, sec. E.

83. Robert Alden, "City Stops Doctor on Birth Control," *New York Times*, July 17, 1958.

84. Alden, "City Stops Doctor."

85. This focus on privacy foreshadows legal logic that will appear in both *Griswold v. Connecticut* and *Roe v. Wade*.

86. "Birth Control Held Right of All in City," *New York Times*, May 23, 1958.

87. "City Edict Sought on Birth Control," *New York Times*, May 22, 1958.

88. "City Edict Sought."

89. "City Edict Sought."

90. Tentler, *Catholics and Contraception*, 2.

91. It is true that many of the married Catholics who would be using contraception by the mid-1960s were using the birth control pill, and that, until *Humanae Vitae* in 1968, many believed that the Pill would come to be seen as acceptable under Catholic teaching in a way that barrier methods were not. That said, even given the differences between the diaphragm and the Pill, Tentler's work shows us that American Catholic attitudes toward contraception were often more in step with those of their fellow Americans than with the teachings of the Church.

92. "Battle Lines Drawn on Birth Control," *New York Amsterdam News*, September 6, 1958.

93. "City Edict Sought."

94. "City Edict Sought."

95. "Birth Control Held Right."

96. Asbury, "Birth Control Issue."

97. Asbury, "Birth Control Issue."

98. For more on the class politics of birth control, and of birth control in publicly funded clinics, see Hajo, *Birth Control on Main Street*; Schoen, *Choice and Coercion*; Tone, "Black Market Birth Control," 435–59; Holz, *Birth Control Clinic*; Sarch, "Dirty Discourse."

99. Alden, "City Stops Doctor."

100. Alden, "City Stops Doctor."

101. Alden, "City Stops Doctor."

102. Asbury, "Birth Control Issue."

103. Alden, "City Stops Doctor."

104. "Jacobs Bars Meeting on Birth Control," *New York Herald Tribune*, July 23, 1958, sec. A.

105. "Birth Control Essential, Park Ave. Pastor Says," *New York Herald Tribune*, July 28, 1958, sec. Religious News.

106. "Dr. Jacobs' Rule Stirs Mail Flood: Most Oppose Ban on Birth Control," *New York Herald Tribune*, September 16, 1958.

107. Mehta, "Family Planning Is a Christian Duty," 153–69.

108. "Harlem Pastors Criticize Jacobs: Commissioner's Stand on Birth Control Is Also Decried by Rabbis," *New York Times*, August 12, 1958.

109. "150 Ministers Ask Talk with Jacobs: Commissioner Agrees but Says He Will Not Drop Birth Control Ban Now," *New York Times*, August 15, 1958.

110. "Harlem Pastors Criticize Jacobs."

111. "Ban on Contraception Called Rights Violation," *New York Herald Tribune*, August 24, 1958.

112. Edith Evans Asbury, "Birth Control Ban Ended by City's Hospital Board," *New York Times*, September 18, 1958.

113. Mehta, "Family Planning Is a Christian Duty."

114. Mary McCarthy, "Dottie Makes an Honest Woman of Herself," *Partisan Review*, February 1954; McCarthy, *The Group*; Roth, "Goodbye, Columbus." Though Roth's novella

refers to McCarthy's 1954 short story, the differences between "Dottie Makes an Honest Woman of Herself" and chapter 3 of *The Group* are minor, particularly as related to the discussion of the diaphragm; therefore, for ease of access, my citations to McCarthy are to *The Group*.

115. Mehta, "Family Planning Is a Christian Duty."

116. May, *America and the Pill*, 81.

117. Laura Jacobs, "Vassar, Unzipped! 50 Years Later, Why *The Group* Still Dazzles as a Generational Portrait," *Vanity Fair*, June 24, 2013, www.vanityfair.com/culture/2013/07/vassar-sex-single-girl-ivy-league-mary-mccarthy.

118. Capo, "Inserting the Diaphragm," 112–13.

119. McCarthy, *The Group*, 66.

120. McCarthy, *The Group*, 66.

121. McCarthy, *The Group*, 63.

122. McCarthy, *The Group*, 63.

123. McCarthy, "Inserting the Diaphragm," 63.

124. McCarthy, "Inserting the Diaphragm," 63, 82.

125. McCarthy, "Inserting the Diaphragm," 68.

126. McCarthy, "Inserting the Diaphragm," 68.

127. McCarthy, "Inserting the Diaphragm," 68.

128. McCarthy, *The Group*, 69, 70.

129. Roth, "Goodbye, Columbus," 56.

130. Roth, "Goodbye, Columbus," 57.

131. Roth, "Goodbye, Columbus," 69.

132. Roth, "Goodbye, Columbus," 70.

133. Roth, "Goodbye, Columbus," 71.

134. The concept of "tri-faith America" came into prominence with Herberg, *Protestant, Catholic, Jew*. More contemporary historiography on the concept includes Schultz, *Tri-Faith America*.

135. To gain a sense of the size of this shift, look at Thompson, "Reasonable (Wo)Man," 771–809, which offers a sense of the reproductive health landscape in the era just prior.

Chapter 2

1. May, *America and the Pill*.

2. Bailey, *Sex in the Heartland*; Bailey and Lindo, "Access and Use of Contraception," D'Emilio and Freedman, *Intimate Matters*.

3. May, *America and the Pill*, 9.

4. "The Pill: How It Is Affecting U.S. Morals, Family Life," *US News and World Report*, July 11, 1966.

5. "The Pill: How It Is Affecting U.S. Morals, Family Life."

6. "The Pill: How It Is Affecting U.S. Morals, Family Life."

7. May, *America and the Pill*; Bailey, *Sex in the Heartland*.

8. Berlant, *Queen of America*, 59.

9. Berlant, *Queen of America*; Jakobsen and Pellegrini, *Love the Sin*.

10. Griswold v. Connecticut, 381 US 479 (1965).

11. Lovett, *Conceiving the Future*.

12. *Collier's* magazine as quoted in May, *America and the Pill*, 23.

13. May, *America and the Pill*, 28.

14. May, chap. 2 in *America and the Pill*; Tone, *Devices and Desires*; Marks, *Sexual Chemistry*; Marsh and Ronner, *Fertility Doctor*.

15. Briggs, *Reproducing Empire*, 129–40.

16. Briggs, *Reproducing Empire*, 131.

17. Briggs, *Reproducing Empire*, 133–34.

18. Briggs, *Reproducing Empire*, 137.

19. Briggs, *Reproducing Empire*, 138.

20. Briggs, *Reproducing Empire*, 138.

21. In its early twenty-first-century usage, the term "responsible parenthood" is most frequently used by the United States Council of Catholic Bishops and Catholics in the natural family planning movement. These groups eschew contraception and believe that to be a responsible parent means "doing nothing to oppose God's gift of human fertility" but rather to "prayerfully discern when to attempt to conceive a new baby or not" through carefully monitoring a woman's cycle. This knowledge can be used to attempt to conceive or attempt to avoid conception, but it is understood as a "valuable help to responsible parenthood" because it "teaches husband and wife to consider each other and the child who may come from their sexual union, not merely their individual desires in the moment." "Responsible Parenthood," United States Congress of Catholic Bishops, accessed December 11, 2023, www.usccb.org/issues-and-action/marriage-and-family/natural-family -planning/what-is-nfp/responsible-parenthood. In contrast to this contemporary usage, the mid-twentieth century usage of "responsible parenthood" by Protestants and by Catholics who were engaging with the contraceptive conversation of the day meant nearly the opposite: the use of birth control to prayerfully plan conception in service of a particular vision of parenting and family life.

22. National Council of the Churches of Christ in the USA, "Responsible Parenthood: Adopted by the General Board February 28, 1961," https://nationalcouncilofchurches.us /common-witness-ncc/responsible-parenthood.

23. National Council of the Churches of Christ in the USA, "Responsible Parenthood."

24. Coffman, "*Christian Century*," 6. For more on the circulation and distribution of the *Christian Century*, see Coffman's work, particularly her introduction.

25. Much has been written about the idea of a "population explosion," and the racial logics underpinning it. We will time thinking about those implications later in the chapter, but, for now, let us work with the assumption that many of the clergymen legitimately believed that the population might outstrip the food supply. "Responsible Parenthood," *Christian Century*, March 29, 1961, 396–98.

26. Fagley, *Population Explosion*, 230.

27. National Council of the Churches of Christ in the USA, "Responsible Parenthood."

28. "Responsible Parenthood," *Christian Century*, March 29, 1961, 396–98.

29. "Responsible Parenthood."

30. Nuriddin, "Engineering Uplift."

31. Estes, *I Am a Man*, 107, 115, 119–20.

32. Martin Luther King Jr., "Family Planning: A Special and Urgent Concern," May 5, 1965, SSC.

33. "PPFA Margaret Sanger Award Winners," Planned Parenthood, accessed September 28, 2025, www.plannedparenthood.org/about-us/newsroom/campaigns/ppfa-margaret-sanger-award-winners.

34. M. King, "Family Planning."

35. I would like to thank Jermaine McDonald for his guidance in thinking about Martin Luther King, and for guiding me to my citations.

36. M. King, "Family Planning."

37. M. King, "Family Planning."

38. M. King, "Family Planning."

39. M. King, "Family Planning."

40. M. King, "Family Planning."

41. M. King, "Family Planning."

42. M. King, "Family Planning."

43. M. King, "Family Planning."

44. M. King, "Family Planning.

45. M. King, "Family Planning."

46. M. King, "Family Planning."

47. The most compelling and complete history of mid-twentieth-century Catholic responses to birth control is the groundbreaking Tentler, Catholics and Contraception.

48. Tone, Devices and Desires, 217.

49. John Rock, "The Scientific Case Against Rigid Legal Restrictions on Medical Birth Control Advice," Clinics 1 (April 1943): 1599.

50. Rock, "Scientific Case," 1599.

51. Rock, "Scientific Case," 1600.

52. Tentler, Catholics and Contraception, 73–74.

53. Tentler, Catholics and Contraception, 176.

54. "From the Allocution of Pope Pius XI to the 'Fronte Della Famiglia,' the Italian Union of Large Families, November 26, 1951: Acta Apostolicae Sedis, Volume 43, Pages 855–60 (1951)," Linacre Quarterly 32, no. 1 (February 1965): 75–79.

55. John Rock, "We Can End the Battle over Birth Control," Good Housekeeping, July 1961.

56. "From the Allocution of Pope Pius XI." The author would like to thank Andrea Ajello for the translation.

57. I have in my head, but cannot find in order to cite, the statistic that 30 percent of the United States birth control market was Catholic, and that part of what motivated Searle to take the risk and fund the research was that Catholics would become a natural market. Other companies declined to develop the Pill in part out of a fear that Catholics would boycott other products.

58. Walter Imbiorski, "What We Should Ask Ourselves," ACT, n.d.

59. McClory, Turning Point, 38–40.

60. Kaiser, Politics of Sex and Religion, 39.

61. Tentler, Catholics and Contraception, 206–7.

62. McClory, Turning Point, 40–41.

63. Kaiser, Politics of Sex and Religion, 38.

64. Tentler, Catholics and Contraception, 207; Kaiser, Politics of Sex and Religion, 38.

65. Tentler, Catholics and Contraception, 207; Paul VI, "Encyclical Letter . . . Humanae Vitae."

66. Genné and Genné, *Christians and the Crisis*, 10–11.

67. Genné and Genné, *Christians and the Crisis*, 10.

68. Genné and Genné, *Christians and the Crisis*, 9.

69. Genné and Genné, *Christians and the Crisis*, 86.

70. Genné and Genné, *Christians and the Crisis*, 86.

71. Genné and Genné, *Christians and the Crisis*, 89–90.

72. Genné and Genné, *Christians and the Crisis*, 90.

73. Anonymous Catholic woman to John Rock, n.d., HMS c161 22:37, CHM.

74. Anonymous Catholic woman to John Rock, January 13, 1964, HMS c161 20:1, CHM.

75. Frances Apice to John Rock, January 22, 1964, HMS c161 20:1, CHM.

76. Anonymous woman, "Letter to John Rock from a Woman Married to a Catholic Man," March 19, 1965, HMS c161 22:37, CHM.

77. Mrs. Alden H. Blake to John Rock, January 13, 1964, HMS c161 20:1, CHM.

78. Blake to John Rock, January 13, 1964.

79. Blake to John Rock, January 13, 1964.

80. Blake to John Rock, January 13, 1964.

81. Robert Brehmer to John Rock, March 8, 1964, HMS c161 20:1, CHM.

82. Fan Mail: 1960s The Personal and Professional Papers of John Rock (1918–1983), HMS c161 22:28, CHM.

83. Russell Burns to John Rock, January 13, 1964, HMS c161 20:1, CHM.

84. Burns to John Rock.

85. John Rock to Russell Burns, January 23, 1964, HMS c161 20:1, CHM.

86. Anonymous Catholic couple, "Survey from a Mobile Couple," n.d. ca.1965, Box 13, Folder 13101A, PPCP.

87. Anonymous Catholic couple, "Survey from a Davenport Couple," n.d. ca. 1965, Box 13, Folder 13101A, PPCP.

88. Anonymous compiled, "April 1966 Survey Part 2 (Crowley)," April 1966, Box 13, Folder 13101A, PPCP.

89. Anonymous Catholic couple, "Survey from Gary, IN Couple," n.d. ca. 1965, Box 13, Folder 13101A, PPCP.

90. Anonymous compiled, "April 1966 Survey Part 2 (Crowley)."

91. Anonymous Catholic couple, "Survey from a Davenport Couple," Davenport, 1965, Box 13, Folder 13101A, PPCP.

92. Anonymous compiled, "April 1966 Survey Part 2 (Crowley)."

93. Anonymous compiled, "April 1966 Survey Part 2 (Crowley)."

94. Anonymous compiled, "April 1966 Survey Part 2 (Crowley)."

95. Anonymous compiled, "April 1966 Survey Part 2 (Crowley)"; anonymous Catholic couple, "Survey from Omaha, NE Couple," Omaha, NE, 1965, Box 13, Folder 13101B, PPCP.

96. Anonymous Catholic couple, "Survey from a San Diego Couple (3)," n.d. ca. 1965, Box 13, Folder 13101A, PPCP.

97. Anonymous Catholic couple, "Survey from a San Diego Couple (3)."

98. Anonymous Catholic couple, "Survey from a San Diego Couple (3)."

99. Anonymous Catholic couple, "Survey from a San Diego Couple (3)."

100. Anonymous Catholic couple, "Survey from a Los Angeles Couple (2)," n.d. ca. 1965, Box 13, Folder 13101A, PPCP.

101. Anonymous Catholic couple, "Survey from a Los Angeles Couple (2)."

102. Perhaps, given the lack of a state, in Connecticut?

103. Anonymous Catholic couple, "Survey from Hartford Couple," n.d. ca. 1965, Box 14, Folder 14108, PPCP.

104. Anonymous Catholic couple, "Survey from Hartford Couple."

105. Anonymous Catholic couple, "Survey from Hartford Couple."

106. "Survey from a Beach Grove, IN Couple," Beach Grove, IN, 1965, Box 13, Folder 13101A, PPCP.

107. Anonymous Catholic couple, "Survey from a Los Angeles Couple (3)," n.d. ca. 1965, Box 13, Folder 13101A, PPCP.

108. "Survey from a Beach Grove, IN Couple."

109. Anonymous Catholic couple, "Survey from a San Francisco Couple," n.d. ca. 1965, Box 13, Folder 13101A, PPCP.

110. Anonymous Catholic woman to Pat and Patty Crowley, September 4, 1965, Box 14, Folder 14108, PPCP.

111. Anonymous Catholic couple, "Survey of a San Francisco Couple (2)," n.d. ca. 1965, Box 13, Folder 13101A, PPCP.

112. Anonymous Catholic woman to Pat and Patty Crowley, September 4, 1965, Box 14, Folder 14108, PPCP.

113. Anonymous Catholic couple, "Survey from a Monterey/Fresno Couple (3)," n.d. ca. 1965, Box 13, Folder 13101A, PPCP.

114. Anonymous Catholic couple, "Survey from a Monterey/Fresno Couple (3)."

115. Anonymous compiled, "April 1966 Survey Part 2 (Crowley)," April 1966, Box 13, Folder 13101A, PPCP.

116. Anonymous compiled, "April 1966 Survey Part 2 (Crowley)."

117. Anonymous compiled, "April 1966 Survey Part 2 (Crowley)."

118. Anonymous compiled, "April 1966 Survey Part 2 (Crowley)."

119. Anonymous compiled, "April 1966 Survey Part 2 (Crowley)."

120. Hamm, *Theologizing the Pill*.

121. Rosemary Ruether, "Speaking Out: Catholic Mother Tells, Why I Believe in Birth Control," *Saturday Evening Post*, April 4, 1964, 12.

122. Ruether, "Speaking Out," 12.

123. Ruether, "Speaking Out," 13.

124. Ruether, "Speaking Out," 13.

125. Alan F. Guttmacher, "Traditional Judaism and Birth Control," *Judaism*, Spring 1967, 159.

126. Guttmacher, "Traditional Judaism," 159.

127. Guttmacher, "Traditional Judaism," 159.

128. Feldman, *Birth Control in Jewish Law*.

129. Feldman, *Birth Control in Jewish Law*, book flap. Onanism is conventionally understood to be masturbation or coitus interruptus, but from the standpoint of Jewish law, it is ejaculation into anything that is not a vagina, including, in many interpretations, a condom.

130. Of course, whether it truly spoke for all Jews was another matter. In general, however, Feldman addresses a range of Conservative and Orthodox relationship to Jewish law. Reform and Reconstructionist Judaism are less tightly tied to the law than are the other

movements, but they form their decisions in dialogue with Jewish teaching, including historical tradition. Feldman's book received attention across the movements and was seen to speak to something of a pan-Jewish understanding of the legal tradition.

131. Fred Rosner, "Birth Control," *Journal of the American Medical Association* 209, no. 12 (September 22, 1969): 1909–10.

132. Feldman, *Birth Control in Jewish Law*, 298.

133. "The Pill: How It Is Affecting U.S. Morals, Family Life," *US News and World Report*, July 11, 1966.

Chapter 3

1. Merchant, *Building the Population Bomb*, 151.

2. Languages included multiple forms of Arabic, Bengali, Cantonese, Farsi, Filipino, French, Hindi, Korean, multiple forms of Malay, Portuguese, Spanish, Swahili, Taiwanese, Tamil, Thai, Turkish, and Urdu. Merchant, *Building the Population Bomb*, 149–50.

3. Gordon, *Moral Property of Women*, 280.

4. Gordon, *Moral Property of Women*, 280.

5. Washington, *Medical Apartheid*, 197; Stern, *Eugenic Nation*, 175.

6. Merchant, *Building the Population Bomb*, 61.

7. Stern, *Eugenic Nation*, 3–4.

8. Stern, *Eugenic Nation*, 4.

9. Connelly, *Fatal Misconception*, 8.

10. I am not the only person to have these concerns. Several popular reviews at the time of the book's publication noted these worries, among them Nicholas Kristof, "Birth Control for Others," *New York Times*, March 23, 2008, sec. Books, www.nytimes.com/2008 /03/23/books/review/Kristof-t.html; "Fatal Misconception: The Struggle to Control World Population," *Times Higher Education*, May 29, 2008, www.timeshighereducation.com/books /fatal-misconception-the-struggle-to-control-world-population/402168.article.

11. In this line of thinking, I very much follow the work of Drake, *To Know the Soul*. Writing about an interwar generation of Black and white social scientists who sought to modernize rural Southern Black communities, Drake calls on his readers to hold in tension the social scientists' earnest desire to help the people whom they studied, the liberalism in their view that such people could be helped, and the racism of their dismissal of rural culture and knowledge of the part of white social scientists and cultural paternalism and class elitism on the part of Black social scientists. While the latter are the result of a white supremacist culture, they often had a qualitatively different inflection than the former in their implementation. Both Drake's written scholarship and our many conversations have helped shape my thinking throughout this project, but most particularly in this chapter.

12. "Bar to War Seen in Birth Control: Harvard Professor, Fosdick Views Simple Contraceptive as Ending H-Bomb Fears," *New York Times*, May 7, 1954.

13. "Bar to War Seen in Birth Control."

14. "Book Briefs," *Christianity Today*, March 28, 1960, www.christianitytoday.com/ct /1960/march-28/books-in-review.html.

15. Fagley, *Population Explosion*, vii.

16. Fagley, *Population Explosion*, 5.

17. Fagley, *Population Explosion*, 13.

18. *Population Explosion* was published in 1960, the same year that opened with a *Time* magazine cover story on the expanding populace. However, Fagley had obviously done much of the writing while population concerns had been growing, but before they had reached the level of panic that they would eventually achieve.

19. Richard M. Fagley, "The Population Explosion Today," *Christian Century*, June 6, 1962, 710–12.

20. Fagley, *Population Explosion*, 6.

21. Paul King Jewett, "A Case for Birth Control," *Christian Century*, May 24, 1961, 651.

22. National Council of the Churches of Christ in the USA, "Responsible Parenthood: Adopted by the General Board February 28, 1961," https://nationalcouncilofchurches.us /common-witness-ncc/responsible-parenthood.

23. National Council of the Churches of Christ in the USA, "Responsible Parenthood."

24. National Council of the Churches of Christ in the USA, "Responsible Parenthood."

25. National Council of the Churches of Christ in the USA, "Responsible Parenthood."

26. National Council of the Churches of Christ in the USA, "Responsible Parenthood."

27. Merchant, *Building the Population Bomb*, 129–30.

28. "Keep Birth Control on UN Agenda," *Christian Century*, October 11, 1961, 1196.

29. "Keep Birth Control on UN Agenda," 1196.

30. "Keep Birth Control on UN Agenda," 1196.

31. "Keep Birth Control on UN Agenda," 1196.

32. "Keep Birth Control on UN Agenda," 1196.

33. "Keep Birth Control on UN Agenda," 1196–97.

34. "Keep Birth Control on UN Agenda," 1197.

35. Fagley, *Population Explosion*, 13.

36. Jewett, "Case for Birth Control," 651.

37. Fagley, *Population Explosion*, 13.

38. Fagley, "Population Explosion Today."

39. Fagley, *Population Explosion*, 13.

40. National Council of the Churches of Christ in the USA, "Responsible Parenthood."

41. "Family Planning Is a Christian Duty," *Christian Century*, September 14, 1960, 1044.

42. Jewett, "Case for Birth Control," 652.

43. Jewett, "Case for Birth Control," 652.

44. Fagley, "Protestant View of Population Control," 471.

45. Fagley, "Protestant View of Population Control," 471.

46. Fagley, "Protestant View of Population Control," 471.

47. Takeuchi-Demirci, "Sexual Diplomacy," 115.

48. Takeuchi-Demirci, "Sexual Diplomacy," 116.

49. Kingsley Davis and Judith Black, "Birth Control and Public Policy," *Commentary*, February 1960, 119.

50. Bess Furman, "Catholics Oppose Use of Aid Funds in Birth Control: Bishops' Statement Attacks 'Propaganda' Drive over 'Population Explosion,'" *New York Times*, November 26, 1959, sec. Archives, www.nytimes.com/1959/11/26/archives/catholics-oppose-use-of -aid-funds-in-birth-control-bishops.html.

51. Furman, "Catholics Oppose Use of Aid Funds."

52. Kingsley Davis and Judith Blake, "Birth Control and Public Policy," *Commentary*, February 1960, 116, ProQuest Central.

53. Davis and Blake, "Birth Control and Public Policy," 116.

54. "Eisenhower Backs Birth-Curb Aids; Changes Stand on U.S. Help for Underdeveloped Lands," *New York Times*, November 10, 1964, sec. Archives, www.nytimes.com/1964/11/10/archives/eisenhowoer-backs-birthcurb-aids-changes-stand-on-ushelp-for.html; Furman, "Catholics Oppose Use of Aid Funds."

55. Furman, "Catholics Oppose Use of Aid Funds."

56. Furman, "Catholics Oppose Use of Aid Funds."

57. Davis and Blake, "Birth Control and Public Policy," 115.

58. Davis and Blake, "Birth Control and Public Policy," 115.

59. Davis and Blake, "Birth Control and Public Policy," 117.

60. Davis and Blake, "Birth Control and Public Policy," 116.

61. Furman, "Catholics Oppose Use of Aid Funds."

62. Furman, "Catholics Oppose Use of Aid Funds."

63. For a very long time, Kennedy was the country's only Catholic president. The second Catholic to hold office, Joseph Biden, was sworn in more than fifty years after Kennedy's death.

64. John F. Kennedy, "Transcript: JFK's Speech on His Religion," September 12, 1960, NPR, December 5, 2007, www.npr.org/templates/story/story.php?storyId=16920600.

65. Davis and Blake, "Birth Control and Public Policy," 119.

66. "Eisenhower Backs Birth-Curb Aids."

67. Anonymous Catholic couple, "Survey of a San Francisco Couple (2)," n.d. ca. 1965, Box 13, Folder 13101A, PPCP.

68. Anonymous Catholic couple, "Survey of Mobile Couple (2)," n.d. ca. 1965, Box 13, Folder 13101A, PPCP.

69. "Survey from a Boston Couple (2)," Boston, MA, 1965, Box 13, Folder 13101A, PPCP.

70. "Survey of a Rockford, IL Couple," Rockford, IL, 1965, Box 13, Folder 13101B, PPCP.

71. "Survey from a Bridgeport, CT Couple," Bridgeport, CT, 1965, Box 13, Folder 13101B, PPCP.

72. Anonymous Catholic couple, "Survey of a San Francisco Couple (2)."

73. "Survey of a Couple from Boston," Boston, MA, 1965, Box 13, Folder 13101A, PPCP.

74. Anonymous Catholic couple, "Survey from a San Diego Couple (2)," n.d. ca. 1965, Box 13, Folder 13101A, PPCP.

75. Anonymous Catholic couple, "Survey from a Mobile Couple," n.d. ca. 1965, Box 13, Folder 13101A, PPCP.

76. "Survey from a Couple in Oakland, CA," Oakland, CA, 1965, Box 13, Folder 13104, PPCP.

77. "Survey from a Couple in Altoona/Johnstown, PA," Pennsylvania, 1965, Box 13, Folder 13101A, PPCP.

78. Anonymous Catholic couple, "Santa Clara Couple," Santa Clara, CA, n.d. ca. 1965, Box 13, Folder 13101A, PPCP.

79. Taylor, *Promise of Patriarchy*, 115.

80. Taylor, *Promise of Patriarchy*, 115.

81. Jill Lepore, "Birth Control in the Cabinet: Planned Parenthood in the Archives," *New Yorker*, November 4, 2011, www.newyorker.com/news/news-desk/birth-control-in-the

-cabinet-planned-parenthood-in-the-archives. Jill Lepore attached to her article a memo to Alan Guttmacher, president of Planned Parenthood, describing this interview. Taylor also writes about this document in *Promise of Patriarchy*, where she reads it much the way that I do here, though in service of a broader point more about the experience of women in the NOI, rather than in service of a broader point about birth control.

82. Lepore, "Birth Control in the Cabinet."

83. Lepore, "Birth Control in the Cabinet."

84. Lepore, "Birth Control in the Cabinet."

85. "Birth Control," *Black Panther*, February 7, 1970.

86. "Birth Control," *Black Panther*, February 7, 1970.

87. Nelson, *Women of Color*, 102.

88. Nelson, *Women of Color*, 102.

89. Brown, *Taste of Power*, 367.

90. Brown, *Taste of Power*, 368.

91. Martin Luther King, "Family Planning: A Special and Urgent Concern," May 5, 1965, SSC.

92. M. King, "Family Planning."

93. M. King, "Family Planning."

94. M. King, "Family Planning."

95. M. King, "Family Planning."

96. Darity and Turner, "Family Planning," 1457–58.

97. Darity and Turner, "Family Planning," 1458.

98. Frances E. Ruffin, "Birth Control, a Choice: Genocide or Survival?," *Essence*, September 1972, 42.

99. Ruffin, "Birth Control, a Choice," 43.

100. Ruffin, "Birth Control, a Choice," 73.

101. Ruffin, "Birth Control, a Choice." Note that the *Essence* article did not identify who had performed the survey or when (nor was it clear whether it was a survey tied to reproductive health care or social services more generally).

102. Ruffin, "Birth Control, a Choice," 43.

103. Ruffin, "Birth Control, a Choice," 43.

104. Ruffin, "Birth Control, a Choice," 43.

105. Ruffin, "Birth Control, a Choice," 43.

106. Ruffin, "Birth Control, a Choice," 43.

107. Ruffin, "Birth Control, a Choice," 43.

108. Ruffin, "Birth Control, a Choice," 70.

109. Ruffin, "Birth Control, a Choice," 70.

110. "Black Women Think That Birth Control Is Aimed at Them," *Chicago Daily Defender*, February 2, 1971.

111. "Black Women Think."

112. In the July 2020 issue of *American Jewish History*, historians Lila Corwin Berman, Kate Rosenblatt, and Ronit Stahl wrote an article called "Continuity Crisis: The History and Sexual Politics of an American Jewish Communal Project," which was an academic expansion of an op-ed that they wrote for the *Forward* in July 2018 called "How Jewish Academics Created a #MeToo Disaster." In that article, they trace much of the history that I trace here and make a similar point about its gendered implications. Yet they do so

in order to make a broader (and vitally important) point about the mutually reinforcing misogyny of the field of Jewish studies and the Jewish communal world for much of the past seventy-five years, rather than to make a point about the role of Jews in the history of contraception in the United States. Their feminist interpretation of this moment in history has been helpful in my own understanding of its history, and Ronit Stahl in particular has been generous in the sharing of primary source material and citations.

113. Irving Spiegel, "Rabbi Deplores Small Families," *New York Times*, January 24, 1974, sec. Archives, www.nytimes.com/1974/01/24/archives/rabbi-deplores-small-families-head -of-board-here-urges-3child.html.

114. Spiegel, "Rabbi Deplores Small Families."

115. Spiegel, "Rabbi Deplores Small Families."

116. "The Disappearing Jews," *Time*, July 14, 1975, https://time.com/archive/6851405 /religion-thedisappearing-jews/.

117. While conventional wisdom in Jewish communal life, long reflected in American Jewish history, suggests that there was a long period of silence around the Holocaust in the decades immediately following World War II, Hasia Diner's *We Remember with Reverence and Love* demonstrates that this is by and large not true. It is, however, the case that the Holocaust was not marshaled in metaphor in quite this way before the 1970s.

118. Staub, *Torn at the Roots*, 253.

119. Beck and Kolankiewicz, *Forsaking Fundamentals*.

120. Fisher, "National Gallup Polls," 123. According to Fisher, Gallup reported 22 percent of Americans had college educations in 1970–71 as compared with 42 percent of Jews, a percentage gap that would stay roughly stable across the decade. (Fisher reported numbers for 1974, 1975, and 1979.)

121. "FG 275 (Commission on Population Growth and the American Future) (White House Central Files: Subject Files)," finding aid, Richard Nixon Presidential Library and Museum, accessed March 4, 2024, www.nixonlibrary.gov/finding-aids/fg-275-commission -population-growth-and-american-future-white-house-central-files.

122. "FG 275 (Commission on Population Growth and the American Future) (White House Central Files: Subject Files)."

123. Rockefeller Commission, introduction and chap. 1 in *Population and the American Future*.

124. Daniel Callahan, "Letter to John D. Rockefeller the 3rd on the Hastings Center Report to the Commission on Population Growth and the American Future," September 3, 1971, 2, Series 3, Subseries 4, Box 69, Folder 456, Rockefeller Family Archives, Rockefeller Archive Center, Tarrytown, NY.

125. Callahan, "Letter to John D. Rockefeller," September 3, 1971.

126. Callahan, "Letter to John D. Rockefeller," September 3, 1971.

127. William Ryan, "Catholic Official Says Population Commission Has Entered Ideo-logical 'Valley of Death,'" March 15, 1972, Series 3, Subseries 4, Box 71A, Folder 472C, John D. Rockefeller 3rd Papers, Rockefeller Archive Center.

128. Ryan, "Catholic Official Says."

129. John Wesley Lord, "Bishop John Wesley Lord to Richard Nixon," April 14, 1972, Series 3, Subseries 4, Box 71A, Folder 472C, John D. Rockefeller 3rd Papers, Rockefeller Archive Center.

130. Lord, "Bishop John Wesley Lord to Richard Nixon," April 14, 1972.

Chapter 4

1. "Components of *The Dinner Party*," Brooklyn Museum, accessed June 19, 2024, www .brooklynmuseum.org/eascfa/dinner_party/home.

2. "Components of *The Dinner Party*."

3. Cobble, Gordon, and Henry, *Feminism Unfinished*, 69–75; Hesford, *Feeling Women's Liberation*, 1.

4. Cobble, Gordon, and Henry, *Feminism Unfinished*, 79–82.

5. Cobble, Gordon, and Henry, *Feminism Unfinished*, 94–95.

6. Gordon, *Moral Property of Women*, 295.

7. Gordon, *Moral Property of Women*, 296.

8. In *Feeling Women's Liberation*, Victoria Hesford focuses on the rhetoric and the constructed memory of the women's liberation movement in order to argue that the rhetorical moves people made about the movement, both in the moment and in historiography, are based in their emotions about women's liberation as much or more than they are based in an analysis of the many movements that made up women's liberation, Hesford also contends that the dominant rhetorical moves at the time both ensured the erasure of women of color and overemphasized the figure of the feminist as lesbian. In turn, these rhetorical tropes or truisms shape how the movement is remembered. Hesford pushes against the idea that one can make declarative or definitive statements about the past. For more on her argument about how we might theorize the history of the women's liberation movement, see Hesford, *Feeling Women's Liberation*. I am trying here to offer a quick gloss of the feminist movement, and one that is no doubt overly reliant on those rhetorical moves, though I have tried my best to avoid their pitfalls. I have depended on Gordon, *Moral Property of Women*, but there are any number of other excellent histories of the feminist movement to which one could turn. Hesford critiques them all in ways that I find deeply compelling. Some of those titles include: Echols, *Daring to Be Bad*; Rosen, *World Split Open*; K. King, *Theory in Its Feminist Travels*.

9. Bailey and Lindo, "Access and Use of Contraception"; Guldi, "Survey of the Literature"; Goldin and Katz, "Power of the Pill," 730–70.

10. "Eisenstadt v. Baird, 405 U.S. 438 (1972)," Justia, accessed April 24, 2024, https:// supreme.justia.com/cases/federal/us/405/438/.

11. "Eisenstadt v. Baird, 405 U.S. 438 (1972)."

12. Berlant, *Queen of America*, 59.

13. Roof et al., *Generation of Seekers*, 250.

14. Winston, "Back to the Future," 974.

15. Winston, "Back to the Future," 974.

16. "Birth-Control Rule Test Due," *Hartford (CT) Courant*, February 14, 1983.

17. "Birth-Control Rule Goes into Effect," *Boston Globe*, January 26, 1983. This article notes Heckler's objections, but also notes that it was unclear what she would do when she took over the department.

18. Best, "Unemancipated Minors' Rights," 220.

19. Best, "Unemancipated Minors' Rights," 221.

20. Best, "Unemancipated Minors' Rights," 221.

21. Best, "Unemancipated Minors' Rights," 221.

22. Best, "Unemancipated Minors' Rights," 221.

23. "900 Groups Oppose Birth Control Rule," *Los Angeles Times*, January 26, 1983, sec. Part I—Late Final; Earl Lane, "Birth-Control Rule Is Published," *Newsday*, January 27, 1983, Nassau edition.

24. "Birth-Control Rule Sidestepped," *Atlanta Constitution*, January 24, 1983.

25. Best, "Unemancipated Minors' Rights," 219–20.

26. Ronald Reagan, "Remarks at the Annual Convention of the National Association of Evangelicals in Orlando, FL," March 8, 1983, Ronald Reagan Presidential Library and Museum, www.reaganlibrary.gov/archives/speech/remarks-annual-convention-national -association-evangelicals-orlando-fl.

27. Reagan, "Remarks at the Annual Convention."

28. Reagan, "Remarks at the Annual Convention."

29. Reagan, "Remarks at the Annual Convention."

30. Reagan, "Remarks at the Annual Convention."

31. Reagan, "Remarks at the Annual Convention."

32. Reagan, "Remarks at the Annual Convention."

33. Reagan, "Remarks at the Annual Convention."

34. "Abortion and the Squeal Rule," *New York Times*, February 26, 1982, sec. Opinion, www.nytimes.com/1982/02/26/opinion/abortion-and-the-squeal-rule.html.

35. "Abortion and the Squeal Rule."

36. Reagan, "Remarks at the Annual Convention."

37. David Robert Carlin Jr., "The Squeal Rule and Lolita Rights," *Commonweal*, September 9, 1983, 465.

38. Carlin, "Squeal Rule," 465.

39. Carlin, "Squeal Rule," 465.

40. Carlin, "Squeal Rule," 465.

41. Carlin, "Squeal Rule," 465.

42. Carlin, "Squeal Rule," 465.

43. Carlin, "Squeal Rule," 466.

44. Staub, *Torn at the Roots*, 242–43.

45. "'Contraceptive Virtuoso' Seen as Survival Threat," *Jewish Week*, February 20, 1975, 1.

46. Himmelfarb, "Fertility Trends," 5–9; Johnson, "Impact of Family Formation Patterns," 1–5.

47. Johnson, "Impact of Family Formation Patterns," 1–2; Himmelfarb, "Fertility Trends," 7.

48. Himmelfarb, "Fertility Trends," 8–9; Johnson, "Impact of Family Formation Patterns."

49. Himmelfarb, "Fertility Trends."

50. Himmelfarb, "Fertility Trends," 8–9.

51. Shirley Frank, "Population Panic: Why Jewish Leaders Want Jewish Women to Be Fruitful and Multiply," in *Lilith*, Fall/Winter 1977/1978, 14.

52. For a more fulsome description of the gendered dynamics of Jewish communal politics, see Berman et al., "Continuity Crisis," 168–94.

53. Tentler, *Catholics and Contraception*, 264.

54. Tentler, *Catholics and Contraception*, 265.

55. Tentler, *Catholics and Contraception*, 266.

56. Tentler, *Catholics and Contraception*, 266.

57. Tentler, *Catholics and Contraception*, 266.

58. Tentler, *Catholics and Contraception*, 267.

59. Tentler, *Catholics and Contraception*, 270–71.

60. Greeley, "Is Catholic Sexual Teaching," 31.

61. Greeley, "Is Catholic Sexual Teaching," 31.

62. Greeley, "Is Catholic Sexual Teaching," 31.

63. Greeley, "Is Catholic Sexual Teaching," 31.

64. Greeley, "Is Catholic Sexual Teaching," 31.

65. Greeley, "Is Catholic Sexual Teaching," 31.

66. Cajka, *Follow Your Conscience*, 119.

67. Cajka, *Follow Your Conscience*, 119.

68. Cajka, *Follow Your Conscience*, 2–3, 13.

69. Miller, *Good Catholics*, 91.

70. Greeley, "Is Catholic Sexual Teaching," 33.

71. Greeley, "Is Catholic Sexual Teaching," 31.

72. Greeley, "Is Catholic Sexual Teaching," 31.

73. Katherine Dugan, "Rejecting the Pill: Catholic Women Reinterpreting Feminism," *The Revealer* (blog), October 4, 2023, https://therevealer.org/rejecting-the-pill-catholic-women-reinterpreting-feminism/; Miller, *Good Catholics*, 26.

74. Marjorie Hyer, "Kung Assailed Church's Stand in Letter to Pope," *Washington Post*, April 4, 1980, www.washingtonpost.com.

75. Hyer, "Kung Assailed."

76. Hyer, "Kung Assailed." While the University of Tübingen is not a Catholic university, and the Church therefore could not fire him, Kung was a Catholic priest, and so the Church would have been within its rights to compel his resignation.

77. Francis X. Murphy, "Of Sex and the Catholic Church," *Atlantic Monthly*, February 1981, 48.

78. Murphy, "Of Sex and the Catholic Church," 48.

79. Murphy, "Of Sex and the Catholic Church," 48.

80. Murphy, "Of Sex and the Catholic Church," 49.

81. "Pope Names Relator General for 2023 Synod," *Crux*, July 8, 2021, https://cruxnow.com/vatican/2021/07/pope-names-relator-general-for-2023-synod/.

82. "Pope Benedict XVI Had Some Pretty Intense Nicknames," *Rare*, December 31, 2022, https://rare.us/people/pope-benedict-xvi-had-some-pretty-intense-nicknames/.

83. Murphy, "Of Sex and the Catholic Church," 49; Hyer, "Kung Assailed"; Xavier Rynne, "The Catholic Church and Contraception," *New Yorker*, October 26, 1968, www.newyorker.com/magazine/1968/11/02/letter-from-vatican-city-13.

84. Murphy, "Of Sex and the Catholic Church," 49.

85. Murphy, "Of Sex and the Catholic Church," 49.

86. Murphy, "Of Sex and the Catholic Church," 49–50.

87. Murphy, "Of Sex and the Catholic Church," 50.

88. Miller, *Good Catholics*, 90.

89. Murphy, "Of Sex and the Catholic Church," 51.

90. Murphy, "Of Sex and the Catholic Church," 44.

91. John Paul II, "Apostolic Exhortation . . . *Familiaris Consortio.*"

92. John Paul II, "Apostolic Exhortation . . . *Familiaris Consortio.*"

93. For more on natural family planning, or NFP, as a Catholic practice, see the work of Dugan, including "*Humanae Vitae*, Natural Family Planning," and "Rejecting the Pill."

94. Miller, *Good Catholics*, 93.

95. Miller, *Good Catholics*, 93.

96. Miller, *Good Catholics*, 93.

97. Miller, *Good Catholics*, 93.

98. Philip J. Hilts, "Foes Rap Reagan Policy on Population Control," *Washington Post*, July 26, 1984, www.washingtonpost.com.

99. Hilts, "Foes Rap Reagan Policy."

100. *U.S. Policy on Population Assistance: Hearing Before the Subcommittee on Census and Population of the Committee on Post Office and Civil Service*, 98th Cong. (1984).

101. Hilts, "Foes Rap Reagan Policy."

102. Susan F. Rasky, "Reagan Restrictions on Foreign Aid for Abortion Programs Lead to a Fight," *New York Times*, October 14, 1984, sec. World, www.nytimes.com/1984/10/14/world/reagan-restrictions-on-foreign-aid-for-abortion-programs-lead-to-a-fight.html.

103. Rasky, "Reagan Restrictions."

104. "U.S. Policy on Population," 1, 3.

105. For more on Reagan and Evangelical manhood, see Du Mez, *Jesus and John Wayne*.

106. Grimes et al., "Epidemic of Antiabortion Violence," 1263–68.

107. Grimes et al., "Epidemic of Antiabortion Violence."

108. Grimes et al., "Epidemic of Antiabortion Violence."

109. Frank, "Population Panic," 14.

110. Durang, *Sister Mary Ignatius*, 2.

111. Durang, *Sister Mary Ignatius*, 5.

112. Durang, *Sister Mary Ignatius*.

113. Frank Rich, "Theater: One-Acters by Durang," *New York Times*, October 22, 1981, sec. Theater, www.nytimes.com/1981/10/22/theater/theater-one-acters-by-durang.html.

114. Kevin Kelly, "Devilish Good Fun with Sister Mary," *Boston Globe*, July 18, 1991, sec. Living/Arts.

115. Kelly, "Devilish Good Fun."

116. Kevin Kelly, "Playwright Durang Wins Kenyon Award," *Boston Globe*, February 15, 1983, sec. Arts and Films.

117. Kelly, "Playwright Durang."

118. Margo Miller, "Flynn's Support of 'Sr. Mary' Pickets Decried," *Boston Globe*, September 26, 1984.

119. Miller, "Flynn's Support."

120. Miller, "Flynn's Support."

121. Christopher Durang et al., "Correspondence: New Republic," *New Republic* 193, no. 14 (September 30, 1985): 6.

122. Durang et al., "Correspondence: New Republic."

123. Evelyn Wolfson, "Play Offers Catholics a Chance to Question," *Boston Globe*, December 6, 1984.

124. Durang et al., "Correspondence: New Republic."

125. Christopher Durang, "Defending 'Sister Mary Ignatius' from Zealots," *Boston Globe*, November 25, 1984.

126. Durang, "Defending 'Sister Mary Ignatius.'"

127. Durang, "Defending 'Sister Mary Ignatius.'"

128. Durang, "Defending 'Sister Mary Ignatius.'"

129. Durang, "Defending 'Sister Mary Ignatius.'"

130. For more on how we might consider how artists, particularly gay artists raised in the Catholic Church, produce work that is best understood as Catholic art, see Petro, chap. 4 in *After the Wrath of God*; Petro, "US Religious History"; Petro, "Ray Navarro's Jesus Camp," 920–56.

131. Evelyn Wolfson, "Play Offers Catholics a Chance to Question," *Boston Globe*, December 6, 1984.

Epilogue

1. "Dobbs v. Jackson Women's Health Organization," Oyez, accessed January 26, 2025, www.oyez.org/cases/2021/19-1392.

2. Lara Freidenfelds, "When the Constitution Was Drafted, Abortion Was a Choice Left to Women," *Washington Post*, May 23, 2022, www.washingtonpost.com/outlook/2022 /05/23/when-constitution-was-drafted-abortion-was-choice-left-women/; Lauren MacIvor Thompson, "Women Have Always Had Abortions," *New York Times*, December 13, 2019, sec. Opinion, www.nytimes.com/interactive/2019/12/13/opinion/sunday/abortion-history -women.html; Thompson, "Abortion, Contraception"; Samira K. Mehta et al., "The Supreme Court's Abortion Decision Is Based on a Myth. Here's Why," *Washington Post*, June 24, 2022, www.washingtonpost.com/outlook/2022/06/24/supreme-courts-abortion -decision-is-based-myth-heres-why/; Samira K. Mehta and Tisa Wenger, "Anti-Abortion Laws Are an Attack on Religious Freedom," *360info*, July 10, 2022, https://360info.org/anti -abortion-laws-are-an-attack-on-religious-freedom/.

3. While many activist organizations were also caught by surprise by the backlash against contraception, and by the overturning of *Roe*, many organizations were not surprised, as they had long been carefully guarding against the small incursions on funding for reproductive health. Even there, however, most of the activism focused on protecting abortion rights, or protecting contraception from being collateral damage in attacks on abortion, rather than on explicitly protecting birth control rights.

4. Pew Research Center, *Where the Public Stands*, 25.

5. Pew Research Center, "Public Opinion on Abortion," May 13, 2024, www.pewresearch .org/religion/fact-sheet/public-opinion-on-abortion/.

6. Pew Research Center, "Public Opinion on Abortion."

7. Smith et al., *Decline of Christianity*, 243.

8. Pew Research Center, *Cultural Issues and the 2024 Election*, 29–36.

9. Michael Tesler et al., "Republican Men and Women Are Changing Their Minds About How Women Should Behave," *New York Times*, February 27, 2025, www.nytimes.com/2025 /02/27/opinion/trump-republicans-masculinity-gender-traditional.html. This is an opinion piece, but it cites many of the relevant studies. I put the word "return" in quotation marks because of the reality that many historians, particularly historians of race and of the family,

have pointed out—the traditional family of male breadwinner and woman homemaker has never been available to the working poor, a group that is disproportionately people of color.

10. Rick Pidcock, "Meet the Theobros, Who Want You to Know They're Right About Everything," *Baptist News Global*, June 28, 2021, https://baptistnews.com/article/meet-the -theobros-who-want-you-to-know-theyre-right-about-everything/.

11. Pidcock, "Meet the Theobros."

12. Kiera Butler, "To Understand JD Vance, You Need to Meet the 'TheoBros,'" *Mother Jones*, November–December 2024, www.motherjones.com/politics/2024/09/theobros-jd -vance-christian-nationalism/.

13. Butler, "To Understand JD Vance."

14. Butler, "To Understand JD Vance."

15. National Women's Law Center, "Don't Be Fooled: Birth Control Is Already at Risk," June 17, 2022, https://nwlc.org/resource/dont-be-fooled-birth-control-is-already-at-risk/.

16. National Women's Law Center, "Don't Be Fooled."

17. Committee on Practice Bulletins–Gynecology and Long-Acting Reversible Contraception Work Group, *Long-Acting Reversible Contraception*; Swan et al., "Physician Beliefs," 237–39.

18. Anna North, "The Trump Administration's War on Birth Control," Center for Public Integrity, September 24, 2020, http://publicintegrity.org/politics/system-failure/the-trump -administrations-war-on-birth-control/.

19. North, "Trump Administration's War."

20. North, "Trump Administration's War"; "Little Sisters of the Poor."

21. "Little Sisters of the Poor."

22. "Little Sisters of the Poor."

23. "Little Sisters of the Poor."

BIBLIOGRAPHY

Archives

American Jewish Historical Society, New York, NY
Center for the History of Medicine, Francis A. Countway Library of Medicine,
    Harvard University
Richard Nixon Presidential Library and Museum, Yorba Linda, CA
Rockefeller Archive Center, Tarrytown, NY
Ronald Reagan Presidential Library and Museum, Simi Valley, CA
Smith College Archives, Northampton, MA
University of Notre Dame Archives, Notre Dame, IN

Periodicals

ACT
Analysis
Atlantic Constitution
Atlantic Monthly
Baptist News Global
Chicago Daily Defender
Christian Century
Clinics
Commentary
Commonweal
Critic

Crux
Essence
Good Housekeeping
Hartford (CT) Courant
Jewish Week
Judaism
Linacre Quarterly
Mother Jones
Negro Digest
New Republic
Newsday
New York Amsterdam News

New York Herald Tribune
New York Times
New Yorker
NPR
Partisan Review
Rare
Saturday Evening Post
360info
Times Higher Education
Vanity Fair
Washington Post

Published Sources

Adams, Carol J. *The Sexual Politics of Meat: A Feminist-Vegetarian Critical Theory*. 25th anniver-
    sary ed. Bloomsbury, 2015.
Anglican Consultative Counsel. *The Lambeth Conference: Resolutions Archive from 1930*. An-
    glican Communion Office, 2005. www.anglicancommunion.org/media/127734/1930
    .pdf.

Bailey, Beth. *Sex in the Heartland*. Harvard University Press, 2002.

Bailey, Martha J., and Jason M. Lindo. "Access and Use of Contraception and Its Effects on Women's Outcomes in the United States." In *The Oxford Handbook of Women and the Economy*, edited by Susan L. Averett, Laura M. Argys, and Saul D. Hoffman. Oxford University Press, 2018. https://doi.org/10.1093/oxfordhb/9780190628963.013.19.

Berlant, Lauren. *The Queen of America Goes to Washington City: Essays on Sex and Citizenship*. Duke University Press, 1997.

Berman, Lila Corwin, Kate Rosenblatt, and Ronit Stahl. "Continuity Crisis: The History and Sexual Politics of an American Jewish Communal Project." *American Jewish History* 104, no. 2/3 (July 2020): 168–94.

Best, Marilyn. "Unemancipated Minors' Rights of Access to Contraceptives Without Parental Consent or Notice—The Squeal Rule and Beyond Notes." *Oklahoma City University Law Review* 8, no. 2 (1983): 220.

Braude, Ann. "Women's History Is American Religious History." In *Retelling US Religious History*, edited by Thomas A. Tweed. University of California Press, 1997.

Briggs, Laura. *Reproducing Empire: Race, Sex, Science, and U.S. Imperialism in Puerto Rico*. University of California Press, 2002.

Brown, Elaine. *A Taste of Power: A Black Woman's Story*. Pantheon, 1992.

Cajka, Peter. *Follow Your Conscience: The Catholic Church and the Spirit of the Sixties*. University of Chicago Press, 2021.

Capo, Beth Widmaier. "Inserting the Diaphragm in(to) Modern American Fiction: Mary McCarthy, Philip Roth, and the Literature of Contraception." *Journal of American Culture* 26, no. 1 (2003): 112–13. https://doi.org/10.1111/1542-734X.00079.

Centers for Disease Control and Prevention. "Differences in Maternal Mortality Among Black and White Women—United States, 1990." *Morbidity and Mortality Weekly Report*, January 13, 1995. www.cdc.gov/mmwr/preview/mmwrhtml/00035538.htm.

Cobble, Dorothy Sue, Linda Gordon, and Astrid Henry. *Feminism Unfinished: A Short, Surprising History of American Women's Movements*. Liveright, 2015.

Coffman, Elesha J. *"The Christian Century" and the Rise of the Protestant Mainline*. Oxford University Press, 2013.

Committee on Practice Bulletins–Gynecology and Long-Acting Reversible Contraception Work Group. *Long-Acting Reversible Contraception Implants and Intrauterine Devices*. In collaboration with Eve Espey and Lisa Hofler. Practice Bulletin no. 186, November 2017. American College of Obstetricians and Gynecologists. www.acog.org /clinical/clinical-guidance/practice-bulletin/articles/2017/11/long-acting-reversible -contraception-implants-and-intrauterine-devices.

Conference of Bishops of the Anglican Communion: Holden at Lambeth Palace July 5 to August 6, 1908; Encyclical Letter from the Bishops with Resolutions and Reports. London: Society for Promoting Christian Knowledge, 1908.

Connelly, Matthew James. *Fatal Misconception: The Struggle to Control World Population*. Belknap Press of Harvard University Press, 2008.

Coontz, Stephanie. *Marriage: A History; How Love Conquered Marriage*. Penguin Books, 2006.

Coontz, Stephanie. *The Way We Never Were: American Families and the Nostalgia Trap*. Basic Books, 2000.

Coontz, Stephanie. *The Way We Really Are: Coming to Terms with America's Changing Families*. Basic Books, 1998.

Darity, William A., and Castellano B. Turner. "Family Planning, Race Consciousness and the Fear of Black Genocide." *American Journal of Public Health* 62, no. 11 (1972): 1457–558.

Davis, Rebecca L. *More Perfect Unions: The American Search for Marital Bliss.* Harvard University Press, 2010.

Davis, Rebecca L., and Michelle Mitchell, eds. *Heterosexual Histories.* New York University Press, 2021.

D'Emilio, John, and Estelle B. Freedman. *Intimate Matters: A History of Sexuality in America.* 2nd ed. University of Chicago Press, 1998.

Drake, Jamil. *To Know the Soul of a People: Religion, Race, and the Making of Southern Folk.* Oxford University Press, 2022.

Dugan, Katherine. "*Humanae Vitae*, Natural Family Planning, and U.S. Catholic Identity: The Founding of the Couple to Couple League," *U.S. Catholic Historian* 39, no. 2 (Spring 2021): 113–32.

Du Mez, Kristin Kobes. *Jesus and John Wayne: How White Evangelicals Corrupted a Faith and Fractured a Nation.* Liveright, 2020.

Durang, Christopher. *Sister Mary Ignatius Explains It All for You; The Actor's Nightmare—Two One-Act Plays.* Nelson Doubleday, 1981.

Echols, Alice. *Daring to Be Bad: Radical Feminism in America, 1967–1975.* 30th anniversary ed. With a foreword by Ellen Willis. University of Minnesota Press, 2019.

Eig, Jonathan. *The Birth of the Pill: How Four Crusaders Reinvented Sex and Launched a Revolution.* W. W. Norton, 2014.

Estes, Steve. *I Am a Man: Race, Manhood, and the Civil Rights Movement.* University of North Carolina Press, 2005.

Fagley, Richard M. *The Population Explosion and Christian Responsibility.* Oxford University Press, 1960.

Fagley, Richard M. "A Protestant View of Population Control." *Law and Contemporary Problems* 25, no. 3 (1960): 470–89.

Feldman, David M. *Birth Control in Jewish Law: Marital Relations, Contraception, and Abortion as Set Forth in the Classical Texts of Jewish Law.* New York University Press, 1968.

Fisher, Alan M. "The National Gallup Polls and American Jewish Demography." *American Jewish Year Book* 83 (1983): 123.

Frazier, E. Franklin. *The Negro Church in America.* Schocken Books, 1966.

Frazier, E. Franklin. *The Negro Family in the United States.* 1939. Rev. and abridged ed. With a foreword by Nathan Glazer. University of Chicago Press, 1966.

Gaston, K. Healan. *Imagining Judeo-Christian America: Religion, Secularism, and the Redefinition of Democracy.* University of Chicago Press, 2020.

Genné, Elizabeth, and William H. Genné. *Christians and the Crisis in Sex Morality: The Church Looks at the Facts About Sex and Marriage Today.* Literary Licensing, 2011.

Goldin, Claudia, and Lawrence F. Katz. "The Power of the Pill: Oral Contraceptives and Women's Career and Marriage Decisions." *Journal of Political Economy* 110, no. 4 (2002): 730–70. https://doi.org/10.1086/340778.

Gordon, Linda. *The Moral Property of Women: A History of Birth Control Politics in America.* University of Illinois Press, 2007.

Greeley, Andrew. "Is Catholic Sexual Teaching Coming Apart?" *Critic* 30, no. 4 (April 1972): 30–35.

Griffith, R. Marie. *Moral Combat: How Sex Divided American Christians and Fractured American Politics*. Basic Books, 2017.

Grimes, David A., Jacqueline D. Forrest, Alice. L. Kirkman, and Barbara Radford. "An Epidemic of Antiabortion Violence in the United States." *American Journal of Obstetrics and Gynecology* 165, no. 5, pt. 1 (November 1991): 1263–68. https://doi.org/10.1016/0002-9378(91)90346-s.

Guldi, Melanie. "A Survey of the Literature on Early Legal Access to the Birth Control Pill and Its Influence on Young Women's Fertility, Education, Career and Labor Supply." In *Research Handbook on the Economics of Family Law*, edited by Lloyd R. Cohen and Joshua D. Wright. Edward Elgar, 2011.

Hajo, Cathy Moran. *Birth Control on Main Street: Organizing Clinics in the United States, 1916–1939*. University of Illinois Press, 2010.

Hamm, Margaret J. "Theologizing the Pill: Christianity, Women's Magazines, and Birth Control, 1960–1972." Master's thesis, Harvard Divinity School, 2021.

Harrison, Peter. *The Territories of Science and Religion*. University of Chicago Press, 2017.

Hedstrom, Matthew S. *The Rise of Liberal Religion: Book Culture and American Spirituality in the Twentieth Century*. Oxford University Press, 2015.

Heinze, Andrew R. *Jews and the American Soul: Human Nature in the Twentieth Century*. Princeton University Press, 2006.

Herberg, Will. *Protestant, Catholic, Jew: An Essay in American Religious Sociology*. Anchor Books, 1960.

Hesford, Victoria. *Feeling Women's Liberation*. Duke University Press, 2013.

Higginbotham, Evelyn Brooks. *Righteous Discontent: The Women's Movement in the Black Baptist Church, 1880–1920*. Harvard University Press, 1993.

Himmelfarb, Harold. "Fertility Trends and Their Impact on Jewish Education." *Analysis* no. 60 (November–December 1976): 5–9.

Holz, Rose. *The Birth Control Clinic in a Marketplace World*. University of Rochester Press, 2014.

Imber, Jonathan B. *Trusting Doctors: The Decline of Moral Authority in American Medicine*. Illustrated ed. Princeton University Press, 2008.

Jakobsen, Janet. "Sex + Freedom = Regulation: Why?" *Social Text* 23, nos. 3–4 (Fall–Winter 2005): 285–308.

Jakobsen, Janet, and Ann Pellegrini. *Love the Sin: Sexual Regulation and the Limits of Religious Tolerance*. Beacon, 2004.

John Paul II. "Apostolic Exhortation . . . on the Role of the Christian Family in the Modern World. Familiaris Consortio." November 22, 1981. The Holy See. www.vatican.va/content/john-paul-ii/en/apost_exhortations/documents/hf_jp-ii_exh_19811122_familiaris-consortio.html.

Johnson, George. "The Impact of Family Formation Patterns on Jewish Community Involvement." *Analysis* no. 60 (November–December 1976): 1–5.

Josephson-Storm, Jason Ānanda. *The Myth of Disenchantment: Magic, Modernity, and the Birth of the Human Sciences*. University of Chicago Press, 2017.

Kaiser, Robert Blair. *The Politics of Sex and Religion: A Case History in the Development of Doctrine, 1962–1984*. Leaven, 1985.

Kennedy, David M. *Birth Control in America: The Career of Margaret Sanger*. Yale University Press, 1971.

Khan, Fahd, Saheel Mukhtar, Ian K. Dickinson, and Seshadri Sriprasad. "The Story of
    the Condom." *Indian Journal of Urology* 29, no. 1 (2013): 12–15. https://doi.org/10.4103
    /0970-1591.109976.

King, Katie. *Theory in Its Feminist Travels: Conversations in U.S. Women's Movements.* Indiana
    University Press, 1995.

King, Martin Luther, Jr. "Advice for Living, December 1957." *Ebony,* December 1957,
    p. 120. The Martin Luther King, Jr. Research and Education Institute, Stanford Uni-
    versity. https://kinginstitute.stanford.edu/king-papers/documents/advice-living.

Klapper, Melissa R. *Ballots, Babies, and Banners of Peace: American Jewish Women's Activism,*
    1890–1940. NYU Press, 2014.

Klepp, Susan E. *Revolutionary Conceptions: Women, Fertility, and Family Limitation in America,*
    1760–1820. Omohundro Institute of Early American History and Culture; University
    of North Carolina Press, 2009.

"*Little Sisters of the Poor Saints Peter and Paul Home v. Pennsylvania.*" *Harvard Law Review* 134,
    no. 1 (November 10, 2020). https://harvardlawreview.org/print/vol-134/little-sisters
    -of-the-poor-saints-peter-and-paul-home-v-pennsylvania/.

Lovett, Laura L. *Conceiving the Future: Pronatalism, Reproduction, and the Family in the United
    States, 1890–1938.* University of North Carolina Press, 2007.

Marks, Lara. *Sexual Chemistry: A History of the Contraceptive Pill.* Yale University Press, 2010.

Marsh, Margaret, and Wanda Ronner. *The Fertility Doctor: John Rock and the Reproductive
    Revolution.* Johns Hopkins University Press, 2008.

May, Elaine Tyler. *America and the Pill: A History of Promise, Peril, and Liberation.* Basic Books,
    2010.

May, Elaine Tyler. *Homeward Bound: American Families in the Cold War Era.* Basic Books,
    2008.

McCann, Carole R. *Birth Control Politics in the United States, 1916–1945.* Cornell University
    Press, 1999.

McCann, Carole R. *Figuring the Population Bomb: Gender and Demography in the Mid-Twentieth
    Century.* Feminist Technosciences. University of Washington Press, 2017.

McCarthy, Mary. *The Group.* 1963. Reissue ed. Mariner Books, 1991.

McClory, Robert. *Turning Point: The Inside Story of the Papal Birth Control Commission, and
    How Humanae Vitae Changed the Life of Patty Crowley and the Future of the Church.* Cross-
    roads, 1997.

Mehta, Samira K. "Family Planning Is a Christian Duty: Religion, Population Control,
    and the Pill in the 1960s." In *Devotions and Desires: Histories of Sexuality and Religion in
    the Twentieth-Century United States,* edited by Bethany Moreton, Gillian Frank, and
    Heather White. University of North Carolina Press, 2018.

Merchant, Emily Klancher. *Building the Population Bomb.* Oxford University Press, 2021.

Miller, Patricia. *Good Catholics: The Battle over Abortion in the Catholic Church.* University of
    California Press, 2014.

Moeller, Andrew. "Eugenics and the Approval of Birth Control at the 1930 Lambeth
    Conference." *Journal of Ecclesiastical History* 75, no. 1 (January 2024): 99–100.

Mokhtarian, Jason Sion. *Medicine in the Talmud: Natural and Supernatural Therapies Between
    Magic and Science.* University of California Press, 2022.

Myers-Shirk, Susan E. *Helping the Good Shepherd: Pastoral Counselors in a Psychotherapeutic
    Culture, 1925–1975.* Johns Hopkins University Press, 2009.

Neis, Rafael Rachel. *When a Human Gives Birth to a Raven: Rabbis and the Reproduction of Species*. University of California Press, 2023.

Nelson, Jennifer. *Women of Color and the Reproductive Rights Movement*. New York University Press, 2003.

Nuriddin, Ayah. "Engineering Uplift: Black Eugenics as Black Liberation." In *Nature Remade: Engineering Life, Envisioning Worlds*, edited by Luis A. Campos, Michael A. Dietrich, Tiago Saraiva, and Christian C. Young. Convening Science: Discovery at the Marine Biological Laboratory. University of Chicago Press, 2021.

Paul VI. "Encyclical Letter . . . on the Regulation of Birth. *Humanae Vitae*." July 25, 1968. The Holy See. www.vatican.va/content/paul-vi/en/encyclicals/documents/hf_p-vi _enc_25071968_humanae-vitae.html.

Petro, Anthony M. *After the Wrath of God: AIDS, Sexuality, and American Religion*. Oxford University Press, 2015.

Petro, Anthony M. "Ray Navarro's Jesus Camp, AIDS Activist Video, and the 'New Anti-Catholicism.'" *Journal of the American Academy of Religion* 85, no. 4 (2017): 920–56. https://doi.org/10.1093/jaarel/lfx011.

Petro, Anthony M. "US Religious History, the Culture Wars, and the Arts of Secularity." *Journal of the American Academy of Religion* 87, no. 4 (2019): 968–81. https://doi.org/10 .1093/jaarel/lfz080.

Pew Research Center. *Cultural Issues and the 2024 Election: Immigration, Gender Identity, Racial Diversity, and Views of a Changing Society*. Pew Research Center, June 6, 2024. www .pewresearch.org/politics/2024/06/06/cultural-issues-and-the-2024-election/.

Pew Research Center. *Where the Public Stands on Religious Liberty vs. Nondiscrimination*. Pew Research Center, September 28, 2016. www.pewresearch.org/religion/2016/09/28 /4-very-few-americans-see-contraception-as-morally-wrong/.

Reed, James. *The Birth Control Movement and American Society: From Private Vice to Public Virtue*. Originally published as *From Private Vice to Public Virtue: The Birth Control Movement and American Society Since 1830* by Basic Books, 1978. Reprint. Princeton University Press, 1984.

Rockefeller Commission. *Population and the American Future: The Report of the Commission on Population Growth and the American Future*. Center for Research on Population and Security, 1972. www.population-security.org/rockefeller/001_population_growth _and_the_american_future.htm.

Roof, Wade Clark, Bruce Greer, and Mary Johnson. *A Generation of Seekers: The Spiritual Journeys of the Baby Boom Generation*. Harper, 1994.

Rosen, Ruth. *The World Split Open: How the Modern Women's Movement Changed America*. Rev. ed. Penguin, 2006.

Roth, Philip. *"Goodbye, Columbus" and Five Short Stories*. Bantam Books, 1959.

Roy, Beck, and Leon Kolankiewicz. *Forsaking Fundamentals: The Environmental Establishment Abandons U.S. Population Stabilization*. Center for Immigration Studies, March 2, 2001. https://cis.org/Report/Forsaking-Fundamentals.

Sarch, Amy. "Dirty Discourse: Birth Control Advertising in the 1920s and 1930s." PhD diss., University of Pennsylvania, 1994.

Schoen, Johanna. *Choice and Coercion: Birth Control, Sterilization, and Abortion in Public Health and Welfare*. University of North Carolina Press, 2005.

Schultz, Kevin M. *Tri-Faith America: How Catholics and Jews Held Postwar America to Its Protestant Promise*. Oxford University Press, 2011.

Sehat, David. *The Myth of American Religious Freedom*. Oxford University Press, 2001.

Smith, Gregory A., Alan Cooperman, Becka A. Alper, et al. *Decline of Christianity in the U.S. Has Slowed, May Have Leveled Off: Findings from the 2023–24 Religious Landscape Study*. Pew Research Center, February 26, 2025. www.pewresearch.org/wp-content/uploads/sites/20/2025/02/PR_2025.02.26_religious-landscape-study_report.pdf.

Staub, Michael. *Torn at the Roots: The Crisis of Jewish Liberalism in Postwar America*. Religion and American Culture. Columbia University Press, 2004. https://doi.org/10.7312/stau12374.

Stern, Alexandra. *Eugenic Nation: Faults and Frontiers of Better Breeding in Modern America*. 2nd ed. University of California Press, 2016.

Stewart, Dianne M. *Black Women, Black Love: America's War on African American Marriage*. Seal, 2020.

Swan, Laura E. T., Abigail S. Cutler, Madison Sands, Nicholas B. Schmuhl, and Jenny A. Higgins. "Physician Beliefs About Contraceptive Methods as Abortifacients." *American Journal of Obstetrics and Gynecology* 228, no. 2 (February 1, 2023): 237–39. https://doi.org/10.1016/j.ajog.2022.09.039.

Takeuchi Demirci, Aiko. "Sexual Diplomacy: U.S. Catholics' Transnational Anti-Birth Control Activism in Postwar Japan." In *Devotions and Desires: Histories of Sexuality and Religion in the Twentieth Century United States*, edited by Bethany Moreton, Heather R. White, and Gillian Frank. University of North Carolina Press, 2018.

Taylor, Ula Yvette. *The Promise of Patriarchy: Women and the Nation of Islam*. John Hope Franklin Series in African American History and Culture. University of North Carolina Press, 2017.

Tentler, Leslie Woodcock. *Catholics and Contraception: An American History*. Cornell University Press, 2004.

Thompson, Lauren MacIvor. "Abortion, Contraception, and the Comstock Law's Original Medical Exemption, 1873–1936." "Anthony Comstock and the Comstock Laws," special issue, *Journal of the Gilded Age and Progressive Era* 23, no. 4 (October 2024): 444–51.

Thompson, Lauren MacIvor. "'The Reasonable (Wo)Man': Physicians, Freedom of Contract, and Women's Rights, 1870–1930." *Law and History Review* 36, no. 4 (November 2018): 771–809. https://doi.org/10.1017/S073824801800041X.

Tone, Andrea. "Black Market Birth Control: Contraceptive Entrepreneurship and Criminality in the Gilded Age." *Journal of American History* 87, no. 2 (2000): 435–59. https://doi.org/10.2307/2568759.

Tone, Andrea. *Devices and Desires: A History of Contraceptives in America*. Hill and Wang, 2002.

Washington, Harriet A. *Medical Apartheid: The Dark History of Medical Experimentation on Black Americans from Colonial Times to the Present*. Doubleday, 2006.

Wells-Oghoghomeh, Alexis. *The Souls of Womenfolk: The Religious Cultures of Enslaved Women in the Lower South*. University of North Carolina Press, 2021.

Wenger, Tisa J. *Religious Freedom: The Contested History of an American Ideal*. University of North Carolina Press, 2017.

White, Heather R. "How Heterosexuality Became Religious: Judeo-Christian Morality and the Remaking of Sex in Twentieth Century America." In *Heterosexual Histories*, edited by Rebecca L. Davis and Michelle Mitchell. New York University Press, 2021.

White, Heather R. *Reforming Sodom: Protestants and the Rise of Gay Rights*. University of North Carolina Press, 2015.

Wilde, Melissa J. *Birth Control Battles: How Race and Class Divided American Religion*. University of California Press, 2019.

Winston, Diane. "Back to the Future: Religion, Politics, and the Media." *American Quarterly* 59, no. 3 (September 2007): 969–89.

Woloch, Nancy. *Women and the American Experience*. 5th ed. McGraw-Hill Education, 2010.

INDEX